HEALTHCARE PAYMENT SYSTEMS

Cost-Based, Charge-Based, and Contractual Payment Systems

HEALTHCARE PAYMENT SYSTEMS

Cost-Based, Charge-Based, and Contractual Payment Systems

Duane C. Abbey

CRC Press
Taylor & Francis Group
Boca Raton   London   New York

CRC Press is an imprint of the
Taylor & Francis Group, an **informa** business
A PRODUCTIVITY PRESS BOOK

CRC Press
Taylor & Francis Group
6000 Broken Sound Parkway NW, Suite 300
Boca Raton, FL 33487-2742

© 2013 by Taylor & Francis Group, LLC
CRC Press is an imprint of Taylor & Francis Group, an Informa business

No claim to original U.S. Government works

Printed in the United States of America on acid-free paper
Version Date: 20120621

International Standard Book Number: 978-1-4398-7299-4 (Paperback)

Library of Congress Cataloging-in-Publication Data

Abbey, Duane C.
    Cost-based, charge-based, and contractual payment systems / Duane C. Abbey.
        p. ; cm.
    Includes bibliographical references and index.
    Summary: "This book provides an overview of a wide range of healthcare payment systems. It compares cost-based systems, charge-based payment approaches, and contractually-based payment processes to fee-schedule payment systems and prospective payment systems. It covers claim adjustment and compliance as well as managed care contracts and various combinations of payment systems used by third-party administrators. Examples illustrate the processes used for capitated contract arrangements. The author also addresses various compliance issues, including statutory, contractual, and overpayment issues"--Provided by publisher.
        ISBN 978-1-4398-7299-4 (pbk. : alk. paper)
    I. Title.
    [DNLM: 1. Reimbursement Mechanisms--United States. 2. Contract Services--United States. W 80]

338.4'73621--dc23

                                                                                                2012013464

Visit the Taylor & Francis Web site at
http://www.taylorandfrancis.com

and the CRC Press Web site at
http://www.crcpress.com

Dedication

This text is dedicated to all of you who have struggled with understanding the explanation of benefits (EOBs) from your insurance company that was sent to you after receiving healthcare services. In some cases, you may be reviewing EOBs for family members and loved ones. These EOBs seem almost unfathomable relative to the way in which claims are paid, or not, for healthcare services.

While this is the fourth text in a series of books devoted to healthcare payment systems, we have really just scratched the surface of a complex and continuously evolving area. Most of the concepts discussed can be grasped by interested laypersons as well as those professionals involved in the healthcare services industry. I invite interested readers to be patient with themselves. You may have to read and then reread certain sections to grasp the concepts presented. Small case studies are used in this text as they were in the preceding three texts. These are used to assist in explaining and illustrating certain issues. My objective is not only to explain; it is to explicate.

I wish to acknowledge the many students who have attended my workshops over the years. We have discussed numerous, intricate topics and attempted to develop policies and operating procedures when guidance from Medicare and other private payers is less than precise. Compliance issues have always loomed large in our discussions, particularly the possibility of inadvertently receiving overpayments for services.

For all our readers, enjoy the technicalities. For healthcare payment, everything seems to be in the fine print.

Contents

Preface

This is the fourth in a series of four books devoted to healthcare payment systems. I address several fee-for-service payment systems and discuss capitation in this book. References are made to the other three books from time to time in our discussions; here are their titles:

- *Healthcare Payment Systems: An Introduction*
- *Fee Schedule Payment System*
- *Prospective Payment Systems*

As feasible, a similar approach and style has been maintained for all four books.

Healthcare payment processes are often quite complicated. At times, there can even be political controversy concerning their use and the payment mechanisms that are included. Discussion surrounding various types of healthcare payment processes can become quite confusing unless there is uniformity in terminology and definitions. Unfortunately, you must sometimes glean the meaning of terminology from the context of the discussion. Also, healthcare payment and associated delivery system discussions involve hundreds of acronyms. An acronym listing has been provided to assist in wading through this alphabet soup.

Because healthcare payment is a statutory issue for the Medicare program and often a contractual issue for private third-party payers, great care must be taken to understand the terminology and the many acronyms that are used in this area. In some cases, healthcare providers file claims to third-party payers with whom the healthcare provider has no relationship. While there should be full payment for the charges made, often the unknown third-party payers will pay on the basis of a predetermined system, including various fee schedules, prospective payment, or other payment systems. Even when there is a contractual relationship, terminology specific to a given third-party payer may seem unorthodox. Always be prepared to ask exactly what certain terms mean.

Many of the adjudication discussions surrounding cost-based and charge-based payment can become quite technical. For example, the Medicare program uses several cost-based payment systems for certain types of healthcare providers. With the Medicare program, there are tens of thousands of pages of rules, regulations, bulletins, transmittals, and other documents that are issued. Thus, as a way to make reading of such materials a little more friendly, the term *small case studies* is used to illustrate various concepts as we discuss them.

Private third-party payers often use contractual payment processes. These are called *managed care contracts,* although our main emphasis is with the payment processes more than with the healthcare management processes. The complexity in the use of contracts lies within the contracts themselves. While these contracts are supposedly negotiated, the contracts tend to be written by the payers and thus incorporate terms and features that are generally advantageous to the payer. Again, small case studies illustrate some of the concepts typically found in contracts. Note that with contracts, the contract itself may be very brief with the actual coding, billing, and reimbursement features being contained in associated companion manuals or links to web sites.

This text has been prepared to address various complexities by iterating certain concepts. This means that we address a concept or topic at a high conceptual level and then revisit the same or perhaps a similar topic and drill down with more detail. Due to the extreme complexities of most payment systems, we are only able to address many topics at a detailed conceptual level. For this text, our goal is to understand many of the features and the way in which payment systems function. When these systems are in use to actually reimburse healthcare providers, they are dynamic and are constantly changing and evolving.

The level of detail provided concerning cost-based, charge-based, and contractual payment arrangements has been balanced with the number of conceptual features that are presented. To fully discuss any of the many issues addressed would take a separate book. For instance, Chapter 5 briefly addresses capitated healthcare payment. To really discuss capitated payment systems, a rather large volume would be needed. The intent is to provide a framework to understand and analyze the characteristics of the payment systems discussed in this text. Thus, the intended level is that of a detailed conceptual discussion. The concepts can then be applied to a wide variety of specific circumstances.

Comments on Terminology and Notation

Acronyms abound in healthcare for coding, billing, and reimbursement. As much as possible, when acronyms are first used in a chapter, the meaning is provided. However, you may find times when you need to go to the acronym listing to verify the meanings. We are at a point where there are sometimes *second-order* acronyms. These are acronyms that can be used in different ways. For instance, the acronym *MAC* can refer to monitored anesthesia care or Medicare administrative contractor.

Special notes are provided throughout the text. These notes convey additional information that is an adjunct to the specific discussion. Almost any rule, regulation, or approach to payment will have exceptions and unusual idiosyncrasies. When possible, further references are provided. Also, alerts are made to topics subject to current change. If healthcare payment systems have any one feature in common, it is that they are in a constant state of change.

Modifiers are indicated in quotations with a leading hyphen, such as "-LT," *Left*. The description of the modifier is indicated in italics. This notation is used to indicate that the modifier is used as a suffix that is appended to a CPT* (Current Procedural Terminology) or HCPCS (Healthcare Common Procedure Coding System) code. This notation really follows from the paper claims. Today, for the most part, modifiers represent data elements that go into a specific location in the electronic format. Thus, the leading hyphen is for human reading purposes, not for actual claims-filing purposes.

Generally, the *Medicare program* is referred to, as opposed to CMS (Centers for Medicare and Medicaid Services). CMS is the administrator for the Medicare program. Thus, various rules, regulations, directives, transmittals, and the like all emanate from CMS. Thus, these various rules and regulations govern the Medicare program and the payment system arrangements that we discuss in this book, at least those applicable to Medicare.

I also use abbreviated descriptions for CPT and HCPCS codes as well as for the various modifiers. For the full descriptions of codes and modifiers, this can become lengthy; see the respective CPT or HCPCS manual.

Case Study Approach

A series of simple case studies or scenarios is used throughout this book to illustrate the concepts presented. For the most part, these case studies are in the context of a fictitious community, namely, Anywhere, USA. The hospital involved is the Apex Medical Center. When a clinic is needed, the Acme Medical Clinic is used. Anywhere, USA, also has a skilled nursing facility, home health agency, hospice, and other types of healthcare providers. The Maximus Insurance Company is also located in Anywhere, USA.

The individuals who present for various services include:

- Sarah: Feisty lady who has been 87 years old for the last 5 years. While she is actually a nonagenarian, Sarah's most endearing characteristic is her speed walker, which has a horn, headlight, and racing wheels. She is also tired of signing forms, so she has had a signature stamp fabricated that hangs from the handle on her walker.
- Sam: Sarah's cousin, who is an octogenarian, semiretired rancher. He also works part time at the local hardware store.
- Susan: Sarah's daughter, who teaches school.
- Sydney and Stephen: Both are elderly Medicare beneficiaries who have a number of chronic health conditions.

While there are other residents who may be used in THE case studies, these are the main characters. Keep in mind that this is a fictitious community that exists only in our imaginations. Also, when necessary for a given case study, the specific circumstances involving a healthcare provider may be altered. For instance, the Apex Medical Center may be an acute care hospital for a given case study and then changed to be a critical access hospital for another case study.

Anywhere, USA, is also home to a regional insurance company, Maximus Insurance Company, which provides health and accident insurance for individuals and companies. As with all third-party payers for healthcare services, Maximus must determine how to pay for healthcare services. We will join in some of their efforts and thoughts relative to different contractual payment systems.

The use of case studies is intended to make the study of sometimes-technical material a little more tractable and enjoyable. Note that for a given case study there may be many issues involved even though these are very short in nature and often without appropriately specific detail. Watch for notes that indicate there may be some hidden issues that are not a part of our immediate discussions.

Medicare Orientation

Several Medicare cost-based payment systems are discussed in this book. Information about these payment systems is publicly available and generally extensive. Specific information about private third-party payer utilization of cost-based, charge-based, and contractual payment is not as readily available. Also, contractual payment systems are highly variable and may involve unusual features. As a result, both Medicare payment approaches are discussed along with myriad charge-based and contractual payment systems. Private third-party payers often adopt modified forms of the different Medicare payment systems. In some sense, the Medicare program leads the way in breaking new ground for innovative healthcare payment processes.

For healthcare providers and patients alike, the way in which private third-party payer payment systems work can be mysterious and sometimes frustrating. The bottom line for payment systems outside the Medicare program is that variability is the norm. This is the reason why, in this series of four books, we tend to start with the Medicare payment systems and then work toward how private payers adapt and use the different payment processes that have been developed by Medicare.

References

References to specific resources are provided on a limited basis. Some of the topics addressed are present in the Medicare program in one form or another. The *Federal Register* update process involves proposed rule changes followed by final rule changes. Other references are to the CMS manuals, *Federal Registers,* or the *Code of Federal Regulations.* The CMS manual system is updated through various transmittals. In some cases, extremely important guidance is made at very informal levels. For instance, there are significant policy statements from CMS through their Question and Answer (Q&A) website (https://questions.cms.gov/). Note that if you are creating policies and associated procedures based on informal guidance, be certain to save a copy of the document or website. Informal guidance can suddenly disappear. Changes to the CMS manuals have to go through a more formal process using the transmittals. Thus, there is official notice of the changes so that when changes are made, everyone knows what is being changed and when.

Note: Even with the transmittal process for updating the Medicare manuals, there are times when complete paragraphs are removed from a manual, but this may not be reflected in the changes indicated in a given transmittal.

While references to non-Medicare, that is, private, third-party payers would certainly be wonderful, most of these resources depend on very specific implementations and guidance that is provided through contractual relationships. The specific guidance for coding, billing, and associated payment may be adjunct to the actual contract. There are often companion manuals and guidance for providers through the Internet or secure intranets.

Note also that you must constantly update yourself on any given implementation or instantiation of a given payment arrangement. For healthcare payment, change is constant. Thus, this text is oriented toward understanding overall systems and implementation parameters for various types of payment systems. Specific details of exactly how a claim should be developed and then adjudicated must be supplied by the specific third-party payer, and this includes the Medicare program as well. There are always gaps in guidance, so questions are always appropriate.

As you read and study the materials in this text, you will probably want to access a number of different resources cited. Here is a list of specific resources and an Internet address for each. These are the general resources. You may need to delve further into a particular manual or book to find specific information and concepts referenced.

1. Social Security Act (SSA): http://www.ssa.gov/OP_Home/ssact/ssact-toc.htm. You will need to know which section to reference specific issues. For example, §1861(s)(2)(A) addresses payment to physicians, including "incident-to" language and noncoverage for self-administrable drugs.
2. *Code of Federal Regulations* (*CFR*): http://www.nara.gov. You will need to know the specific citation, such as 42 CFR §413.65 for the provider-based rule.

3. *Federal Register*: http://www.archives.gov/. You will need to know the date or the formal legal citation, such as 74 FR 60315, which refers to page 60315 (and following) of the November 20, 2009, *Federal Register* and discusses physician supervision requirements.

4. CMS Manual System: CMS has a series of very large manuals that provide all of the rules and regulations. Go to https://www.cms.gov/manuals/iom/list.asp to start. You will need to know which manual, such as Publication 100-04, *Medicare Claims Processing Manual* (MCPM), and then the chapter and section number within a given manual.

5. CMS Transmittals: CMS uses frequently issued transmittals to update their manual system. Go to https://www.cms.gov/transmittals/. You will need to know the number of the transmittal and the manual to which it applies. Typically, if you have the number and date, you will be able to find the correct transmittal.

6. CPT Manual: This is published annually by the American Medical Association. Go to http://www.ama-assn.org/ to obtain more information.

7. HCPCS Manual: The HCPCS code set is published by CMS and is available at https://www.cms.gov/medhcpcsgeninfo/. This code set is also republished by different healthcare publishing companies. Note that this code set is updated quarterly.

8. AHA Coding Clinic˚ for *ICD-10*: Official guidance from the American Hospital Association on *ICD-10* (*International Classification of Diseases, Tenth Revision*). See http://www.ahacentraloffice.com/.

9. AHA Coding Clinic for HCPCS: Official guidance from the American Hospital Association on HCPCS coding. See http://www.ahacentraloffice.com/.

10. UB-04 Data Specifications Manual: See the National Uniform Billing Committee at http://www.nubc.org.

11. 1500 Health Insurance Claim Form Reference Instruction Manual: See the National Uniform Claims Committee at http://www.nucc.org.

12. SNF (Skilled Nursing Facility) PPS: The SNF PPS is RUGs. Go to http://www.cms.gov/snfpps/ for additional information.

13. Home Health Agency (HHA) PPS: Information on the HHA PPS can be found at https://www.cms.gov/HomeHealthPPS/.

14. Long-Term Care Hospitals (LTCHs): The LTCH MS-DRGs represent a modification to MS-DRGs (Medicare Severity Diagnosis Related Groups) for long-term care hospitals. See http://www.cms.gov/longtermcarehospitalpps/.

15. Inpatient Rehabilitation Facilities (IRFs): Information for the IRF PPS can be found at http://www.cms.gov/InpatientRehabFacPPS/.

16. Inpatient Psychiatric Facilities (IPFs): Further information concerning the IPF-PPS can be found at http://www.cms.gov/InpatientPsychFacilPPS/.

17. Hospice: See https://www.cms.gov/Hospice/ for additional information.

18. Pricer Information for all Medicare PPSs: See http://www.cms.gov/PCPricer/.

19. MedPAC (Medicare Payment Advisory Commission): See http://www.medpac.gov.

20. Medicare Physician Fee Schedule (MPFS): Go to https://www.cms.gov/PhysicianFeeSched/ to download the large MS Excel spreadsheet that constitutes the MPFS.

21. Medicare Provider-Supplier Enrollment and CMS-855 Forms: Go to https://www.cms.gov/MedicareProviderSupEnroll for information and the five different forms.

22. Medicare HPSA (health personnel shortage area) and PSA (physician scarcity area): Go to https://www.cms.gov/hpsapsaphysicianbonuses/ for additional information.

23. Clinical Laboratory Fee Schedule (CLFS): Go to https://www.cms.gov/ClinicalLabFeeSched/.

24. Ambulance Fee Schedule (AFS): Go to https://www.cms.gov/AmbulanceFeeSchedule/.

25. Medicare Secondary Payer (MSP): Go to https://www.cms.gov/MedicareSecondaryPayerand You/.
26. National Correct Coding Initiative (NCCI) Coding Policy Manual: Go to https://www. cms.gov/NationalCorrectCodInitEd/. In this book, specific references may be to chapter and page numbers along with the version of the policy manual that is referenced.
27. Critical Access Hospitals (CAHs): See https://www.cms.gov/center/cah.asp. For Method II billing, the hospital bills the professional component for physicians and practitioners on the hospital facility component on the UB-04 claim form.

While the information in the *CFR* is official, this information is often rather cryptic. More detail can be found in the CMS manual system. The two manuals that are most often referenced relative to payment systems are

■ The *Medicare Claims Processing Manual* (MCPM), Publication 100-04, and
■ The *Medicare Benefit Policy Manual* (MBPM), Publication 100-02.

For instance, Chapter 3 of MCPM is devoted to inpatient hospital billing. These manuals are updated through rather frequent transmittals, sometimes called *change requests* (CRs). The transmittals are sometimes only a few pages long; in other cases, they can comprise a hundred pages or more.

References to the *Federal Register* and the *Code of Federal Regulations* may also be provided. Generally, the date and page number for the *Federal Register* will be provided along with a notation like 76 FR 42914. This is Volume 76, page 42914, which was issued on July 19, 2011, and addresses proposed rules for the MS-DRG Pre-Admission Window. A reference like 42 CFR §413.65 refers to Title 42 of the *CFR* and then Section 413.65. This is the provider-based rule (PBR). For the *CFR*, there are also volume, chapter, and part indicators, but the section numbers appear most commonly.

For the Medicare program, there are tens of thousands of pages of manuals, *Federal Register* entries, and less-formal guidance that Medicare refers to as *subregulatory*. Technically, *subregulatory* refers to guidance that appears below the *CFR* level. The *CFR* actually has the force and effect of law and is the equivalent, at the federal level, to state administrative law.

For private third-party payers, specific information about their payment systems is not nearly as readily available. Your healthcare provider may enter into contractual arrangements with a private third-party payer and thus come under several different payment systems for various types of healthcare services. The information on billing, claims adjudication, and payment will probably not be in the contract itself. Most likely, there will be companion manuals that go along with the contract. Also, these payment arrangements tend to be individualized to the needs of the payer. Specific information on these payment arrangements, using various payment methodologies, is not always readily available.

Compliance

Throughout our discussions of various contractual payment systems, compliance issues will arise. This is also true for the cost-based and charge-based payment systems. While we will discuss cost-based payment under the Medicare program, issues surrounding the cost reporting process are subject to compliance concerns from the Medicare program. Cost reports involve statutory compliance.

For most of the other payment systems discussed in this text, compliance issues involve contractual compliance because generally there will be some sort of a contract in place. While contractual compliance is less severe than statutory compliance, great care must be taken to meet any and all contractual obligations. The biggest difference with statutory compliance is that criminal prosecutions can result, whereas with contractual compliance, cases are normally in the civil courts, and often arbitration can resolve any issues that might arise.

In *Healthcare Payment Systems: An Introduction,* various compliance concerns are discussed. Compliance is inherent throughout the overall process of providing services, filling claims, and receiving payment. This process is referred to as the *revenue cycle.* Because we are interested in claims that are paid through some sort of payment system, the phrase *reimbursement cycle* is more appropriate. This implies that reimbursement is occurring based on a filed claim.

From a compliance perspective, what steps in the overall adjudication process could possibly yield any sort of compliance concerns? Here are the generalized steps in the reimbursement cycle:

- Covered Individual
- Covered Service or Item
- Ordered by a Physician or Qualified Practitioner
- Medically Necessary
- Provided by Qualified Facility or Healthcare Personnel
- Appropriate Written Documentation
- Billing Privileges
- Proper Claim Filed Timely

While each of these steps can create compliance concerns, even for contractual payment, the main area of concern is the proper development and timely filing of the claim for the services provided or items dispensed. For instance, while issues such as medical necessity or covered individual are important, the adjudication of claims should not even get to the point of calculating a payment unless these sorts of conditions are satisfied. The payment systems discussed in this text are highly varied, and there can be significant differences in third-party payer requirements for filing claims. A provider may find that even for the same services, two different payers may have different claims-filing requirements.

There are definitely instances when the healthcare provider may not properly code services and thus generate incorrect payment. This can occur for a number of reasons, not the least of which is that some claims-filing guidance can become confusing and complex. Today, the Medicare program uses a number of different audit and recovery programs, the latest of which is the Recovery Audit Contractor or RAC program. This is a recovery program with regional RACs paid a percentage of any incorrect payments, mainly overpayments, made by the Medicare program.

Note: See the *Medicare Recovery Audit Contractor Program: A Survival Guide for Healthcare Providers*, published by CRC Press (2010). This book is an adjunct to a more general compliance book for healthcare providers, *Compliance for Coding, Billing & Reimbursement: A Systematic Approach to Developing a Comprehensive Program*, also published by CRC Press (2008).

Contents and Approach

The first chapter is devoted to providing important background material concerning types of healthcare providers and associated organizations, along with a review of the main types of healthcare payment systems. Chapter 2 addresses healthcare costs and cost-based reimbursement systems.

This is the oldest of the payment systems. Cost-based reimbursement is still used by the Medicare program for critical access hospitals (CAHs) and RHCs (rural health clinics) and FQHCs (federally qualified health centers). At a very localized or micro level, cost-based reimbursement is used in almost all payment systems for special or expensive items on a pass-through basis.

Chapter 3 discusses healthcare charges and charge-based reimbursement. Healthcare costs and charges have become rather contentious issues over the last decade. Charge-based reimbursement and cost-based reimbursement are actually closely related, presuming that healthcare providers establish their charges based on their costs.

Contractual payment is generally a combination of several different types of payment processes or systems. Healthcare providers and payers often enter into contractual arrangements. Chapter 4 provides a discussion of some of the features and pitfalls with these contractual arrangements.

Chapter 5 discusses a very different type of payment system, namely, capitation. Capitated payment involves a healthcare payer making fixed payments in advance. The payments are often made on a per member per month arrangement, with payments on a per capita or per head basis. A significant paradigm change occurs with capitation in that the risk for excessive services is transferred from the payer to the healthcare provider.

The operational implementation of a healthcare payment system lies in the processing of claims and the determination of payment. Chapter 6 delves into some of the intricacies involved with adjudication of claims. The adjudication process often involves rather complicated logic structures that are programmed into the healthcare payers' claims-processing systems. Whenever there are complex logical constructs used to adjudicate claims, compliance becomes an issue. Payment system interfaces have been discussed throughout this series of texts. An additional payment system interface involves secondary payer issues. For Medicare, a separate effort in this area is the MSP or Medicare secondary payer program.

Chapter 7 briefly discusses where healthcare payment systems are headed in the future. This is a very dynamic area with constant change. Currently, there are very clear attempts to ensure the quality of healthcare while reducing overall costs on the part of healthcare payers.

An appendix is provided that outlines the various Medicare payment systems. References to the previous three books in this series are also provided.

Enjoy the Technicalities

This book addresses what most would consider as technical, convoluted, and boring. Granted, the *Federal Register* entries from CMS are not always scintillating, but make the process fun by looking for inconsistencies and obtuse and sometimes misleading language in the various rules and regulations. Also, reading contracts that establish contractual payment processes is not always that interesting until you realize that significant financial and medical care issues are at stake.

Watch for the definitions. Often, words are used and phrases are invented that are never really defined. Discussing any topic without having precise definitions is a misunderstanding waiting to happen. Also, watch for words like *clarification* and *restatement* as opposed to *changes* in rules and regulations.

Look for words like *believe*. What are people allowed to believe? Basically, anything! This word is often used when an individual does not know something for certain; the person simply thinks it is true or might be true. Is it not interesting how often this word appears in the *Federal Register*?

This book, and the other three books in this Healthcare Payment Systems series, is intended for anyone who is interested in learning more about the specific systems and processes that are used to make (or not) payment for healthcare services. Thus, this text is for motivated laypersons along with those who are entering the healthcare field or find themselves in healthcare without a reasonable understanding of how healthcare payment systems actually work. The one most important guiding factor is that healthcare payment processes are constantly changing and evolving. This is a dynamic area. Be prepared to be surprised every day as changes occur.

Duane C. Abbey, Ph.D.
Ames, Iowa

About the Author

Duane C. Abbey, Ph.D., CFP, is a management consultant and president of Abbey & Abbey Consultants, Inc. Based in Ames, Iowa, Abbey & Abbey specializes in healthcare consulting and related areas.

Dr. Abbey, whose work in healthcare now spans more than 25 years, earned his graduate degrees at the University of Notre Dame and Iowa State University. Today, he spends about half of his time developing and teaching workshops (for students who affectionately quip that the *Federal Register* is his favorite reading material) and making presentations to professional organizations. He devotes the other half to consulting work that involves performing chargemaster reviews, compliance reviews, providing litigation support, and conducting reimbursement studies.

Dr. Abbey also uses his mathematical and financial background to perform financial assessments, develop complex financial models, and conduct various types of statistical work. His studies in the field of neurolinguistic programming have enhanced his ability to provide organizational communication facilitation services for healthcare organizations. He also provides litigation support services for attorneys representing healthcare providers in legal proceedings.

Dr. Abbey can be contacted by e-mail at Duane@aaciweb.com. The main website for his company is at http://www.aaciweb.com.

Chapter 1

Introduction

Preliminary Comments

Fee schedule payment systems and prospective payment systems (PPSs) are addressed in the second and third books in the *Healthcare Payment Systems* series. We now address a number of other types of payment systems, including cost-based and charge-based payment. In actual practice, third-party payers tend to integrate multiple approaches for healthcare payment. These different payment mechanisms are included in various contracts that are established between the third-party payer and the healthcare providers. As with previous payment systems that we have addressed, these are classified fee-for-service payment; that is, payment is made based on the services provided. Fee for service means the greater the volume and complexity of services, the greater the payment on the part of the healthcare payer.

Capitated payment systems represent a paradigm shift in thinking. The amount that the healthcare provider receives is fixed in advance; typically, the payment is on a monthly basis for each covered individual. The healthcare provider addresses medical issues that the covered individuals may need. If a covered individual needs no services, then the monthly payment is mostly profit. For capitated payment, the more services that are provided, the less likely there will be any profits. This means that the risk for excessive services shifts from the payer who is making the monthly payments to the healthcare provider who is providing necessary services. Capitated payment systems have developed more slowly than anticipated over the last several decades. While there are probably many reasons for this slow growth, a major reason has to be that healthcare providers (e.g., hospitals, clinics, physicians, etc.) do not know what kinds of risks are being assumed in such capitated arrangements. The knowledge of incidence of services for various populations is in the domain of insurance companies and other private payers.

Private payers often establish contractual arrangements with those healthcare providers in those areas where the payer's covered individuals are located. We use the term *managed care contracts* for these situations. Our focus is mainly on the payment mechanisms in the contracts as opposed to the management of care, although these two issues merge to some extent. Now, these contracts are not actually payment systems in and of themselves, but they tend to use various payment mechanisms that must be carefully integrated. One of the main issues with these payment contracts is that both parties must fully understand their benefits and obligations. Because there are various payment systems, sometimes unique payment mechanisms, being utilized, coding, billing and claims filing becomes important. Often, these contracts are relatively brief and do not contain explicit coding and billing guidance. The specific guidance may be in companion manuals or sometimes the guidance can be accessed through the private payers' websites.

Review of Healthcare Payment Systems

Many innovative approaches have been developed to pay for healthcare services. The general objective of healthcare payment systems is to reimburse healthcare providers appropriately for services provided. Given the tremendous growth in expenditures for healthcare services, the mechanisms for payment must be designed to properly pay for such services. While healthcare providers complain about inappropriately low payments, conversely healthcare payers claim that there are significant overpayments. Thus, healthcare payment systems must be designed to provide proper payment for necessary services.

Today, most healthcare payment is based on what is termed *fee for service*. In other words, the third-party payer reimburses the healthcare provider based on the services provided. Presumptively, the services provided were medically necessary, ordered by a physician, performed by qualified personnel, and so on. Note that on a fee-for-service basis, the more services that are provided, the more the third-party payer will pay out for the services.

Healthcare payment based on *capitation* is diametrically the opposite of fee for service. With capitation, the risk moves to the healthcare provider from the third-party payer. The basic idea is that the healthcare provider receives a fixed payment and then provides whatever services are required. The fixed payment is often on a per member per month (PMPM) basis for each covered individual. This payment is made regardless of the number and type of healthcare services required. If more services than anticipated occur, then the healthcare provider will probably incur a loss. If the demand for services is low, then the healthcare provider will make a profit.

The oldest and most fundamental healthcare payment system is cost-based reimbursement. For a third-party payer (e.g., insurance company or Medicare) to reimburse for services on a cost basis, the healthcare provider's costs must be known. This is not an easy task. The Medicare program uses a complicated cost-reporting process to determine costs. Obviously, there are differences of opinion regarding which costs are allowable. Also, there is a significant overhead cost for developing a cost report and then auditing the cost report to make certain that there is no overreporting of costs. The cycle to fully develop, audit, and settle a cost report takes three to four years.

One step removed from cost-based payment is charge-based payment. With this approach, the healthcare provider is generally paid a percentage of whatever is charged or in some cases the allowed charge. Typical percentages range from about 70 percent on up to 95 percent. An underlying, often unstated, principle is that the charges are presumed to consistently reflect the costs incurred by the healthcare provider.

Fee schedule payment systems tend to use highly delineated classifications of services provided or items dispensed. The basic idea is that if you have a code set that describes the various services, then a payment rate can be attached to each of the services in the classification system. Probably the best known, and most complex, fee schedule payment system is the Medicare

Physician Fee Schedule (MPFS). This fee schedule payment system uses a combination of CPT® (Current Procedural Terminology) and HCPCS (Healthcare Common Procedure Coding System). Other examples of fee schedule payment are the Ambulance Fee Schedule (AFS) and a fee schedule for DME (durable medical equipment). See the companion book, *Fee Schedule Payment System*, for a more detailed discussion.

Prospective payment systems, which are discussed in the companion book *Prospective Payment Systems*, were developed to help contain healthcare costs. For prospective payment, payment rates are fixed in advance, generally for the period of a year. Each year, adjustments in the payment rates can be made based on predetermined processes that involve costs and resource utilization. The most complex and common PPSs are the Medicare MS-DRGs (Medicare Severity Diagnosis Related Groups) for hospital inpatient services and APCs (Ambulatory Payment Classifications) for hospital outpatient services.

There are many different approaches to healthcare payment. A few of the major systems have been mentioned. In some cases, a third-party payer may contract with a healthcare provider and use a combination of approaches depending on the specific types of services provided. Thus, healthcare providers enter into contractual arrangements to provide services and then receive payment. While the nomenclature is not really accurate, these contracts are often referred to as managed care contracts. In some cases, the third-party payer does manage care (e.g., medical necessity, frequency limitation, surgery preauthorization), but in other cases these managed care contracts involve primarily payment mechanisms.

Using a fee-for-service approach, a healthcare provider must file a claim for services provided or items supplied. The claim is then adjudicated by the third-party payer, and payment is made through a reimbursement process. For fee-for-service payment systems, there are two main processes that must occur:

- Claim adjudication
- Payment calculation

For example, with PPSs, claims are basically adjudicated through a *grouper*. Then, the information generated by the grouper goes through what is called the *pricer*. Both the grouper and pricer are embedded in computer software. Other fee-for-service payment systems also use computer software to adjudicate claims. The logic in all these systems can become quite complex.

Claims Filing and Payment

As discussed in *Healthcare Payment Systems: An Introduction*,* there are numerous mechanisms for providing payment to healthcare providers. While the simplest involves having the patient pay directly for the services, often there is a third party involved. In other words, the third party makes the payment or some portion of the payment on behalf of the patient. The most typical example of this is with health and accident insurance. However, there are many different types of third-party payers, including liability insurance when accidents are involved. Another example is when a third-party administrator makes payment from some sort of trust fund.

When third parties become involved, including cases in which there may be more than one third-party payer, there must be a mechanism to request payment and then a way for the third-party

---

* See *Healthcare Payment Systems: An Introduction*, Duane C. Abbey (CRC Press, Boca Raton, FL, 2009, ISBN 978-1-4200-9277-6).

payer to make payment. Requests for payment are made through a claims-filing process. There are two main claim forms for healthcare:

- Professional claims: 1500 or CMS-1500 for the Medicare program
- Technical claims: UB-04 or CMS-1450 for the Medicare program

The acronym *UB* stands for *Universal Billing,* and the 04 refers to the year that the last major update to the form was made, in this case, 2004. Professional claims are typically associated with physicians and practitioner services. The technical or facility claims are associated with facilities such as hospitals, nursing facilities, home health, and the like.

While both of these forms exist in paper format, today these claims are typically developed through a more extensive computer-based process. Thus, we have the HIPAA 837-P and 837-I formats. The *P* stands for *professional,* and *I* stands for *institutional.* HIPAA refers to the Health Insurance Portability and Accountability Act of 1996. Within HIPAA was a congressional directive to move healthcare into the realm of electronic data interchange or EDI. From time to time in this book, we will refer to the HIPAA TSC or Transaction Standard/Standard Code Set rule. Implementation of the HIPAA mandate in this area has resulted in extensive development of forms, formats, and various code sets that are used to describe healthcare services and file claims for payment.

Healthcare providers code and file claims in standardized ways so that various third-party payers can provide payment by adjudicating and processing the claims. This is the point at which healthcare payment systems become involved.

There are literally hundreds of different mechanisms for providing payment for healthcare services. Among the systems are cost-based and charge-based reimbursement. Also, contracted payment may involve the use of several integrated payment systems. Whatever the case, claims must be developed and adjudicated by the payer. Thus, there must be some type of standard way to develop the claims so that the claims can be correctly adjudicated and paid.

Of course, there are some complicating factors that come into play. First, there must be some uniform way in which to describe the services provided or the items dispensed. This raises the need to develop a *classification system* for services and items. Generally, this involves developing a set of codes that can be used to describe services and items. In turn, the code set must have coherence for accurately describing services and items. When we have a coding system, a process is then needed to translate the services into the appropriate code or codes. This involves the process of *coding.* If the coding system is complex, then the process of coding becomes complex. Specially trained personnel are needed and the propriety of the codes can generate compliance concerns.

Particularly, for some of the more recent PPSs, the classification of services involves acuity levels that are determined from some sort of patient assessment instrument (PAI). These assessment instruments are lengthy and involved. The information from the PAI is then used to determine a code that represents the acuity level or level of service. Due to the detail and complexity of these forms, the key data is input to a computer program, which then determines the proper code.

Assuming that services can be properly classified, then second there must be some way to determine the proper amount to pay for a service provided or items dispensed as described through the code set. Should payment be based on costs? Resources utilized? Skill level? Effort? Risk? The list of ways to determine the payment amounts can become rather extensive.

The third concern can be the most complicated. A basic question that arises is whether every service provided or item dispensed should be separately paid. This takes us into the whole area of what we call the *adjudication logic.* The logical constructs used in adjudicating claims under PPSs can, and do, become enormously complex. Even simple encounters at a hospital can raise questions about appropriate payment.

The short case studies are used throughout this book to illustrate how decisions must be made relative to separate payment versus bundling payments in various ways.

Case Study 1.1: Emergency Department Visit Involving Finger Splint

An individual has presented to a hospital's emergency department (ED) after twisting the right index finger. The emergency room (ER) physician performs a general examination to make certain there are no other problems except for the twisted finger. The physician examines the finger. Routine laboratory tests are performed just for safety. Based on x-rays, there is no fracture, only a sprain, so the physician applies a finger splint to protect the finger during the healing process. The patient is discharged home with a supply of analgesics for pain control.

Case Study 1.1 is an outpatient hospital encounter. There are two different claims that will be filed: one for the physician or professional component (i.e., 1500 claim) and then one for the hospital, which is the technical component (i.e., UB-04 claim). Technically, this is what is called a *provider-based* situation. The physician claim form will be adjudicated and, most likely, paid under some sort of fee schedule payment system. For the Medicare program, this will be the MPFS. The hospital claim is on an outpatient basis, and most likely a PPS will be used. For Medicare, this will be APCs. The claim will involve charges for drugs, routine supplies, the finger splint, laboratory, the x-ray of the finger, the application of the finger splint, and the resources utilized for the examination of the patient by both the physician and the nursing staff.

Note: Because this was an ED encounter, a general medical screening examination (MSE) is required by EMTALA (Emergency Medical Treatment and Labor Act). Payment for MSE for both the physician and the hospital can sometimes be problematic.

For Case Study 1.1, we know how the Medicare program will adjudicate and pay for these services. What about other private payers? The simple fact is that other private payers may approach adjudication and payment in vastly different ways. While fee schedules are common for physician services, there are other methods, including some sort of flat payment amount for different levels of ED encounters. Also, the adjudication logic may pay separately for the evaluation and management services and the therapeutic service (i.e., application of the finger splint). A different private payer may decide that payment for the evaluation and management is to be bundled into payment for the splint. In the meantime, another private payer may decide that the application of the splint is really a part of the evaluation and management service.

Thus, there may be different payment mechanisms, and even within a single payment approach, there may be significantly different payment rules. The same situation occurs on the hospital, or technical component, side for these services. For hospital outpatient services, Medicare uses a PPS, namely APCs, while private third-party payers may approach payment in very different ways. For instance, a given private payer may decide to pay 85 percent of the hospital outpatient charges. Of course, the claims may have to be adjudicated to make certain that all the services are medically necessary, and there may even some bundling of services so that the charges may be reduced based on the adjudication logic.

Note: The way in which a private payer adjudicates claims may give rise to the hospital, in this case, altering the way claims are developed and charged. If, in the previous discussion, the payer drops the evaluation and management service and pays only for the application of the finger splint, then the hospital may alter the claim so that both the charges appear under the application of the finger splint.

Deductibles and Copayments

Almost all third-party payers, including Medicare, use deductibles and copayments as part of their overall payment process. Generally, deductibles and copayment do not directly enter into the adjudication of claims using various payment systems. After the payment amount is calculated, then any deductibles or copayments are removed from the payment that is made by the third-party payer. The individual receiving the services is liable for the deductible and any copayments that might apply. In some cases, there are special supplemental insurance policies that cover items such as deductibles and copayments. In addition, some individuals will have more than one health insurance policy. Having multiple policies gives rise to another complicated area referred to as *coordination of benefits*.

Note that the two terms *coinsurance* and *copayment* may be different depending on the third-party payer involved. Coinsurance generally refers to the percentage of the payment determined after adjudicating the claim, which constitutes the copayment. While this is a little convoluted, the coinsurance is a percentage, while the copayment is an actual dollar amount.

In this text, the deductible and copayment concepts are addressed only on a cursory basis. Only if there is something unusual will these processes be raised. Similarly, coordination of benefits, which can become quite complex, is addressed in Chapter 6. For the Medicare program, there are major compliance concerns because Medicare is often secondary, but Medicare may often end up being the primary payer.

> **Case Study 1.2: Injured While Visiting a Neighbor**
>
> Sarah was visiting one of her neighbors in the middle of the winter. Upon leaving the neighbor's house, she slipped on the steps and fell. She made it back home, but several hours later she was experiencing significant pain, and an ambulance was called. She was taken to the Apex Medical Center and admitted with a fractured hip. The ambulance report indicated that she fell on her steps.

At issue in Case Study 1.2 is the fact that Sarah's medical coverage, Medicare or otherwise, will be treated as the primary payer. Based on the facts briefly described in the case study, the neighbor's property and casualty insurance is actually primary. In this case, there would probably be a payment from the medical payments portion of the policy, with the main liability residing with the liability coverage. Medicare and other health insurance carriers are very sensitive to these secondary-payer situations. Thus, when considering whether a given individual is covered, there is also the question of whether the given insurance policy is primary, or secondary or tertiary for that matter.

Fee Schedule Payment Systems

Fee schedule payment systems use a detailed classification system for services provided or items dispensed. The classification generally involves some sort of coding system. Payment is made for each of the classifications according to the fee schedule. Of course, there is still the process of taking a claim through the adjudication logic. In some cases, there may be reduced payment for a given classification based on other services. For example, if two surgical procedures are performed, then the higher-paying service is paid at 100 percent of the fee schedule. However, the second (or third or fourth) surgical procedure may be paid at only 50 percent. This is called *discounting*.

The calculation of fee schedule payment may also include bundling of services. Two related services may be provided, with only one of the services being paid. The payment for the other service is bundled into the payment for the first service.

One of the major issues with fee schedule payment is the determination of the payment rate. Third-party payers using fee schedule payment generally try to base the payment on the cost or resources utilized. For private payers, this is often the UCR or usual, customary, and reasonable payment amount. Needless to say, there can be significant differences of opinion regarding what the UCR amount should be.

Fee schedule payment systems are discussed in the companion book *Fee Schedule Payment Systems*.

Prospective Payment Systems

Prospective payment systems represent the most complicated payment systems in use. The Medicare program has led the way in developing several different PPSs. Private payers often use the Medicare-developed PPSs by piggybacking onto them along with possible modifications. Prospective payment involves some sort of classification system. The classification can be a highly detailed coding system or a data-driven PAI. The results from the classification are then grouped into categories, which are then processed for payment.

One of the hallmarks of PPSs is that there is a great deal of bundling. While multiple services may be provided, these services may all ultimately be grouped into a single category for payment. Thus, payment for a given category is an averaged payment. The healthcare provider may receive a payment that is higher than costs, or the payment may be lower than the provider's costs. In theory, the payment amount should average out over a range of services in the given category.

The use of prospective payment has grown significantly in the last two decades. The reason for the popularity of this approach is that the payers have more control of the overall payments being made. In most cases, the total payments made by a healthcare payer can be adjusted by changing a single number, namely, the conversion factor. Due to the significant bundling that occurs in these systems, there is an incentive for the providers to be as efficient as possible in the provision of services.

Prospective payment systems are addressed in the companion book, *Prospective Payment Systems*.

Cost-Based Payment Systems

Cost-based payment is discussed in this book. The basic idea is simple: The payer simply pays the healthcare provider based on the cost of providing a service. The amount paid is generally on a cost-plus basis, that is, a percentage somewhat over 100 percent. For instance, the payment might be set at 110 percent of the cost for the service. This allows for some profit margin on the part of the healthcare provider.

Cost-based reimbursement can be provided at significantly different levels. This type of payment system may be used on a macro basis, which can provide payment for a wide range of services. This approach is used with critical access hospitals (CAHs). There is also a micro level; specific services and items may be paid individually on a cost basis. This micro approach for cost-based reimbursement is used in virtually all payment systems. For instance, there may be a particularly expensive drug or unusual device in use. The payment for these unusual items is carved out from the main payment approach, and a cost-based payment is applied.

To use cost-based reimbursement, at least at a macro level, two mechanisms must be established:

1. Determining the costs for providing healthcare services
2. A way to pay for services, possibly on an interim basis, until the true costs are known

Determining the overall costs incurred by a provider in furnishing healthcare services is typically accomplished through a cost-reporting process. Because there is a delay in developing cost reports, an interim payment mechanism is needed. One approach to the interim payment is to pay a percentage of the charges (i.e., the interim rate) until the cost report can be settled.

The challenges for cost-based payment are discussed in Chapter 2.

Case Study 1.3: Expensive Pacemakers

The Maximus Insurance Company (MIC) uses a variety of payment mechanisms for its health insurance products. An area of great concern is the increasing number of pacemaker insertions. There seems great variability in the costs and associated charges for these items. As a result, Maximus has decided to carve out these items and pay them on a cost plus 10-percent basis.

Case Study 1.3 is an example of a micro approach to cost-based reimbursement. There will be some operational challenges. Maximus, in its contracts or other billing requirements, will have to require the hospital, ambulatory surgery center (ASC), or clinic to bill the actual costs of the pacemakers. On a postpayment audit basis, Maximus may require the healthcare provider to keep receipts for costs. In some cases, the receipts may have to be filed with the claim.

Charge-Based Payment Systems

Charge-based payment is one step removed from cost-based reimbursement. Healthcare providers generally develop their charges based on their cost of providing services or the cost of items provided. While there can be significant variability in the way charges are developed, the presumptions is that the charges are consistently based on costs.

As an example, hospitals typically have what is called a *chargemaster*. Different names may be used, such as charge description master (CDM) or service master. This document is actually sometimes a huge file that lists all of the charges for services, supplies, drugs, and the like. Because there are many different hospital service areas and because there are different philosophical approaches to designing and developing a chargemaster, the presumption that the charges are consistently based on costs can certainly be questioned.

The payer that uses charge-based payment will typically pay a percentage of the charges. In the simplest approach, a percentage such as 80 percent might be adopted. Thus, the payer will simply pay the stated percentage of whatever the healthcare provider charges. In some cases, there may be different percentages paid for different types of services or items provided.

Case Study 1.4: Supply Item Payment

The Maximus Insurance Company uses charge-based reimbursement with hospital services. While the general percentage payment rate is 80 percent of the charges, there are a number of special categories in which different percentages are paid. For instance, routine, sterile supply items are paid only at 50 percent, while expensive implantable devices are paid at 90 percent.

In Case Study 1.4, Maximus recognizes that hospitals tend to mark up routine supplies items more than they mark up expensive implantable devices. Thus, a different percentage is paid for these two categories of items.*

---

* The process is not that difficult because there are different revenue codes (RCs) that are used in hospital charge-masters to describe these items. These revenue codes appear on the claims.

Charge-based payment can be used with virtually all types of healthcare providers, although the percentages that are used may vary considerably.

Note: Charge-based payment is often used with hospitals. Compliance issues are raised in using the charge-based approach. If a hospital is willing to accept, say, 85 percent of its charges as full payment, does this mean that the 85-percent payment level can be imputed to be their charges? On the surface, this appears almost a ridiculous interpretation, but the OIG (Office of the Inspector General) has discussed this possible interpretation.*

Capitation Payment Systems

Capitated payment is a major shift from the many different kinds of fee-for-service payment systems in use today. Normally, the risk of increased payments due to increases in services provided lies with the insurance company or third-party payer. With capitation, the location or locus of risk shifts to the healthcare provider. Unfortunately, healthcare providers need some way to assess the risk that they are assuming in agreeing to a capitated payment arrangement. Generally, healthcare providers do not have extensive historic data on the relative incidences of services for various types of populations that might be under such an arrangement.

Conceptually, the idea of capitation is fairly simple. The healthcare provider receives a fixed, generally PMPM payment. The healthcare provider then provides any services that might be necessary. If few services are needed, the capitated payment is basically profit. However, if significant services are required, then the cost of providing these services may outstrip the capitated payment significantly. When more services must be provided than anticipated, there can be significant financial risk.

Capitated payment arrangements tend to become quite complicated. This is particularly true if there is a range of different services provided, such as for an integrated delivery system (IDS). Hospital services along with primary care physicians and specialty physicians might all need to be addressed. Different assumptions for volumes of services or extraordinary situations must be considered. Stopgaps for an unusually expensive situation may create the need for special reinsurance or risk pools.

Contractual Payment Systems

Using the phrase *contractual payment system* is a misnomer. What is being referenced is the fact that private third-party payers, such as insurance companies, establish payment mechanisms through contractual arrangements. The contracts that are established generally involve more than one type of payment system. At the very least, there may be a main approach with exceptions or with special payment features. Contracts also tend to contain many provisions concerning billing and filing claims.

Case Study 1.5: Contracting for Surgical Services

The Maximus Insurance Company routinely establishes contracts with surgeons in the geographic areas where they have coverage. The main approach is a fee schedule using CPT for surgical services and attendant hospital and clinic visits. However, there is an extensive global surgical package that encompasses all services provided one week before the surgery and then for 60 days after the surgery.

---

* For instance, see the September 15, 2003, *Federal Register* (68 FR 53939).

Maximus will also have numerous provisions in the contract relative to timely claims filing, proper coding, preauthorization requirements, and the like.

The phrase *managed care contracts* will also be used. There are many different aspects to these contracts, which may also involve management-of-care and quality-of-care concerns. We are interested primarily in the payment aspects of these contracts. Of particular interest is the process of using various combinations of different payment systems.

Keep in mind that healthcare providers often file claims when there is no contract with a third-party payer. In these cases, there are default requirements generally through state laws, including the uniform commercial code or UCC. Also, the HIPAA TSC places requirements on overall claims development and processing. However, if there is no contractual relationship, the amount of reimbursement that a healthcare provider will receive can be highly variable and may be based on unknown claims adjudication processes.

Healthcare Provider Concepts

The number and type of healthcare providers is significant and continues to grow, as does the general provision of healthcare services. Healthcare payment systems of all types must be designed for use by the providers themselves as well as the specific types of services. Because we will be discussing several different payment approaches and various contractual arrangements, virtually every type of healthcare provider may be included. While our focus is on individuals and organizations that actually file claims and receive reimbursement, there are other healthcare providers that are not directly reimbursed for services. These providers are typically employees of healthcare organizations. For instance, nurses, medical assistants, technicians, phlebotomists, pharmacists, and many others are involved in providing healthcare, but it is their employing organization that is reimbursed.

We briefly discuss the general classes of healthcare providers, starting with individuals such as physicians and various practitioners. These individuals can establish solo practices, typically using a business structure of the sole proprietor. Moving from the individual healthcare provider that is reimbursed, we have various size organizations that extend to nationwide systems of hospitals and large IDSs. Note that business structuring can also become quite complex.

Note: As is often the case, terminology must be carefully studied when considering different types of healthcare providers. For the Medicare program, the two words *provider* and *supplier* have formal definitions that are different from common usage. Billing privileges for Medicare are gained by filing appropriate CMS-855 forms and following the rules generally found at 42 CFR §424. The word *provider* refers to organizations that have provider agreements with Medicare, such as hospitals and skilled nursing facilities (SNFs). Most other healthcare providers are classified as *suppliers*. Thus, physicians are classified as suppliers and not providers. This certainly goes against the grain of common usage. Take care to understand the context of any discussion or guidance because terminology differences can significantly influence the understanding of a particular situation.

Business structuring complexity leads to significant requirements on the part of payment systems, particularly the interface between payment systems that are reimbursing for different kinds of services or to different types of organizations. Contractual payment systems must also address the issue of different kinds of healthcare services within differing business structures. While we will discuss various types of payment arrangements, a full discussion of all the possible payment arrangements even for a modest IDS is well beyond the scope of this text.

However, third-party payers may use comprehensive contracts that do address various types of services. We concentrate on individual payment system interfaces. For example, in the previous books in this series that address fee schedule payment systems and PPSs, we discussed the concept of provider-based clinics under the Medicare program and the interface between hospital outpatient payment and physician fee schedule payment. This same type of issue may arise with private payers as well, particularly if they recognize the Medicare concept of a provider-based clinic as opposed to recognizing only freestanding clinic operations.

We start our discussions at the individual practitioner level and then work up to more complex organizations. Keep in mind that for all payment systems for which there is any sort of a contractual arrangement, there is the issue of credentialing the practitioners or associated organizations. There are two aspects for credentialing:

■ Clinical credentialing
■ Billing credentialing

Billing credentialing is a process of a third-party payer accepting the credentials of a healthcare provider to bill the given third-party payer and be reimbursed for the services. This aspect of credentialing still involves clinical requirements, but for payment we are more concerned with billing and reimbursement aspects of credentialing. For instance, a clinical nurse specialist (CNS) is a practitioner recognized by the Medicare program for separate payment for certain services. Private third-party payers may not recognize this type of practitioner for separate billing and reimbursement.

Physicians

For the Medicare program, the word *physician* is used only for two categories:

1. MDs (medical doctors) or allopathic physicians
2. DOs (doctors of osteopathy) or osteopathic physicians

Where does this leave categories such as chiropractors, podiatrists, optometrists, and clinical psychologists? These individuals hold doctorates and are licensed through state laws, but are they considered physicians? The simple answer, at least for Medicare, is no. Typically, there are limitations on the scope of practice for these other designations. However, the word *practitioner* may be applied to all of these individuals. Be careful with physicians; sometimes they may take offense at being referred to as a practitioner because this can carry the connotation of something less than a physician.

This may seem an innocuous issue, but the distinction can become important. For instance, under the Medicare rules and regulations, physician supervision may be a requirement for certain services. In other cases, hospital services, particularly for payment purposes, must be incident to a physician's service. Can anyone other than an MD or DO meet the physician supervision requirement or incident-to requirement?*

Generally, physicians are paid through fee schedule arrangements for Medicare and most other private third-party payers. This includes chiropractors, podiatrists, optometrists, and clinical

---

* Incident-to and physician supervision requirements are Medicare requirements. See the provider-based rule at 42 CFR §413.65 to investigate current rules and regulations. A major issue for physician supervision is qualifying a nonphysician practitioner to meet the physician supervision requirement.

psychologists, among others. However, there are instances when physicians and practitioners are paid based on charges or other arrangements. Physicians are often included in various types of capitation contracts. Also, over the years the concept of combining physician and hospital reimbursement into a single package, possibly for surgical procedures, has been raised. At this time, physicians and practitioners are generally paid separately from any sort of global facilities payment.

Nonphysician Practitioners and Providers

For the very large number of healthcare providers who do not hold doctorates, the general term *nonphysician provider* is used. This category includes nurses, medical assistants, radiology technicians, and physical therapists, and a long list can be developed. Even within the classification of a nurse, there can be many different types of nurses and associated specialty certifications. Some nurses have gained doctorates in nursing, so be careful with the terminology particularly as it relates to payment for healthcare services.

Important subsets of nonphysician providers are the *nonphysician practitioners*. Using the word *practitioner* implies that the individual can gain billing privileges from the Medicare program and, theoretically, from other third-party payers. Thus, practitioners can file claims, and separate reimbursement can be gained. As with physicians, nonphysician practitioners must be credentialed to provide services and to gain billing privileges.

However, a given practitioner may be employed and the employer may choose not to file claims separately for the practitioner.

> **Case Study 1.6: Clinical Nurse Specialist versus Nurse Practitioner**
>
> The Apex Medical Center employs a clinical nurse specialist (CNS) who is devoted to oncology services. The CNS works closely with specialty physicians in providing oncology services. Apex has decided not to file professional claims for the CNS. However, there is a nurse practitioner (NP) who works in two different provider-based clinics, and Apex has decided to file professional claims for the NP.

The decision in Case Study 1.6 is not necessarily related to the two different types of NPPs (nonphysician providers/practitioners). The decision is based on the fact that professional billing and filing claims for qualified NPPs is optional. In this case, both the CNS and NP are employed by Apex, a hospital. The difference in choosing to file claims or not will have an effect on the hospital's cost report. For instance, if a professional claim is not filed for the practitioner's services, then the cost of employing the practitioner will be included in the hospital's cost report. The converse is true; that is, if there is professional billing, then the practitioner's cost to the hospital will not be on the cost report.

> **Case Study 1.7: Critical Access Hospital Use of Nurse Practitioner**
>
> Critical access hospitals are cost-based reimbursed for Medicare. Two nurse practitioners (NPs) are employed by the hospital basically as hospitalists to provide various types of services throughout the hospital. The decision has been made not to bill separately for these services but to allow payment for their services to be made through the cost-based reimbursement.

While the facts in Case Study 1.7 seem fairly simple, there are many more questions and considerations that lie below the surface of this case study. Presumably, this CAH addresses mainly Medicare patients with relatively few non-Medicare cases. Also, a careful cost-benefit study should be conducted to determine which arrangement (i.e., bill separately vs. not bill separately) will generate the greater reimbursement. In Chapter 2, for CAHs we discuss what is called Method II reimbursement, which provides for even greater reimbursement for physicians and practitioners for outpatient services through professional billing on the hospital claims.

The listing of qualified NPPs can and does vary depending on the specific context of various rules and regulations, particularly from the Medicare program. For instance, a listing of qualified NPPs for providing telemedicine services may be different from the NPPs who qualify for separate reimbursement. The most common NPPs qualified for separate reimbursement are:

- Nurse practitioners
- Clinical nurse specialists
- Physician assistants
- Clinical psychologists
- Clinical social workers
- Nurse midwives

On a limited basis, this list can be augmented by qualified individuals providing medical nutrition therapy (MNT), diabetes self-management training (DSMT), and kidney disease education (KDE). In the anesthesia area, there are also CRNAs (certified registered nurse anesthetists) who can be separately paid under certain circumstances.

As with physicians, if qualified NPPs decide to file claims or have claims filed for them, their payment usually derives from a fee schedule, whether from Medicare or some other third-party payer. While the process for credentialing for billing purposes is well defined in the Medicare program, gaining billing privileges from private third-party payers can be challenging.

Note: When it comes to payment, the world of nonphysician practitioners is quite dynamic. Over time, more and more practitioners are moving into the realm of being able to receive reimbursement and file claims, or have claims filed on their behalf, for professional services. For instance, RNFAs, registered nurse first assistants, provide surgical support services. Such support services are separately payable for certain surgeries to other practitioners, such as physician assistants and NPs. In time, RNFAs will probably be recognized for such professional reimbursement.

Case Study 1.8: Nurse Practitioner and Clinical Nurse Specialist

Among other practitioners, the Apex Medical Center employs both a nurse practitioner (NP) and a clinical nurse specialist (CNS). The CNS works in the hospital's cancer center, while the NP provides outpatient clinical services. Apex is in a quandary because its largest private third-party payer recognizes the CNS for separate billing but does not recognize the NP for separate billing and claims filing.

Case Study 1.8 illustrates the fact that certain midlevel practitioners may or may not be recognized for separate reimbursement. While the Medicare program has gone to significant lengths to delineate which nonphysician practitioners are recognized for separate payment and the process by which they are to be paid, many private payers may or may not choose to recognize these practitioners for separate payment. For healthcare providers such as hospitals and clinics, the inclusion of separate professional payment can be an issue when negotiating contracts.

Clinics

The word *clinic* can be variously interpreted, resulting in confusion unless the context of the discussion is well defined. Almost everyone is familiar with the doctor's office where physicians, and possibly qualified NPPs, provide services. The most common example is a physically freestanding office arrangement where patients come to seek services. This is typically an example of a *freestanding clinic*. Sometimes, the fact that these clinics are physician based will also be emphasized.

Another type of clinic is the *provider-based clinic*. This is a Medicare concept that has significant payment implications. A provider-based clinic is owned and fully integrated into a main provider, which is generally a hospital.* For a hospital to have and operate a clinic as provider based, a number of criteria must be achieved as delineated in the *Code of Federal Regulations*, namely, 42 CFR §413.65. The financial advantage for provider-based clinics is that two claim forms are filed:

1. The 1500 Claim Form for Professional Services
2. The UB-04 Claim Form for Technical Component Services

The Medicare program recognizes provider-based clinics and pays for the services in a provider-based clinic differently from freestanding clinics. For Medicare, the main provider, typically a hospital, is paid, and then the physician payment is reduced.† Some private third-party payers may also recognize provider-based clinics. In these cases, a careful check must be made to determine just how payment is made.

Be careful with the use of the freestanding clinic terminology. This may appear as a physically distinguishing characteristic, but the difference between freestanding and provider based is actually a logical or organizational distinction, not a physical location distinction. Consider the following case study:

Case Study 1.9: Freestanding Clinic inside the Apex Medical Center

A new internal medicine physician has come to Anywhere, USA. The physician wants to start an independent practice. The Apex Medical Center offers to rent space to the new physician and the rent includes nursing and clerical staff. A suite of offices and examination rooms is provided on the third floor of the hospital.

In Case Study 1.9, the physician will file, or possibly the hospital will file for the physician, only 1500 claim forms with place of service (POS) as "11" for physician office. Even though the clinic is located inside the hospital, due to the fact that the physician pays rent, this clinic is the physician's office for billing purposes.

Case Study 1.10: Hospital-Owned and -Operated Clinics

The Apex Medical Center has acquired two different family practice clinics, both of which are about 20 miles away in opposite directions. Apex decides to operate one of the clinics as provider-based by filing two different claims, one for the professional and one for the technical component. Due to competitive pressures, the other clinic is operated as a freestanding clinic and files only the 1500.

---

* Technically, a Medicare provider can establish provider-based facilities such as clinics. Thus, an SNF could establish provider-based clinics.
† This is the Medicare site-of-service (SOS) differential.

Most likely, both of these clinics meet all of the provider-based requirements. However, Apex can choose to operate one of the clinics as freestanding, while the other is treated as provider based. Billing for the two clinics will be distinctly different, with the POS adjusted based on the type of clinic.

Note: Watch for additional distinctions that the Centers for Medicare and Medicaid Services (CMS) may make with freestanding clinics. There have been some hints of differentiating physician-owned freestanding clinics from hospital-owned freestanding clinics.* You may also see the phrase *physician clinic,* which would seem to imply physician ownership, but this phrase may simply indicate that only a 1500 claim form is filed.

While the word *clinic* generally implies physician services, various practitioners, if allowed by state law, can establish independent practices. A group of physical therapists may establish an independent physical therapy practice, including radiology services. NPs can also establish independent practices, although some states require that NPs have a collaborative agreement with a physician. These types of clinics or practices are generally paid through a fee schedule arrangement just as with physicians. However, there can be significant variations under managed care contracts that are outside the Medicare program.

In Chapter 2, we take a closer look at two special types of clinics that are recognized under the Medicare program. These are the rural health clinics (RHCs) and federally qualified health centers (FQHCs). These two types of clinics are also generally recognized by the various state-level Medicaid programs. These two special types of clinics are cost-based reimbursed. The reimbursement is based on an average payment for visits or encounters. These clinics can be provider based or freestanding, although the terminology for freestanding is typically the word *independent.* Recognition of RHCs and FQHCs by private third-party payers for special payment processes is not the norm. Typically, FHCs and FQHCs are simply considered clinics.

Hospitals

Hospitals come in a variety of sizes, locations, and specialties. Some are publically owned, not for profit, while others are privately owned and thus are for profit. In some cases, physicians will own a hospital, and this type of business arrangement has raised issues within the Medicare program relative to referral of patients to such a physician-owned hospital. With increasing frequency, we are also seeing hospitals devoted to specialty services such as orthopedics or cardiology. These types of specialty hospitals are often owned wholly or partially by physicians.

Case Study 1.11: Orthopedic Specialty Hospital

The Apex Medical Center is a general short-term acute care hospital. Two years ago, a specialty hospital addressing only certain types of orthopedic surgeries was established about two miles down the road. The specialty hospital does not have an ED. Apex views the specialty hospital as siphoning off the more common orthopedic services, such as knee replacements and hip repairs, which are being performed at the specialty hospital.

Case Study 1.11 illustrates the fact that hospitals can and do sometimes become competitors. Also, such a specialty hospital will probably have Medicare patients along with significant

---

* See CMS Transmittal 87, dated May 2, 2008, to CMS Publication 100-02, *Medicare Benefits Policy Manual.* This transmittal has been withdrawn, but it does provide some insight into clinic issues.

numbers of patients who are under private payer contracts. Is it possible that such a specialty hospital could provide a limited number of specialized services less expensively than a general acute care hospital?

Other interesting questions can also arise with circumstances such as those in Case Study 1.11. For instance, if an individual were brought to the Apex Medical Center's ED with a severe orthopedic issue, could Apex transfer the patient to the orthopedic specialty hospital even though the specialty hospital does not have an ED? Interestingly, under current EMTALA (Emergency Medical Treatment and Labor Act) directives, the answer to this question is "yes."*

Hospitals are generally licensed at the state level, and their business structuring is based on a combination of state rules and regulations along with significant considerations for tax issues. Layered on top of this are national payment systems, such as those from Medicare that generate special hospital designations, which then further complicates the payment systems in use. For instance, consider the following special Medicare designations for hospitals:

- Critical access hospital (CAH)
- Sole community hospital (SCH)
- Medicare dependent hospital (MDH)
- Disproportionate share hospital (DSH)
- Rural referral center (RRC)

With the exception of the CAHs, all of these hospitals are paid through the Medicare inpatient PPS, MS-DRGs, and the outpatient prospective payment system APCs.

The CAHs are reimbursed on a cost basis; this process is discussed in greater detail in Chapter 2. Keep in mind that being a CAH is a Medicare concept relative to certain conditions of participation (CoPs) and then also for payment. Outside Medicare, these hospitals are just hospitals and most likely will be paid on the basis of a variety of payment systems used by various third-party payers. Note that for CAHs there are some further special payment processes in terms of integrating physician/practitioner payment for outpatient services into the payment of the CAH.†

The other designations do provide additional reimbursement for Medicare under both the inpatient and the outpatient PPSs. Beyond these special Medicare designations, there are also a limited number of very special hospitals, such as cancer hospitals and children's hospitals. For Medicare, these are generally cost-based reimbursed. Private third-party payers may or may not recognize these hospitals for special payment mechanisms.

Most often, hospitals are reimbursed for services through prospective payment for both inpatient and outpatient services. This is particularly true for the Medicare program with the MS-DRG and APCs. For private third-party payers, PPSs are also used, although there can be a much wider variety of payment systems, particularly for inpatient services.

Case Study 1.12: Per Diem Payment for Inpatient Services

The Apex Medical Center is reviewing a contract with a private insurance company. The payment methodology for inpatient services is quite simple. There is a per diem payment rate for medical cases and another higher per diem payment rate for surgical cases.

---

* For instance, see 42 CFR §489.20 for more information on EMTALA.
† See the Method II billing and payment process for CAHs discussed in Chapter 2.

When payment systems are simple, like Case Study 1.12, there are typically a number of other questions that arise. In this case study, the insurance company is going to be concerned about the medical necessity of the patient being in the hospital for a given period of time. Apex will probably be concerned about extensive surgeries for which there may not be a correspondingly long in-hospital recovery period. Conversely, there may be accident cases that require extensive stays in the hospital for extended rehabilitation. Also, there may be cases in which the surgery is performed and then the patient is transferred to another hospital. All of these are legitimate concerns relative to receiving proper payment.

Hospitals can become quite creative in the way in which they are organized. For instance, we have the concept of a *hospital within a hospital*. As the terminology implies, there is a hospital inside another hospital. An example of this kind of arrangement would be to have a specialty hospital located inside a general acute care hospital. The specialty hospital might occupy two floors of the main hospital. What advantage is there to such an arrangement? The primary purpose for such an arrangement is to take advantage of economies of scale. The specialty hospital can piggyback on the main hospital for facilities, utilities, maintenance, nursing staff, and the like. Otherwise, the specialty hospital would have to develop the entire support infrastructure separately.

From a payment system perspective, would a hospital within a hospital require special attention? The answer is most likely yes. For the Medicare program, there would be concern about appropriate cost-sharing arrangements through formal rental agreements. Without specific guidelines in place, the cost report preparation for the two hospitals could be inappropriately skewed.

Case Study 1.13: Long-Term Care Hospital inside a Short-Term Acute Care Hospital

A large metropolitan hospital has discovered that it has numerous long-term patients, some staying for up to two months or even longer. Better reimbursement as a long-term care hospital (LTCH) appears to offer a solution. As a result, the hospital is reorganizing one floor of the hospital to accommodate a hospital within a hospital. The new hospital will be an LTCH actually inside the short-term acute care hospital.

Whether the strategy illustrated in Case Study 1.13 will bear fruit is an interesting question. However, this case study does illustrate the organizational complexity that can evolve in lieu of different kinds of payment mechanisms for hospitals.

Hospitals and Integrated Delivery Systems

Over the past several decades, there has been significant movement to consolidate various types of healthcare providers into seamless delivery systems. Even smaller hospitals may have clinics, an SNF, and a home health agency (HHA) and provide DME. As you might imagine, IDSs are paid through a variety of payment systems, including various prospective payment and fee schedules.

Hospitals often provide the core element in IDSs. In addition, hospitals also form systems, and associated with each hospital there may also be a separate IDS. Or, the hospital system may decide to have a system of HHAs that are associated with the hospitals in the system, but the organizational structuring and reporting are separate for the hospitals and the HHAs.

In other words, in the real world of healthcare, there can be many different types of organizational structuring. The way in which payment systems accommodate these various organization structures can become quite complicated. In turn, the way payment systems are established may actually drive the way services are organized.

Case Study 1.14: Apogee Healthcare System

The Apex Medical Center has been invited to join the Apogee Healthcare System. Currently, Apogee has three hospitals in the region along with half a dozen skilled nursing facilities (SNFs), eight home health agencies, two dozen physician clinics, and a reference laboratory. One of the attractions for joining Apogee is that there are sophisticated billing processes that can for used by Apex.

The basic information given in Case Study 1.14 would suggest that Apex is joining a rather loosely organized IDS. It appears that the IDS may actually function as a management services organization (MSO) that provides various administrative functions for the various member providers of the IDS.

In other cases, an IDS or system of hospitals may be hierarchically structured with tight ownership and highly structured management. Regardless of the specifics of the IDS, there will be many different payment mechanisms used, including various contractual arrangements.

With the enactment of the Affordable Care Act of 2010, a new type of organization is now being developed. These are accountable care organizations or ACOs. Generally, these organizations will be IDSs that have the possibility to share in savings generated from more efficient delivery of healthcare under the Medicare program. The payment systems for the individual parts of the ACO may not really change, but the accounting for services will certainly need to be changed to identify savings that could possibly be shared.

Special Provider Organizations

There are a number of provider organizational structures that provide limited services or products. Variable types of payment systems are used for these special organizations.

DME Suppliers

Durable medical equipment, or using the full acronym, DMEPOS for DME, prosthetics, orthotics, and supplies, represents a major area for healthcare.* The range of products is extensive, including crutches, canes, walkers, commodes, braces, and diabetic shoes, and the list can go on extensively. While there are many compliance issues surrounding DME, particularly medical necessity, the payment process can also become complicated.

Most communities have stand-alone DME suppliers along with providers like hospitals that also have DME companies. Medicare has an extensive DME fee schedule through which DME for Medicare beneficiaries is paid. Many private third-party payers also use a fee schedule or some modified form of a fee schedule. In addition, some DME is provided by physicians, hospitals, home health, and even SNFs.

DME is different from other aspects of healthcare, even those aspects providing some sort of a product or supply item. DME can be new, used, rented, or rent to own. Thus, the ability of healthcare payers to provide payment must be quite adaptable to these different ways of dispensing DME.

Case Study 1.15: Competing DME Suppliers

Anywhere, USA, has the distinction of having nearly a dozen DME suppliers in the immediate area. The Apex Medical Center has attempted to use selected DME suppliers, but the competition is so fierce that Apex has decided to become a DME supplier itself to avoid complaints concerning favoritism from local suppliers.

---

* DME is also an area with significant compliance concerns, including fraudulent activities.

While there are many variations on the theme illustrated in Case Study 1.15, being a DME supplier attracts many organizations. For hospitals, compliance issues can complicate the ways in which DME is supplied to hospital patients.

Skilled Nursing Facilities

SNFs are abundant in most communities. They may be freestanding SNFs, or they may be integrated into a hospital setting. For small, generally rural hospitals, we have the concept of swing beds; a hospital bed can be used for inpatient care and then transferred over to providing skilled nursing care. The patient stays in the same bed, but the services and associated payment process change.

While SNF payments, at least under Medicare, use a PPS, fee schedules are still used by the physicians and practitioners providing services. Also, there are nursing facilities (i.e., not at the skilled level), assisted living, and other arrangements that provide varying degrees of less-acute care. Outside the more typical fee schedules and prospective payment, there are numerous contractual arrangements that are used by private third-party payers.

Home Health Agencies

Home health agencies are used extensively with the Medicare population and to a more limited extent with the population covered by private insurance. While physicians and practitioners must order and substantiate medical necessity for home health services, the payment system used for these services is a special HHA PPS. Also, home health services are often provided after an inpatient discharge, so there can be a payment interface between MS-DRGs for the hospital and the PPS used by HHAs.

> **Case Study 1.16: Private Pay Home Health Services**
>
> The Apex Medical Center has established a home health service as a part of its integrated services strategy. Most of the patients are Medicare beneficiaries, and payment is made through the Medicare home health PPS. However, there is increasing difficulty in qualifying patients for these services under the Medicare program. As a result, there are requests for these services on a private basis, with direct payment from the patients.

Case Study 1.16 illustrates some of the frustrations that healthcare providers encounter when they are actually trying to provide needed services. Qualifying for home health services under Medicare can be an involved process. For example, there is the issue of being homebound. What, exactly, does it mean to be homebound? Also, when a healthcare provider provides services to a Medicare patient, there is generally an expectation that the healthcare provider will bill the Medicare program. In this case study, there are individuals requesting the services on a private pay basis. Do you think this might present some special challenges?

Independent Diagnostic Testing Facilities

Independent diagnostic testing facilities (IDTFs) generally provide a limited range of mainly radiological diagnostic tests. This is a provider entity recognized by the Medicare program, and payment is made through the MPFS. There are special supervision requirements mandated by the

Medicare program for diagnostic tests. Also, the MPFS has a mechanism to separate the radiological services into a technical component, professional component, and total component. Thus, the MPFS can accommodate different arrangements by different providers.

Case Study 1.17: IDTF Billing for Radiology Services

Anywhere, USA, has an IDTF across town from the Apex Medical Center. Due to its location, many patients and physicians find that it is convenient to use. In some cases, physicians near the IDTF simply use it as a place to have radiology services provided. The ordering physician may elect to bill for the professional interpretation, while the IDTF bills only for the technical component. In other cases, a radiologist at the IDTF interprets the test so the IDTF bills for the total component—both the professional and technical components.

For Medicare and many other private payers, IDTFs are paid through a physician fee schedule. For the circumstances delineated in Case Study 1.17, a fee schedule payment system will have to be able to pay for the professional only, the technical component only, and then the combined total of both professional and technical.

For non-Medicare patients, you may find that what is recognized by Medicare as an IDTF for a limited range of diagnostic services may provide a much wider range of services delimited only by state, local, or professional guidelines. Payment processes for these expanded IDTFs can become quite complex.

Case Study 1.18: IDTF Acquired by Apex and Converted to Provider-Based

The Apex Medical Center has decided to purchase the IDTF that is located across town (see Case Study 1.17.) The hospital takes the necessary steps to convert this into a hospital-based facility. This means that the radiology services are now provided as an extension of the radiology department of the hospital.

When a change like that described in Case Study 1.18 occurs, the entire billing and payment process may change. In this case, with the change to provider based, the payment system will switch from MPFS over to the outpatient PPS, namely APCs. Of course, this is for Medicare. How will such a change be addressed by other third-party payers? The answer to this question can be quite variable depending on the type of payment mechanisms used by a given third-party payer for the specific services involved.

Comprehensive Outpatient Rehabilitation Facilities

As the name implies, comprehensive outpatient rehabilitation facilities (CORFs) provide outpatient rehabilitation services. These are generally freestanding facilities, although hospitals can establish CORFs. For hospital-based CORFs, the provider-based rule does not directly apply because the same fee schedule payment is made as with freestanding CORFs. Payment for services comes from the MPFS utilizing the nonfacility RVUs (relative value units). Various services, such as physical and occupational therapy, are typically provided, utilizing a comprehensive multidisciplinary approach.

Clinical Laboratories

Laboratory services abound in many different settings. Hospitals and clinics typically have clinical laboratories, although the range of tests may be more delimited for a physician office laboratory

(POL). There are freestanding laboratories, some of which may be used as reference laboratories for other health care providers who do not offer certain tests. Generally, payment for clinical laboratory services is made by fee schedule arrangements both for Medicare and for private payers alike.

Ambulatory Surgical Centers

Ambulatory surgical centers are a Medicare concept, although hospitals, physicians, and joint ventures of hospitals and physicians also develop and use the ASC concept for non-Medicare patients as well. ASCs are generally physical freestanding entities, although often they are located relatively close to a hospital. In some cases, ASCs are right on the campus of a hospital. Also, while unusual, an ASC could literally be located inside a hospital through some sort of rental agreement.

As the name implies, ambulatory or outpatient surgeries are provided in this setting. For the Medicare program, outpatient surgical services are divided into three categories:

1. Surgeries that must be provided in a hospital setting
2. Surgeries that can be performed in an ASC
3. Surgeries that can be performed in a physician's clinic

Clearly, any outpatient surgical procedure can be performed in a hospital, and certainly any medical office procedures can also be performed in an ASC. These three categories are hierarchical. For ASC Medicare payment, there is a complicated payment formula that is a hybrid of MPFS and APCs.

> **Case Study 1.19: ASC across the Street**
>
> A group of surgeons has decided to establish an ASC right across the street from the Apex Medical Center. A wide variety of less-complicated surgical services is provided at the ASC. The ASC opens at 6:00 a.m. six days a week and closes promptly at 5:00 p.m. each day.

Even if not organizationally connected, why would an ASC be physically located next to a hospital? Keep in mind that the ASC closes at 5:00 pm. What happens if there is a patient at the ASC who is not fully recovered?

If you look around your community, assuming that you are someplace close to a metropolitan area, you may start recognizing ASCs that may be highly specialized.

> **Case Study 1.20: Cataract Surgery ASC**
>
> Anywhere, USA, has the distinction of having a specialized ASC in the community. While this is not a metropolitan area, there is a sizable number of retirees on Medicare. This ASC specializes in one, and only one, surgery: cataract surgery with IOL (intraocular lens) implantation. While there is a single ophthalmologist, there are three operating bays that have plate glass windows so that friends and relatives of the patient can observe the operation. Also, the ASC has several small buses that will go out, pick up, and then return the patients after the surgery.

If you take a little time to think about the arrangements in Case Study 1.20, you will probably realize that there are some complicating factors. At this ASC, only the surgical procedure is performed. What happens if there are complications following the surgery? One approach is to have the community physicians and the Apex Medical Center address any follow-up care. For the overall payment processes, this type of situation makes demands on being able to address separate payment for postoperative services (i.e., the follow-up care) versus the actual operation (i.e., intraoperative care).

Note that, as for IDTFs, for non-Medicare patients, ASCs may perform significantly increased numbers and types of surgical services. The main delimitations are at the state level and then also within professional guidelines developed by different specialty societies at the national level. In some cases, patients may even be kept overnight.

Claim Adjudication and Payment Processing

For the fee-for-service payment systems, itemized statements and associated claims must be developed and filed with the third-party payer for payment. The processing of these claims is referred to as *claim adjudication*. Even when we move to other types of payment systems (e.g., cost based, capitated, etc.), itemized statements and claims are most often still generated, but their use changes somewhat. For instance, in the case of capitated payment systems, the generation of itemized statements and claims is to account for resource utilization as opposed to filing the claim for payment. In cost-based payment, claims may still be needed so that charges can be used to generate some sort of interim payment.

The factors that must be included in the overall claims adjudication and payment are as follows:

a. The patient must be covered.
b. The services rendered and items dispensed must be covered.
c. The services are ordered and provided by qualified medical persons.
d. The services are medically necessary.
e. The services must be appropriately documented.
f. A correct claim is filed on a timely basis.

Each of these six items can be discussed at significant length. When managed care contracts provide for payment, each of these factors must be addressed. A major factor for all types of payment systems is the concept of a qualified medical person. Individual healthcare providers (e.g., physicians, practitioners, technicians, etc.) must be qualified just as different healthcare organizations (e.g., clinics, hospitals, SNF, etc.) are. As mentioned in this chapter, this qualifying process is called credentialing. For our purposes, we divide credentialing into two categories:

1. Clinical credentialing
2. Billing credentialing

For physicians and practitioners, the process of clinical credentialing is a detailed process that involves verifying the qualifications of the individual to provide services that fall under their credential, licensing, and personal capabilities. Billing credentialing is our main focus. Both individual providers and healthcare organizations must gain billing privileges with a given third-party payer to file claims and generally be considered for entering into contractual arrangements with a given third-party payer.

Clinical and billing credentialing are not at all discrete, and often the process of credentialing will address both issues. Credentialing is used in conjunction with virtually all the different types of payment systems. The Medicare program uses an extensive, and sometimes bureaucratic, process through their CMS-855 forms.* Larger third-party payers may use somewhat similar processes.

---

* There are six different CMS-855 forms that are enrollment forms. These forms are sometimes quite lengthy, and gaining Medicare billing privileges can be challenging.

Note: In some cases, healthcare providers may have to file claims with third-party payers with whom they have no relationship. Technically, it is the patients who have the responsibility to make payment in these cases. However, as a practical matter, healthcare providers will generally file claims on behalf of their patients. Because there is no statutory or contractual relationship between the provider and the third-party payer, issues such as credentialing and the amount of payment that will be received can become significant issues.

Another issue within these six aspects is that of *medical necessity*. With fee-for-service payment systems, third-party payers want to pay only for those services that are really medically necessary. Overpayment allegations are often made on the basis that the services provided were not really necessary. However, with capitated payment arrangements, the healthcare provider will only want to provide services that are really necessary. In the case of capitation, the third-party payer may allege that the quality of care is substandard because medically necessary services were not provided.

Note: The whole issue of medical necessity is subjective. For healthcare payment, the question of medical necessity is a constant source for allegations of overpayment and assertions of fraudulent claims.

Summary and Conclusion

In this introductory chapter, we have reviewed the main types of healthcare payment systems along with the typical healthcare provider organizations. There are two fundamental aspects in the world of healthcare payment systems:

■ Variability in organizational structuring and relationships
■ Significant ongoing changes

Part of the reason for the variability and change is that the provision of medical and clinical services is also rapidly evolving. While new technology, new pharmaceuticals, and new surgical techniques all enhance the quality and efficacy of healthcare, these advances constantly challenge the payment systems to provide proper payment for medically necessary services.

The most common healthcare payment systems are fee for service. This simply means that the third-party payer makes payment for services as they are provided. The greater the volume and level of complexity of services, the greater are the payments. In contrast to fee for service is the capitated payment approach. In this capitated, or per-head, approach, the healthcare provider receives a fixed, periodic payment. Typically, the payment is on a PMPM basis. For the fixed payment, the healthcare provider agrees to provide necessary healthcare services for covered members (i.e., patients) for the given period of time. While the concept is straightforward, the actual implementation of capitated payment arrangements is extremely complex. For capitation, note particularly that the risk for increased services now lies with the healthcare provider, not the third-party payer.

As we discuss the cost-based, charge-based, and contractual payment systems in this text, keep in mind that there are additional ancillary concerns. Claims adjudication and subsequent payment are key financial issues. Proper coding, billing, and claims development must occur on the part of the healthcare provider. Proper adjudication of the claims is in the purview of the payer. Due attention on both parties is necessary for healthcare payment to occur in a proper and expeditious manner. The overall claims adjudication process is governed by statutory and contractual directives. These directives and requirements are driven by the type of payment system or systems that are being used by the given payer. For any sort of complex services, there will probably be more than one payment process being used. Thus, in any given managed care contract, there will be a variety of payment mechanisms delineated.

In the next chapter, we start our discussions with cost-based reimbursement, which is closely aligned with charge-based payment processes, discussed in Chapter 3.

Chapter 2

Healthcare Provider Costs and Cost-Based Payment Systems

Introduction

Healthcare costs are definitely in the news as national healthcare expenditures continue to rise precipitously. While we can all debate whether the monies spent go into the provision of healthcare itself or into administrative overhead for paying for healthcare services, there is little controversy concerning the fact that healthcare costs are rising.

Our primary focus in this chapter is to look at provider costs in general and then to discuss cost-based payment systems. Cost-based payment is one of the oldest approaches for healthcare payment. Because of a number of shortcomings, cost-based payment has now been bypassed by newer payment systems, including fee schedule payment and prospective payment systems (PPSs). As we will discuss, even these newer payment systems still involve costs, and charges, to some degree. One of the primary reasons that payers do not like cost-based reimbursement is that there is no incentive for cost containment. If a healthcare provider is being paid at cost or at a percentage above cost, then there is no incentive to delimit services.

Within the mechanics of cost-based reimbursement, a major issue is determining exactly what costs are incurred in the provision of services or dispensing various items. Cost-based payment can be used at two very different levels: at a global or macro level and then at a very detailed specific or micro level. The global level involves paying for a wide range of services based on costs such as with a critical access hospital (CAH). At a much more local level, certain individual items or groups of items may be paid on a cost basis. Often, these are referred to as *pass-through payments*. For instance, relatively expensive radiopharmaceuticals may be individually paid at cost or at some percentage above cost.

Note: We will encounter this same concept with charge-based payment. Certain items may be paid, at cost, on a pass-through basis. The challenge with using charges to drive the process is that the charge must somehow be converted into the appropriate cost to determine payment.

Let us consider two simple case studies to illustrate the challenge with identifying costs for healthcare services.

Case Study 2.1: Dr. Brown, a Sole Practitioner

Dr. Brown is a sole practitioner in a small rural community. His clinic is about two blocks from a small rural hospital that is a CAH for Medicare purposes. Dr. Brown has a nurse, a medical assistant, a receptionist, and one person who does the billing and files claims. He owns his clinic building, which was constructed about 20 years ago.

In Case Study 2.1, if you were a payer interested in paying Dr. Brown on a cost or cost plus a percentage basis, what would you need to know? The big question would revolve around what costs Dr. Brown incurs in providing healthcare services. This would involve services at the clinic as well as at the hospital or at other locations, such as a skilled nursing facility. Also, would these costs be at a general or gross level, or would they be at a visit or specific procedure level? Some thought would also involve distinguishing operating costs from capital costs.

As you should discern from Dr. Brown's situation, costs at this clinic are probably not really known. Dr. Brown provides services, keeps his overhead to a minimum, maintains the clinic building, purchases supplies, files claims, and then hopes that there is a profit at the end of the year. If careful cost calculations were to be performed, how much time and effort would be involved in determining the actual costs?

A more global approach for Dr. Brown is actually to calculate the costs for an entire year. Of course, some concern must be given to which costs are really a part of the clinic activities versus other costs that are not directly related. If we calculate all the costs, including a reasonable salary for Dr. Brown, we can then analyze all the services provided. Fortunately, because claims are developed using CPT (Current Procedural Terminology) codes, we can associate the costs back to the actual visits and procedures performed. Of course, some services are much more cost intensive than others. For instance, a brief follow-up visit is less intensive than the removal of a lesion from the arm.

A mechanism to categorize services at various levels is needed to assess properly the relative cost of providing the services or dispensing various items. If all of these elements are in place, then cost-based reimbursement can take place. Further in this chapter, we return to this case study when we discuss cost-based reimbursement for rural health clinics (RHCs).

Case Study 2.2: Pharmacy Items at the Apex Medical Center

The main pharmacy at the Apex Medical Center stocks thousands of pharmacy items. For most of the payment systems, particularly prospective payment systems (PPSs), the payment for these pharmacy items is bundled, and no separate payment occurs. However, for expensive items such as chemotherapy drugs and nuclear medicine radiopharmaceuticals, a number of healthcare payers want to pay cost plus a percentage.

Case Study 2.2 illustrates the concept of pass-through payment. The actual percentage above cost will be negotiated and appear in the contract. Percentages generally range in the area of 5 percent up to 15 percent. The percentage above costs should be influenced by overhead costs and any special costs for compounding certain pharmacy items.

As with Dr. Brown's clinic, the issue is to determine the cost of a particular drug and then have payment properly made at the contractual percentage above cost. Various arrangements can be made in this area, some of which are quite cumbersome. For instance, Apex may be required actually to charge the cost, and then when the claim is adjudicated, the proper percentage will be added on by the payer through the claim adjudication system. Or, Apex may be required to charge the cost plus the percentage for proper payment.

Note: In Chapter 3, we discuss establishing charges with particular attention to hospitals' charge-masters. Chargemasters list all the charges made by the hospital, including charges for pharmaceutical items. Because there may be very different contractual arrangements, pharmaceutical charges can become complicated.

In this particular area, there are sources of external cost data. For pharmacy items, there are two sets of data generally available:

■ average wholesale price (AWP)
■ average sales price (ASP)

Cost-based payment on a pass-through basis can be established using either or both of these pricing structures. Note that even with this external data, pricing can change over time. Also, particularly for hospitals, certain pharmacy items may be available on a bulk or discounted basis below the AWP or ASP. Thus, the true acquisition cost may be lower by virtue of such discounts.

These two case studies start our discussions of cost-based reimbursement. One case study is at a global level, that is, making payment for a wide range of services. The second case study illustrates the concept of pass-through payments based on the cost of a specific item or groups of items. Further in this chapter, we discuss the Medicare cost report that is used to make cost-based reimbursement in a limited number of cases. Note that in the third volume of this series, *Prospective Payment Systems*, the use and impact of the Medicare cost report on various PPSs has already been examined.

Costs and Cost Accounting

The concept of *cost* from an accounting perspective has filled many lengthy volumes. We simply touch lightly on this concept and then relate the concept of costs back into the healthcare payment arena. Thus, we examine only a limited part of a very large subject. Let us first look at two relatively simple concepts:

■ Acquisition costs
■ Fully loaded costs

Acquisition cost is simply the amount that was paid for some item. In healthcare, this is particularly applicable to pharmacy items (i.e., drugs), durable medical equipment (e.g., crutches, canes, walkers), and various medical devices (e.g., pacemakers, stents, implants). Even within these examples, determining the exact acquisition cost can become complicated.

Case Study 2.3: Volume Purchasing of Pharmacy Items

The Apex Medical Center's pharmacy has been working on establishing contracts with pharmaceutical suppliers for volume discounting. There are hundreds of common drugs, including intravenous solutions, which Apex uses in significant quantities. While there has been some significant success, even within the contracts themselves, there is some variability in pricing over the course of a year.

In Case Study 2.3, if we asked the pharmacy personnel about the cost of a specific drug, they would be hard pressed to give an exact answer, and the answer may depend on a given time period.

Now, is acquisition cost the best way to determine cost? Accounting personnel would be quick to point out that we really should consider the acquisition cost along with the *overhead costs* that are associated with the item. You may see the phrase *fully loaded cost*. Continuing with our discussion of pharmacy items, what kind of overhead costs are involved? After a few moments' thought, you will come up with items such as:

■ Ordering
■ Receiving
■ Stocking
■ Storing
■ Tracking
■ Retrieving
■ Delivering
■ Administering
■ Billing

There are probably more costs involved, including verification of orders/prescriptions along with drug reconciliation activities. Also, in some cases the administration of a drug, particularly injections or infusions, may be paid separately from the drug itself.

What we have done with this simple drug example is to move beyond the acquisition cost by developing additional cost drivers to calculate the fully loaded costs. In essence, this involves the topic of *cost accounting*. As you might guess, there are different approaches to cost accounting. Here are a few terms that you will encounter when you study cost accounting:

■ Standard cost accounting
■ Activity-based costing (ABC)
■ Lean cost accounting
■ Resource consumption accounting

All of these approaches address the fundamental question of what a service provided or an item rendered actually costs a healthcare provider. Depending on the specific cost accounting approach used, you may find different costs being reported.

Let us review a few more examples to illustrate some of the challenges that almost all healthcare providers face when addressing the issue of costs and then the accounting for costs.

Case Study 2.4: High-Technology Pacemakers

The Apex Medical Center is performing an increasing number of pacemaker implants. These are high-technology items that can be programmed and then periodically interrogated to make certain they are functioning properly. Also, these devices may need to be swapped out due to manufacturer recalls. These high-technology pacemakers cost well into the tens of thousands of dollars.

Case Study 2.4 illustrates a situation in which the acquisition cost (i.e., tens of thousands of dollars) represents the main cost associated with the items. Issues such as stocking, tracking, and preparation do not significantly add to the cost. In Chapter 3, we discuss charging for these items for which the markup is generally limited.

Note: In the third volume of this series, *Prospective Payment Systems*, we did discuss that PPSs, such as Ambulatory Payment Classifications (APCs) and Diagnosis Related Groups (DRGs), payment for these expensive implantable medical devices (IMDs) that is on an averaged basis. Thus, an issue is the variability of the costs of these items and whether hospitals are actually being properly paid. See *device-dependent* MS-DRGs (Medicare Severity Diagnosis Related Group) and APCs discussed in the third book, *Prospective Payment Systems*.

When you start analyzing costs, particularly overhead costs, there are some additional costs that may be incurred relative to items such as expensive implantable devices. Let us join the financial analysts at the Apex Medical Center.

Case Study 2.5: Expensive Stent Wastage

Apex is starting to perform more cardiac and vascular catheterization, both outpatient and inpatient. A problem has been encountered with the expensive stents. There have been several instances when an attempt to place a stent was not successful because the stent was the wrong size. Thus, there may be several stents that are wasted. A similar situation is occurring with the expensive catheters that are used for angiographies and stent placement; sometimes, a given catheter may not be adequate and must be discarded.

If you were a financial analyst at Apex, what kind of concerns would you have? What kinds of questions need answers? Will the company supplying the stents or catheters absorb the loss? While a complete analysis of this type of situation can become complex, the type of situation illustrated in Case Study 2.5 will influence costs, which in turn may also influence charges.

In Case Study 2.6, we start to consider more complex situations relative to identifying costs.

Case Study 2.6: Acme Medical Clinic Examination Room

The Acme Medical Clinic has eight examination rooms. These rooms are all virtually the same. An examination table, equipment, and supply items along with chairs and a desk are all included.

Trying to assess the cost of the use of an examination room is interesting. First, we better delimit the timeframe and consider this examination room use for, say, an hour. Second, we start to encounter concerns about *capital* costs versus *operating* costs. How much did it cost to construct an examination room? Do we need to amortize the capital cost over several years? What about the equipment? Is this a capital or operating cost? Should we include various supply items? Are there different kinds of supply items, that is, routine versus special? What about maintenance and cleaning along with heating, ventilating, and air conditioning (HVAC) costs?

Even with a simple case study involving the cost of the use of an examination room, it can become a challenge for determining costs and for cost accounting in general. In the next case study, we elevate these very same questions in a more complex setting.

Case Study 2.7: Apex Medical Center Operating Room

The Apex Medical Center has three different operating suites. Each of them is designed to handle different types and levels of surgical procedures. Thus, the equipment in each room is different, the numbers of nursing staff and technicians assigned to each room are different, and the type and level of supply items are different.

As with the examination room, let us consider the cost for one hour. An operating suite involves significant capital expense. Also, the equipment that is located in an operating suite involves significant capital investments. One of the issues for operating rooms is the personnel that are typically assigned and utilized for operating procedures. Surgical supply items can range from a minor cost on up to thousands of dollars. Should supplies be included in the cost of an operating room, and if so, which supplies?

Note: The Medicare program differentiates between *routine* and *ancillary* costs and charges. For example, in establishing hospital room costs and charges, routine nursing services are included in the room charge and thus cost. This same concept and terminology carries over into areas such as charging for supply items. (See Chapter 3 relative to hospital chargemasters.)

To pursue this discussion a little further, let us consider surgical nursing staff. What is the cost for a surgical nurse for an hour? We can certainly determine hourly wages and fringe benefits. We must also include vacation time, sick leave time, continuing education time, administrative overhead time, and so on. Also, while a surgical nurse will be paid for hours on the job, how many hours are actually spent in the operating suite or in activities directly associated with surgical services?

This same discussion can be extended relative to different costs that might be associated with an operating suite. One of the issues that immediately arises when determining the cost of more complex situations is exactly what should be included in the calculation of the cost.

Note: We will encounter this same issue in Chapter 3 when we discuss the development of charges for healthcare services and items. In some cases, the charge for a particular service may bundle several items together into a single charge. Given that charges are generally based on costs, the degree of bundling that is present in determining costs then affects the development of charges.

Cost accounting is a standard discipline within the accounting world. Some larger healthcare providers do have cost accounting systems that can assist significantly in determining the actual costs for providing healthcare services. Even with our brief discussion of some simple case studies, cost accounting takes time and resources, some would say significant resources. As a result, smaller healthcare organizations have difficulty justifying the costs to have cost accounting. This means that costs are really known only in limited cases. This lack of definitive cost information also delimits healthcare providers from developing charge structures that are reasonably based on their costs.

This lack of cost information is why healthcare payers such as the Medicare program have developed rather extensive alternative mechanisms to create payment systems that bear some resemblance to costs. We discuss the Medicare cost report in this chapter. Also, the Medicare physician fee schedule (MPFS) uses a resource-based approach to paying physicians and others on fee schedules. Separate, extensive studies over the years have been conducted to determine physician resource utilization for providing services.

There is much public discussion concerning the rapidly escalating healthcare costs. Our main concern is with determining what costs are involved with providing healthcare services. The number and types of services seem to be increasing. Also, new technologies bring wonderful medical advancements, but at the same time they bring significantly increased costs. Elderly patients are living longer, and there seems almost a vicious cycle that is driving the whole process of increases in the costs of healthcare. Most of the payment systems discussed in this four-volume series are *fee-for-service* payment systems. This simply means that the more services that are provided, the more payment is made to the healthcare provider. The only payment system that does not pay more for increased services or increased costs of services is capitation. This type of payment has been slow to develop because of the risks involved to healthcare providers. Capitated payment is discussed in Chapter 5.

Medicare Cost Report

In Case Study 2.1, we discussed actually calculating the overall cost at Dr. Brown's clinic over the period of a year. One issue that was raised is that there might be certain costs that are not appropriate for inclusion in calculating overall costs. The Medicare program has long used what is called the *Medicare cost report*. To state that preparing the Medicare cost report is a complex, detailed, and time-consuming process is a major understatement.

The Medicare cost report is actually a process that generally takes about three to four years from the time the report is prepared and submitted to the time that final settlement takes place. Specially trained analysts are necessary to gather the necessary data, analyze the data, and then prepare the report. The Medicare administrative contractor (MAC) also analyzes the report. The MAC may request more information or request that changes be made. One of the areas of greatest concern is that of *allowable costs*. Only costs that are deemed appropriate by the Medicare program can be included in the cost report.

The Medicare cost report also is generally used by the state Medicaid programs depending on specific circumstances. Note that each state Medicaid program tends to have unique features. If you are working with a state Medicaid program, be certain to check for state-level rules and regulations.

Now, which healthcare providers and entities are required, by Medicare, to develop and file a cost report? Here is the list:

- Hospitals: CMS-2552-96
- Home health agencies (HHAs): CMS-1728-94
- Skilled nursing facilities: CMS-2540-96
- Renal facilities: CMS-265-94
- Hospices: CMS-1984-99
- Outpatient rehabilitation providers: CMS-2088-92
- Organ procurement organization/histocompatibility laboratory providers: CMS-216-94
- Home office cost statement: CMS-287-92
- Health maintenance organization: CMS-276

Further in this chapter, we discuss RHCs and federally qualified health centers (FQHCs). RHCs can be independent or provider based. Similarly, FQHCs can be freestanding or provider based. In this case, provider based generally means hospital based; that is, the RHC or FQHC is really organizationally integrated into the hospital.* If the RHC or FQHC is provider based, then Worksheet M of the hospital cost report must be filed. If the RHC or FQHC is independent or freestanding, respectively, then the CMS-222-92 must be filed by the RHC of FQHC.

Note the following:

1. As with all Centers for Medicare and Medicaid Services (CMS) forms, there are periodic updates. As this text is prepared, the CMS-2552-96 is being updated to the CMS-2552-10. The "10" in this case refers to the year 2010.
2. CMS has a system that addresses the cost-reporting process, namely, HCRIS, which stands for Healthcare Provider Cost Reporting Information System.

---

* Note that physically the RHC may be some distance from the hospital. The organizational structuring determines whether the RHC is provider based or independent.

3. The CMS website that is devoted to cost reporting can be found at https://www.cms.gov/CostReports/.
4. The directions and associated rules and regulations can be found in the *Provider Reimbursement Manual—Part 2*. See https://www.cms.gov/Manuals/PBM/list.asp.

We now review the main components of the hospital cost report. This is intended as a brief overview only. The intent is to give you an idea of the kinds of data that are required. Always be certain to check for the latest information. As with almost everything involving the Medicare program, change is rampant.

■ Section One: Provider Identity—Worksheet S
  – Worksheet S: Hospital and Hospital Health Care Complex Cost Report Certification and Settlement Summary
  – Worksheet S-2: Hospital and Hospital Health Care Complex Identification Data
  – Worksheet S-3: Hospital and Hospital Health Care Complex Statistical Data and Hospital Wage Index Information
  – Worksheet S-4: Hospital-Based Home Health Agency Statistical Data
  – Worksheet S-5: Hospital Renal Dialysis Department Statistical Data Statistical Data Outpatient Providers
  – Worksheet S-6: Hospital-Based Outpatient Rehabilitation Provider Data
  – Worksheet S-8: Provider-Based RHC/Federally Qualified Health Center Provider Statistical Data
  – Worksheet S-9: Hospice Identification Data
  – Worksheet S-10: Hospital Uncompensated Care Data
■ Section Two: Cost Allocation/Expenses—Worksheet A
  – Worksheet A: Reclassification and Adjustment of Trial Balance of Expenses
  – Worksheet A-6: Reclassifications
  – Worksheet A-7: Analysis of Capital Assets
  – Worksheet A-8: Adjustments to Expenses
  – Worksheet A-8-2: Provider-Based Physician Adjustments
  – Worksheet A-8-4: Reasonable Cost Determination for Therapy Service
■ Section Two: Cost Allocation/Expenses—Worksheet B
  – Worksheet B, Part I: Cost Allocation: General Service Cost
  – Worksheet B-1: Cost Allocation: Statistical Basis
  – Worksheet B, Part II: Allocation of Old Capital-Related Costs
  – Worksheet B, Part III: Allocation of New Capital-Related Costs
■ Section Three: Charges—Worksheet C
  – Worksheet C: Computation of Ratio of Cost to Charges and Outpatient Capital Reduction
    • Part I: Computation of Ratio of Cost to Charges
    • Part II: Calculation of Outpatient Services Cost to Charge Ratios Net of Reductions
    • Part III: Computation of Total Inpatient Ancillary Costs: Rural Primary Care Hospitals
    • Part IV: Computation of Inpatient Operating Cost: Rural Primary Care Hospitals
    • Part V: Computation of Outpatient Cost Per Visit: Rural Primary Care Hospitals
■ Section Three: Charges—Worksheet D
  – Worksheet D: Cost Apportionment
    • Part I: Apportionment of Inpatient Routine Service Capital Costs

- • Part II: Apportionment of Inpatient Ancillary Service Capital Costs
- • Part III: Apportionment of Inpatient Routine Service Other Pass-Through Costs
- • Part IV: Apportionment of Inpatient Ancillary Service Other Pass-Through Costs
- • Part V: Apportionment of Medical and Other Health Services Costs
- • Part VI: Vaccine Cost Apportionment
  - – Worksheet D-1: Computation of Inpatient Operating Cost
  - – Worksheet D-2: Apportionment of Cost of Services Rendered by Interns and Residents
  - – Worksheet D-4: Inpatient Ancillary Service Cost Apportionment
  - – Worksheet D-6: Computation of Organ Acquisition Costs and Charges for Hospitals Which Are Certified Transplant Centers
  - – Worksheet D-9: Apportionment of Cost for Services of Teaching Physicians
- ■ Section Four: Payments and Settlements—Worksheet E
  - – Worksheet E: Calculation of Reimbursement Settlement
    - • Part A: Inpatient Hospital Services Under PPS
    - • Part B: Medical and Other Health Services
    - • Part C: Outpatient Ambulatory Surgical Center
    - • Part D: Outpatient Radiology Services
    - • Part E: Other Outpatient Diagnostic Procedures
- ■ Section Four: Payments and Settlements
  - – Worksheet E-1: Analysis of Payments to Providers for Services Rendered
  - – Worksheet E-2: Calculation of Reimbursement Settlement: Swing Beds
  - – Worksheet E-3: Calculation of Reimbursement Settlement
- ■ Section Five: Special Subunit Cost Reports
  - – Worksheet K: Analysis of Provider-Based Hospice Costs
  - – Worksheet H: Analysis of Provider-Based Home Health Agency Costs
  - – Worksheet J-1: Allocation of General Service Costs to Outpatient Rehabilitation Provider Cost Centers
  - – Worksheet I: Analysis of Renal Dialysis Department Costs
  - – Worksheet M-1: Analysis of Provider-Based Rural Health Clinic Federally Qualified Health Center Costs
  - – Worksheet M-2: Allocation of Overhead to RHC/FQHC Services
  - – Worksheet M-3: Calculation of Reimbursement Settlement for RHC/FQHC Services
  - – Worksheet M-4: Computation of Pneumococcal and Influenza Vaccine Cost
  - – Worksheet M-5: Analysis of Payments to Hospital-Based RHC/FQHC Services Rendered to Program Beneficiaries
- ■ Section Six: Financial Statements
  - – Financial Statements: Worksheets G, G-1, G-2, and G-3

Even this relatively extensive outline is not complete. For instance, Worksheet L is for capital costs. Regardless of understanding all of the terminology presented in this outline, clearly the cost report is quite complex and can constitute hundreds of pages. However, the overall intent of the cost report can be seen from the types of data that are required. The main financial data that is needed falls into two categories:

- ■ Costs
- ■ Charges

From the cost and charge data, the cost report can then determine the cost-to-charge ratios (CCRs). The calculation of the CCRs is generally found in Worksheet C. These ratios and their use are discussed further in Chapter 3.

Notice also that accommodation is made for provider-based operations such as clinics, physicians, RHCs, HHAs, and the like. For payment purposes under the Medicare program, provider-based operations are important. As we discuss in the following material, certain clinics such as RHCs and FQHCs are cost-based reimbursed. Also, CAHs are cost-based reimbursed along with the CAHs' provider-based operations.

Of course, there are many other accounting processes that must be addressed, including various allocations, apportionment, and other financial analyses. Generally, when there is cost-based reimbursement, interim payments are made on some basis, and then after the cost report is settled there is a final reconciliation of costs to the interim payments made. For the Medicare program, this generally takes three and sometimes four years.

While the Medicare program, and to some extent Medicaid programs, is the main payer that utilizes cost-based reimbursement at a global level, it is the Medicare cost report that provides the necessary mechanism for determining costs on which reimbursement can be made. Also, at least for Medicare, pass-through payments use the CCRs as developed from the cost report.

Note: By just reading through the general outline of topics for the hospital report, you should be able to discern that the cost report is quite complicated and requires a great deal of time and effort to prepare correctly. A good analogy is a complicated income tax form in which there are rather inexplicable instructions to add certain lines together then multiply by 80 percent and then subtract from some other line.

Cost-Based Payment: Key Features

Cost-based payment is conceptually simple with some significant operational challenges. The greatest challenge is for the payer to know and be able to verify what costs have been incurred for providing the service or dispensing an item. If the final determination of the costs is on a retrospective basis, there is also a need to provide interim payment until the costs can be calculated and verified.

Cost-based payment generally is used in two different ways:

1. On a local basis for individual, generally special, services or items
2. On a global basis for a wide variety of services and items

We refer to the first as being at the micro level and the second at the macro level. Many payment systems carve out certain services or more generally certain items. Cost-based payment for these individual items is useful when the item or class of items is relatively expensive or there is wide variation in the cost of the items. A good example is pacemakers and related devices that are implanted. There can be enormous differences in the cost of these items. Thus, for a payer to make reasonable and appropriate payment, each individual item will require consideration.

Case Study 2.8: Expensive Pacemakers

The Maximus Insurance Company is encountering more cases in which expensive devices are being used to treat cardiac conditions. These devices vary from about $5,000.00 to more than $25,000.00. Because of this variability, Maximus has decided to start paying the actual acquisition cost plus 10 percent.

As with many aspects of healthcare payment, the concept illustrated in Case Study 2.8 is simple, but actually implementing such a process can create some significant challenges. The Maximus contract will probably require the healthcare provider to charge the acquisition cost plus 10 percent. This will allow Maximus then to adjudicate the claim and simply pay the amount charged. For auditing purposes, Maximus may require the actual invoices to be retained to verify that payment is correct. Another possibility is that Maximus may require prior authorization based on the medical necessity for the use of a specific device, at which time cost can be determined.

We encounter this same case study in the next chapter when we discuss charge-based payment (see Case Study 3.18).

A second reason for cost-based reimbursement involves new items or services. Particularly for PPSs, the process of integrating a new expensive device or even drug into the PPS may take several years to develop enough data for integration. In cases like this, payment may be made based on a pass-through basis, that is, on a cost basis.

Going beyond the micro level, there is the macro or global level, where virtually all the services at a given healthcare facility are cost-based reimbursed. A good example of this type of cost-based payment is Medicare payment for CAHs. We will discuss RHC and FQHC reimbursement, which is also cost based.

The basic idea for the macro level is twofold:

- On an annual basis, provide estimated interim payment for services
- Retrospectively determine the actual costs and settle final payments, up or down, based on the final costs

At a conceptual level, this is a relatively simple process. In actual practice, the process can become quite complicated. Besides the complexity of the cost report preparation, there is a time delay, measured in years, in making the final settlement with the cost report. Thus, interim payments may be made based on outdated cost data.

Case Study 2.9: Increasing Costs at the Apex Medical Center

The Apex Medical Center has experienced significant growth over the period of three years. While inpatient services have grown modestly, outpatient services have expanded dramatically in both volume and the level of complexity of services. This outpatient growth is due mainly to the recruitment of a gastroenterologist and a cardiologist along with several specialty nurse practitioners (NPs). Apex is a CAH for Medicare, and it appears that the interim payment rate is significantly out of date and lower than it should be.

In Case Study 2.9, because of several years between completing and settling the cost report, certain cost data may be out of date. Similarly, if Apex were also increasing its overall charge structure during the same period, then there could be added pressure on currency and accuracy of the cost report. Keep in mind that for cost-based reimbursement on any sort of a global basis, there must be an interim payment process that is eventually compared to the actual costs incurred. Interim payment is often based on charges.

At the micro level, in which we are dealing with individual or small groups of items, the actual cost can generally be determined in real time. This cost-based payment generally involves some sort of pass-through payment; that is, the payer will pay for the actual cost of the item or the cost plus a percentage above the cost. While this is a simple approach, there is still a question of exactly what cost is involved.

Case Study 2.10: Pass-Through Payments for Intraocular Lenses

There is an ambulatory surgery center (ASC) located in Anywhere, USA, that specializes in cataract surgeries. While most of the patients are Medicare beneficiaries, there is an increasing number of patients covered under a local insurance company. The insurance company is proposing to pay separately for the intraocular lenses (IOLs) at cost.

The big question in Case Study 2.10 is the same question that we have for virtually all cost-based reimbursement. What is the cost of the IOLs? Certainly, acquisition cost can be used, but should there be some sort of a markup for overhead expenses involved with obtaining the IOLs? Also, some sort of mechanism to bill correctly and be paid will have to be established. For IOLs, or more accurately NTIOLs (new technology IOLs), there is the issue of vision-correcting IOLs. These are more expensive, and then the question of coverage enters the discussion. For Medicare, the base IOL is covered, but the extra cost for vision correction is not covered.

Medicare and other healthcare payers use this pass-through payment process to some degree. There are so many new items appearing and being placed into use that payment systems cannot adequately adjust the payment processes to accommodate the new, and generally more expensive, items.

In the third volume in this series, *Prospective Payment Systems*, the concept of cost outliers for both MS-DRGs and APCs was discussed. Cost outliers tend to be used with most PPSs. PPSs tend to pay for a range of service categories on an averaged basis. While this average payment may be adequate for the usual services in the given category, there can be cases that are unusually expensive. If the given case becomes too costly, then there are mechanisms (i.e., algorithms) that will make extra payment.

The cost outlier calculation is basically a cost-based payment mechanism. As usual, the big issue is how to determine the actual costs for the services provided and then how to structure the additional payment. While PPS hospitals are not cost-based reimbursed at a macro or overall levels, there is still a need for the cost report and the CCRs that are calculated through the cost report. A cost outlier calculation involves converting the charges for a case to costs by using the CCRs. While a gross oversimplification, if the charges for a hospital inpatient case are $90,000.00 and the inpatient CCR is 0.6000, then the (presumed) costs would be 0.6000 * $90,000.00 or $54,000.00. The cost outlier formula can then use this calculated cost to determine any additional cost outlier payment.

The all-important CCRs are discussed further in Chapter 3. Note that because there is a lag time in preparing and filing the cost report to the time of final settlement, the CCRs can become outdated. This is particularly true if the given hospital or hospital system is dramatically increasing charges over a three- to five-year time period. If the CCRs become outdated, then incorrect calculation of costs can occur, and inappropriate cost outliers might be paid.

Critical Access Hospitals

The CAH designation is purely a Medicare, and possibly a Medicaid, concept. In Chapter 1, we briefly mentioned a number of other special designations that are used by the Medicare program, such as the sole community hospitals (SCHs), Medicare-dependent hospitals (MDHs), and rural referral centers (RRCs). Each of these designations involves and affects payment to the hospital. The CAH designation is unusual because it moves Medicare payment from prospective payment to cost-based payment. The other designations typically provide increased payment by providing certain add-ons or increases in payment mechanisms.

Note: The CAH designations as well as the others mentioned are Medicare designations. If a non-Medicare patient goes to one of these hospitals, then the hospital is just like any other duly licensed hospital. While it is possible that a private payer might recognize a hospital as being a small, rural hospital and then providing some payment adjustment, generally this is not the case.

The CAH designation has developed over several decades. The main intent of this designation is to provide special payment incentives to guarantee that hospital services (i.e., emergency services, outpatient services, and limited inpatient services) are available for individuals in rural, less-populated areas. To qualify for this designation, and thus be cost-based reimbursed, the hospital must meet a series of requirements. Here is a partial list to give you some idea of the kinds of requirements:

- Must be at least 35 miles from the nearest hospital. This requirement can be reduced to 15 miles if located in a mountainous area.
- Can have no more than 25 inpatient beds. These beds can be used for skilled nursing services if swing-bed approval is granted.
- The average length of stay cannot be more than 96 hours. This means that lower-acuity inpatient services are provided.
- Emergency services are available 24/7/365. The availability of emergency services is one of the key factors for having CAHs.
- The CAH must have agreements in place for the transfer of patients. This is generally so that a quick transfer for emergency cases can take place.

Given that for a hospital to gain the CAH designation a number of special requirements must be attained, what is the benefit? One of the benefits is that CAHs have a distinctly different set of Medicare conditions of participation (CoPs) relative to acute care hospitals. Generally, the CAH CoPs are less stringent than those for acute care hospitals. As an example, let us examine the CoP requirement relative to providing emergency services. The emergency services requirements for CAHs are found at 42 CFR §485.618. The following are selected excerpts only:

- The CAH provides emergency care necessary to meet the needs of its inpatients and outpatients.
  a. *Standard: Availability.* Emergency services are available on a 24-hours a day basis.
  b. *Standard: Equipment, supplies, and medication.* Equipment, supplies, and medication used in treating emergency cases are kept at the CAH and are readily available for treating emergency cases. The items available must include the following:
    1. *Drugs and biologicals* commonly used in life-saving procedures, including analgesics, local anesthetics, antibiotics, anticonvulsants, antidotes and emetics, serums and toxoids, antiarrythmics, cardiac glycosides, antihypertensives, diuretics, and electrolytes and replacement solutions.
    2. *Equipment and supplies* commonly used in life-saving procedures, including airways, endotracheal tubes, ambu bag/valve/mask, oxygen, tourniquets, immobilization devices, nasogastric tubes, splints, IV therapy supplies, suction machine, defibrillator, cardiac monitor, chest tubes, and indwelling urinary catheters.
  c. *Standard: Blood and blood products.* The facility provides, either directly or under arrangements, the following:
    1. Services for the procurement, safekeeping, and transfusion of blood, including the availability of blood products needed for emergencies on a 24-hours a day basis.

2. Blood storage facilities that meet the requirements of 42 CFR part 493, subpart K, and are under the control and supervision of a pathologist or other qualified doctor of medicine or osteopathy. If blood banking services are provided under an arrangement, the arrangement is approved by the facility's medical staff and by the persons directly responsible for the operation of the facility.

d. *Standard: Personnel.*
   1. Except as specified in paragraph (d)(3) of this section, there must be a doctor of medicine or osteopathy, a physician assistant, a nurse practitioner, or a clinical nurse specialist, with training or experience in emergency care, on call and immediately available by telephone or radio contact, and available on site within the following timeframes:
      i. Within 30 minutes, on a 24-hour a day basis, if the CAH is located in an area other than an area described in paragraph (d)(1)(ii) of this section; or
      ii. Within 60 minutes, on a 24-hour a day basis, if all of the following requirements are met: [frontier area, state determination, other criteria].
   2. A registered nurse with training and experience in emergency care can be utilized to conduct specific medical screening examinations only if:
      i. The registered nurse is on site and immediately available at the CAH when a patient requests medical care; and
      ii. The nature of the patient's request for medical care is within the scope of practice of a registered nurse and consistent with applicable State laws and the CAH's bylaws or rules and regulations.
   3. A registered nurse satisfies the personnel requirement specified in paragraph (d)(1) of this section for a temporary period if:
      i. The CAH has no greater than 10 beds;
      ii. The CAH is located in an area designated as a frontier area or remote location as described in paragraph (d)(1)(ii)(A) of this section;

e. *Standard: Coordination with emergency response systems.* The CAH must, in coordination with emergency response systems in the area, establish procedures under which a doctor of medicine or osteopathy is immediately available by telephone or radio contact on a 24-hours a day basis to receive emergency calls, provide information on treatment of emergency patients, and refer patients to the CAH or other appropriate locations for treatment.

If you compare these CoPs with those of an acute care hospital,* you will find that these CoPs have been tailored to small, rural hospitals. In summary:

1. CAHs must provide emergency services 24/7/365;
2. CAHs must have the appropriate drugs, equipment, supplies and blood products;
3. A physician or qualified practitioner must be immediately available by communication and must be able to come to the hospital within 30 minutes (60 minutes for certain situations);
4. A registered nurse can meet the practitioner requirement under certain circumstances; and
5. There must be coordination with emergency response systems.

---

* See 42 CFR §482 for acute care hospital CoPs.

Note that CAHs are still subject to EMTALA (Emergency Medical Treatment and Labor Act) requirements and other requirements, such as physician supervision.

While the specially designed CoPs are a benefit for CAHs, probably the biggest benefit is that CAHs are cost-based reimbursed, generally at 101 percent of costs. Why is this of benefit? If cost-based reimbursement was not used, then the CAHs, like other hospitals, would be paid through prospective payment (i.e., MS-DRGs and APCs) along with a variety of fee schedules. Because of the relatively low volume of services, the PPSs may not even cover the costs, let alone generate any sort of profit margin. Given the popularity of this designation, cost-based reimbursement must certainly provide a financial incentive over the other payment mechanisms. At the time this text was prepared, there were more than 1,300 CAHs across the country.

Case Study 2.11: Advantage of Cost-Based Reimbursement

The Apex Medical Center has been a CAH for some 10 years and is more than financially viable. However, there is increasing demand, and Apex is considering adding more beds, which will move them beyond 25 beds and outside the maximum number of beds for being a CAH. The plan is to double the bed capacity in the next two years and then move to being a sole community hospital (SCH).

If you were a financial analyst at Apex, would you be running financial models to determine the financial impact of moving from cost-based reimbursement to prospective payment? The answer is certainly in the affirmative. Let us take another example of this difference in payment levels using ambulance services. Note that CAHs, like any hospital, can have provider-based entities such as clinics, ambulance services, and RHCs.

Case Study 2.12: Provider-Based Ambulance Services

Anywhere, USA, has an ambulance service located about 15 miles away in another small community. This ambulance service is having difficulty maintaining a financially viable operation. Currently, payments are made through various fee schedules, and even with increased payment amounts for a rural area, the reimbursement is not enough. The suggestion has been made that the Apex Medical Center acquire the ambulance services and then arrange for payment to be made on a cost basis, at least for Medicare.

In Case Study 2.12, Medicare ambulance services can be paid through the Medicare ambulance fee schedule (AFS)* or paid on a cost basis through the CAH. At issue for this particular ambulance service is which would pay more. Again, if there is relatively low volume so that economies of scale cannot be attained, then the cost-based reimbursement may yield significantly greater benefit.

The financial incentives for CAHs can also be extended to physician and practitioner payment. This is referred to as Method II payment. For Medicare, when physicians and practitioners provide services at the hospital or in provider-based clinics, there is a reduction in the professional reimbursement. This is called the site-of-service (SOS) differential. This is a part of the Medicare Physician Fee Schedule (MPFS) payment system.† For CAHs, if the physicians agree to reassign their Medicare payments, the professional payment is 115 percent

---

* The AFS is discussed in *Fee Schedule Payment Systems*.
† The MPFS is discussed at some length in *Fee Schedule Payment Systems*.

of the reduced professional payment. To a certain extent, this 15-percent increase makes up for the SOS reduction.

Note also that physicians and practitioners may qualify for additional payments from physician scarcity areas (PSAs) or health personnel shortage areas (HPSAs). Because CAHs tend to be in rural, less-populated areas, the PSA and HPSA bonuses may apply.

> **Case Study 2.13: Acme Medical Clinic Conversion**
>
> The Acme Medical Clinic is a small family practice clinic with two physicians and a nurse practitioner. It is located about a block away from the Apex Medical Center, which is a CAH. The physicians at Acme have approached the hospital about purchasing the practice and then hiring the physicians and nurse practitioner as employees.

Assuming that Apex does proceed with this process, a decision will need to be made regarding whether to make the clinic provider based, that is, a part of the hospital. If the clinic is left freestanding, then full MPFS reimbursement will be received for professional services at the clinic itself. Billing in this manner for CAHs is referred to as Method I.

However, if the clinic is established as provider based, then there will be a technical component reimbursement to the hospital along with reimbursement for the physician services. While the Medicare SOS will reduce the payments, the Method II reimbursement process will bring back 15 percent of that reimbursement for the physicians. Even at a very high level financial analysis, the use of the provider-based approach is very attractive.

For Medicare, CAHs code and file claims just like other hospitals. While there are some differences in claims filing, adjudicable claims must be filed; that is, the claims must be able to be processed through the various code editors that are used by Medicare for inpatient and outpatient claims.

For cost-based reimbursement, there must be a mechanism for making interim payments, which are then finally reconciled to the cost report for the given year. For CAHs, the interim payment calculations are made on the following bases:

- Inpatient: Per diem for covered days
- Swing bed: Per diem for covered days (separate from inpatient)
- Outpatient: Percentage of charges

The actual calculations are based on the most current settled cost report. Because there is a three- to four-year delay in preparing and finally reconciling the cost report, the Medicare program has made provisions so that the interim rates can be adjusted to some degree to accommodate current circumstances (e.g., increasing costs, changes in charge structure, etc.).

Rural Health Clinics and Federally Qualified Health Centers

We address RHCs and FQHCs together because their respective payment mechanisms are similar and are based on costs. This is not to imply that these two types of entities are the same; there are some very distinct differences. Our discussion focuses on RHCs, with comments on how FQHCs are similar or dissimilar.

There are two types each for RHCs and FQHCs:

Provider-based RHCs
Independent RHCs
Provider-Based FQHCs
Freestanding FQHCs

Because both RHCs and FQHCs are cost-based reimbursed, there must be a cost-reporting process and an interim payment process. As with CAHs, interim payments are made over the course of a year and then eventually reconciled with the cost report.

For provider-based (i.e., generally hospital-based) RHCs and FQHCs, the cost-reporting process is integrated into the hospital cost report (CMS-2552-96). See Worksheet M-1 through M-5 as listed in the hospital cost-reporting section. A special cost report, the CMS-222-92, is used for independent RHCs and freestanding FQHCs.

Now, what about the interim payment methodology? For RHCs and FQHCs the interim payment mechanism is based on a visit or patient encounter. You should immediately realize that there can be very different services provided for a given encounter. A patient may be presenting for a cold and sinus congestion, while another patient may be presenting with several lacerations or a fracture that needs attention. The resources and thus costs associated with these two visits will be quite different. However, the interim payment will be exactly the same. The only time any sort of overpayment or underpayment will be reconciled is through the cost report process.

The interim payment rate is called the all-inclusive reimbursement rate (AIRR) and is set by Medicare each year. Given the variability of services provided during an encounter or visit, there is great sensitivity regarding what is or is not included in the visit. For our next case study, let us assume that there is an AIRR rate of $80.00 per visit.

Case Study 2.14: Differences in RHC Visits

Two different patients present to an RHC on the same day. The first patient requires only a level 3 evaluation-and-management (E/M) service (i.e., CPT 99213) relative to a cold and nausea. The second patient presents with two lacerations after a fall. There is a general examination, and then the two lacerations, both simple lacerations on the same arm, are repaired. Here are the comparative payments relative to the MPFS:

	Regular Clinic Payment	*Rural Health Clinic per Visit Payment*
Patient One	$45.00	$80.00
Patient Two	$120.00	$80.00

While we are dealing only with the interim payment, for the first patient there is a $35.00 profit, while for the second patient there is a $40.00 loss. Of course, at the time of cost report reconciliation, the interim per visit payment may have been too low because there were too many extensive clinic visits, and everything will be adjusted to actual costs.

Note: In Case Study 2.14, there was no consideration of the fact that a nonphysician practitioner (NPP) may be providing the service, so that there is a reduction in the regular MPFS clinic for the

NPP. Also, no consideration has been made for any deductible or coinsurance. Coinsurance for clinic services is generally 20 percent.

For both RHCs and FQHCs, the definition of what is included in a visit and then also what constitutes a visit become important. For the most part, RHC services are premised on being mainly medical visits, that is, primary health care services. In some cases, particularly for provider-based RHCs, the RHC will be located in fairly close proximity to the hospital to which the RHC is provider based. If there is a hospital with emergency room (ER) services, most likely the second patient in Case Study 2.14 would go to the hospital ER instead of the RHC. However, there are cases when RHCs are not in close proximity to a hospital. These RHCs will have a tendency to have higher-level services provided at the RHC itself.

In both the second and third volumes in this series of books, the concept of an encounter or visit was discussed relative to the MPFS and outpatient prospective payment, namely, APCs. We have the same types of situations with the RHC encounter. Consider Case Study 2.15:

Case Study 2.15: Two Visits on the Same Day

Stephen, a Medicare beneficiary, visited the local RHC in the morning to address a cough and some congestion. Late in the afternoon, he returned to the RHC because of abdominal pain.

The question in Case Study 2.15 is whether there were two distinct visits versus a single visit that occurred at different times of the day. If there were two separate visits, then two separate per visit payments will be made. If the two encounters are related, then there was a single visit for payment purposes. Also, RHCs may provide services involving more than one health care professional, such as an NP and then also a clinical social worker (CSW). Ostensibly, in this type of case there are two different visits; however, the payment system will have to have directives in place to make appropriate decisions when adjudicating claims.

There are special requirements for establishing an RHC and even more requirements for an FQHC. The RHC must be located in a rural (i.e., nonurbanized) area where there are shortages of services. For example, a primary care HPSA or a medically underserved area (MUA). Here are some additional requirements:

■ Employ an NP or physician assistant (PA).
■ For 50 percent of the time the RHC is operating, there must be an NP, PA, or certified nurse midwife (CNM) working.
■ Routine diagnostic and laboratory services must be directly available (i.e., not under arrangements).
■ For emergencies, certain drugs and biologicals are to be available.
■ Furnish on site the following laboratory tests:
   – Urine test by stick or tablet
   – Hemoglobin or hematocrit
   – Blood sugar
   – Occult blood of stool specimens
   – Pregnancy tests
■ Primary culturing for transmittal to a certified laboratory

Services that RHCs provide include the following healthcare providers:

■ Physicians
■ NPs, PAs, CNMs, clinical psychologists (CPs), and CSWs

- Services incident to those of physicians and NPPs
- Medicare Part B covered drugs furnished by and incident to RHC providers
- Visiting nurse services for homebound patients where there is a shortage of HHAs

Interestingly, the various state Medicaid programs must recognize RHCs. Payment by the Medicaid programs can be on a cost basis, as with Medicare, or there can be alternative PPSs utilized.

FQHCs are different from RHCs in a number of aspects. Both are cost-based reimbursed using the Medicare cost report and an interim payment process based on visits. FQHCs tend to be broader in scope of services. For instance, FQHCs involve pharmacies, preventive health services, preventive dental services, case management, and primary care for all life-cycle ages. Interestingly, RHCs must use NPPs, while FQHCs do not have a similar requirement. However, because FQHCs are in rural underserved areas, there is a definite tendency to use midlevel practitioners. Another distinction is with emergency services. RHCs are required to provide emergency medical procedures as a first response to life-threatening injuries and acute illnesses. These services are basically the same as would be found in any physician's office or physician clinic. FQHCs are held to a higher standard in that they must either provide the emergency services or have well-defined access to emergency care on a 24/7/365 basis.

Note that for RHCs it is possible to obtain waivers relative to some of the requirements. For instance, an RHC may have difficulty recruiting a midlevel practitioner. A wavier relative to this requirement can be obtained for up to a year. Another situation that might arise is that an established RHC may have started in a shortage area, but over the period of several years, the shortage area designation may no longer be in effect. In a case of this type, the RHC may continue as a RHC.

Summary and Conclusion

Cost-based reimbursement for healthcare services is one of the oldest payment approaches. Cost reimbursement is a fee-for-service type of payment system; that is, the more services that are provided, the greater the costs and thus the greater the payments. Over the past several decades, cost-based reimbursement has been supplanted with PPSs and fee schedule payment systems. The intent of using these newer payment systems is their apparent ability to constrain healthcare payments as costs continue to escalate.

Cost-based reimbursement occurs at two levels, which we have called the micro and macro levels. Almost all healthcare payment systems use cost-based reimbursement at a micro or individual item level. There are certain drugs, biologicals, implantable medical devices, and expensive supply items that are highly variable in cost. These items also tend to come into the healthcare arena unexpectedly, so any sort of payment system that uses averaging to determine payments cannot properly address these new and ever-more-costly items. Thus, healthcare payers tend to pay for these items on a cost or cost-plus basis. Of course, there must be a way to determine the actual cost of these items before a payer can make payment. Determining cost is not a straightforward process. There are different approaches and a wide range of concepts when it comes to cost or to the process of costing items. Whenever possible, standard cost information is used as the basis for cost-based reimbursement for specific items. For example, for expensive pharmacy items, there is readily available information, such as the ASP and AWP. Even here, there is concern about including overhead costs as a part of the cost-based reimbursement.

At the macro or more global level, there a three special Medicare payment processes that are used with:

- CAHs
- RHCs
- FQHCs

When dealing with cost-based reimbursement for a wide range of healthcare services, there are two requirements:

- Determining overall costs for the services
- Utilizing an interim payment process until final costs can be determined

For the Medicare program, there is a complex Medicare cost-reporting process. Only allowable costs can be included on the cost report. Because of the extreme complexity of the cost report, specially trained financial analysts and accountants must gather cost and organizational data and then prepare the cost report. For Medicare, it takes about three to four years to prepare, submit, and then settle the cost report with the Medicare program. Because of this time lag, there must be some way to make interim payments. Once the cost report is finally settled, then the sum total of interim payments made can be compared to the sum total costs. If the costs are greater, then Medicare pays the difference. If the interim payments are more than the costs, then the provider must address the difference.

For CAHs, the interim payments depend on the type of service. The three general categories are:

- Inpatient: Per diem for covered days
- Swing bed: Per diem for covered days (separate from inpatient)
- Outpatient: Percentage of charges

Because of the lag in cost report settlement, there are mechanisms by which the interim payments can be adjusted to address ongoing changes in either costs or charges.

For RHCs and FQHCs, the interim payment is based on the concept of a visit or encounter. Because there can be significantly different services provided in a typical clinic visit, the interim payment rate can also vary. In addition, great concern must be given to what is included in a visit and what is or should be paid separately.

CAHs, RHCs, and FQHCs are all special Medicare designations that allow these entities to be cost-based reimbursed. There are rather stringent requirements to attain any of these designations. The Medicare program has developed these special designations over several decades to ensure that healthcare services are available to generally rural, underserved areas. Overall, these designations and associated cost-based reimbursement have become fairly popular.

Chapter 3

Healthcare Provider Charges and Charge-Based Payment Systems

Introduction

Charges made by healthcare providers of all types have an impact on overall healthcare payments and payment mechanisms. Sometimes, the charges directly affect payment. For instance, a patient without insurance must contend with the charges made for services. In another instance, a third-party payer may contract to pay 85 percent of the charges made by a hospital. In these two cases, along with others, there is a direct relationship between the charges made and the payments.

In some other cases, the influence of charges is relatively indirect. For example, the Medicare Physician Fee Schedule (MPFS) is based on a relative value scale that uses resource utilization as the determining factor for developing relative values and thus payment. So, at least in theory, physician charges have little to do with payments under the MPFS. However, there are other fee schedules that utilize the usual, customary, and reasonable (UCR)* charges to develop payments, particularly for physicians. In these cases, there is a more direct relationship between charges and healthcare payment.

Over the past decade, charges for healthcare services have become a major issue and are receiving much public attention. Most of the public attention focuses on what are perceived as excessive charges. Even with increased public scrutiny, those who are insured often have little concern with the charges that are made for healthcare services because they are protected. Let us join Sydney, who has the luxury of having a very nice employer-sponsored health plan.

---

* See the concept of UCR in *Fee Schedule Payment Systems*.

Case Study 3.1: Charge Sensitivity for Insured Patients

Sydney recently had some outpatient surgery performed. He has just received the explanation of benefits from his insurance company. Even though the hospital charged over $10,000.00, the insurance company allowed only $2,800.00 of the charges. The insurance company paid $2,520.00, and Sydney's copayment amount was $280.00.

In Case Study 3.1, Sydney may well complain about the $280.00 copayment, but there will be little concern about the overall charges from the hospital. The only issue that Sydney will relate to is his copayment amount. There may also be some deductible to satisfy as well. Let us take this same example for a Medicare beneficiary who has one of the standard Medicare supplemental policies (i.e., Medigap coverage).

Case Study 3.2: Charge Sensitivity for Medicare Beneficiary

Sarah, an elderly lady who resides in Anywhere, USA, recently received outpatient surgical services at the Apex Medical Center. She has received both her Medicare statement of benefits and the benefit statement from the supplemental insurance company. While the charges were more than $10,000.00, Medicare allowed only $2,100.00. Medicare paid $1,680.00, and the supplemental coverage paid the $420.00 copayment. Sarah owes nothing out of pocket.

In Case Study 3.2, do you suppose that Sarah will be concerned about the overall charges? Or, will she simply be pleased that she does not have to pay anything?

In this chapter, we discuss various payment mechanisms that involve charges. In some cases, we examine localized situations such as pass-through payment for expensive drugs, radiopharmaceutical sources, and medical devices. For other cases, the charge-based payment processes will be much more global, involving wide ranges of healthcare services. This micro versus macro approach is the same as we discussed in Chapter 2 for cost-based payment.

Charge-Based Payment: Key Features

Conceptually, charge-based payment for healthcare services is very simple. The third-party payer agrees to pay the healthcare provider a certain percentage of the charges on the claim form. The percentages generally range from about 65 percent to 95 percent. Of course, the actual percentage payment will have to be negotiated. Note that if the healthcare provider's charges are uniformly based on costs, then charge-based payment is really one step removed from cost-based reimbursement.

Note: In theory, charges are supposed to be uniformly based on the healthcare provider's costs. For hospitals under the Medicare program, charges must be uniformly based on costs.* How this requirement can be interpreted is open to question. However, as a general rule, charges are based on costs for healthcare providers. How much the charges are marked up from costs is another very real question.

Charge-based payment is typically considered in the context of some sort of insurance contract that a healthcare provider negotiates with an insurance company or some other third-party payer.

---

* See the concept of the *Medicare charging rule* as found at 42 CFR §1001.701 and the CMS *Provider Reimbursement Manual* (Publication 15-1) §2203.

There are instances when this concept is used in a more basic manner. The fundamental business arrangement for healthcare is that an individual presents to a healthcare provider, services are provided, and the healthcare provider bills (charges) the patient for services provided. The individual who received the services then pays the billed amount. This is basically a 100 percent of charges payment mechanism. In this case, there is no third-party payer involved.

In Case Study 3.3, we consider a slight variation on this overall theme.

Case Study 3.3: Negotiated Payment for Services

Shaun, middle-aged resident of Anywhere, USA, has only a major medical policy that will pay only for services that exceed $10,000.00 per year. Once the $10,000.00 deductible has been reached, the policy will pay 75 percent of the charges. Recently, Shaun fell in his yard while mowing the lawn and sustained several lacerations. He went to the Apex Medical Center's emergency department (ED), where services were provided. Shaun received the bill several days later and discovered a long list of services, supplies, and pharmacy items, all of which totaled $1,500.00. Shaun's deductible was nowhere close to being attained. Shaun decided to go to the hospital to see if he could negotiate a reduction in payment.

Do you think that Shaun will be successful in negotiating a reduction in payment? What if Shaun offered to pay 75 percent of the bill if an immediate cash payment was made? While it came as a surprise, Shaun was able to negotiate a reduction of 20 percent, that is, he paid 80 percent of the $1,500.00 or $1,200.00. Now, we can all argue about whether Shaun received a good deal, and there are some other associated questions that can be considered:

1. Did Apex lose money on this transaction? This question relates to how Apex charges and whether there is more than a 20-percent markup on costs that are used to develop the charges.
2. On Shaun's insurance policy, will he receive $1,500.00 in credit toward his insurance deductible (i.e., the charges), or will he receive $1,200.00 in credit (i.e., the payment)?
3. Is it generally possible to negotiate payments to healthcare providers for the amounts owed personally by patients?

As you can probably surmise, this little case study can engender some significant discussion. For instance, the last question can be raised in many different contexts, but the general answer is that a patient can always try to negotiate a reduction in payment. As we will discuss, healthcare providers of all types tend to mark up their charges significantly. The main point of this case study is to illustrate that charge-based payment to healthcare providers can occur at a localized level as opposed to an overall payment system level.

Among the many variables, the percentage-of-charges payment may vary depending on the type of services provided or items supplied. In some cases, charge-based and cost-based approaches may be combined in a single contract.

Case Study 3.4: Mixed Charge-Based and Cost-Based Arrangements

The Apex Medical Center is negotiating a contract with a smaller third-party payer in its local region. While the proposal is generally to pay Apex 88 percent of charges, for pharmaceutical items the third-party payer wants to pay 10 percent above the average wholesale price (AWP). Thus, pharmacy items will be on a cost-plus basis of cost plus 10 percent. In addition, Apex will be required to bill separately for all pharmacy items, and the charges for pharmacy items should be set at 10 percent above AWP.

We will revisit Case Study 3.4 further in this chapter when we discuss the concept of the hospital chargemaster. For hospital billing, there can be some unusual requirements, particularly through contractual arrangements.

While charge-based payment systems are most common with hospitals, they can also be used with physicians and other types of healthcare providers. All types of healthcare providers have charge structures, although they may masquerade with different names. For instance, for physicians and clinics the charges are often referred to as the *fee schedule* of charges.

Third-party payers that make payments based on a percentage of charges are *extremely sensitive* to the charge structure. Another key factor is how the healthcare provider changes and updates its charge structures, particularly for new services, pharmaceuticals, devices, and the like. Healthcare is highly dynamic, with many technological advances, many of which can be quite expensive. If unusually high charges are suddenly instituted, then the third-party payer will end up paying significantly more than may have been anticipated.

As a result of this sensitivity to charges, a number of contractual considerations will be made relative to charge structures, instituting new charges, and updating charges. Note that while the charge structures are a focus, there may also be very specific rules relative to coverage, medical necessity, and preauthorization for certain types of services. In this way, the third-party payer may be better able to control overall charges and thus the total payments when charge-based payment is made.

Case Study 3.5: Charge-Based Payment to Medicare Plus Percentage Payment

The Apex Medical Center has a contract with a smaller regional insurance company that pays 85 percent of charges for both inpatient and outpatient services. This insurance company has been aggressively marketing, so their market share is gaining. Now, the regional insurance company is maintaining that Apex is overcharging, and the insurance company wants to move to a payment process of whatever Medicare pays plus 25 percent. This would mean using Ambulatory Payment Classifications (APCs) for outpatient services and Medicare Severity Diagnosis Related Groups (MS-DRGs) for inpatient services.

The motivation on the part of the regional insurance company is that it, the insurance company, wants to reduce payments to Apex. As you can probably ascertain, the insurance company has probably run all of the financial models before making this new offer. Apex will certainly have to perform some careful financial analyses as well to determine whether the proposed payment process is appropriate and profitable.

Charge Structures for Healthcare Providers

Over the last several decades, charges made by healthcare providers of all types have generally become inflated. The basic reason charges have increased is called *cost shifting*. As insurance companies and government programs such as Medicare have instituted payment systems such as fee schedules and prospective payment, the actual amounts paid to healthcare providers has, relatively, been reduced. To make up some of the real or perceived losses, healthcare providers have tended to increase their charges for private-pay patients, those patients who have payers that will pay the full charges, those patients who do not have insurance coverage or are not under some sort of federal or state payment system.

Individuals who have insurance coverage of some sort may not even look carefully at the actual charges being made for the healthcare services. Instead, because insurance is paying, the only real interest is in how much the given individual must pay out of pocket. This means that for insured individuals, there is little sensitivity to the overall actual charges.

Case Study 3.6: Realization Rate

Sarah was recently in the hospital for outpatient surgery. She is a Medicare beneficiary and has a supplemental policy. After Sarah received all of her explanations of benefits and payments made by Medicare and her supplemental policy, she was surprised to learn that even though there were total charges of $15,500.00, the hospital only received total payment of $8,000.00 from both Medicare and her supplemental policy.

In Case Study 3.6, for this case, what is the hospital's realization rate? In this case, the calculation is to divide $8,000.00 by $15,500.00, which is about 52 percent. If you were the chief financial officer (CFO) at a hospital, what kind of a realization rate would you desire? The answer to this question really relates to your charge structure and relative costs. If you are at a hospital with a relatively high charge structure, then a realization rate of 60 percent might be more than adequate. This would mean that for each dollar charged, there would be payment at 60 cents. If your general markup formula is twice your cost, then 60 percent of the double cost would result in an overall return of 20 percent above costs. This calculation is an oversimplification but illustrates the concept of realization under charge-based payment.

Case Study 3.7: Conservative Hospital Pricing

Over the years, the Apex Medical Center has been very conservative in marking-up their charges. Generally, no more than a 50-percent markup above cost is made. Other hospitals in the general area have developed charges that are often more than two to three times their costs. There is a local insurance company that wants to establish a 70-percent-of-charges payment process. The other hospitals in the area have agreed to such contracts with little negotiation. Apex is balking at 70 percent and wants something more in the 90-percent range.

Case Study 3.7 illustrates that when there are very different charging structures, particularly if a given hospital is too low or too high relative to other hospitals, then difficulties can ensue. In theory, the hospital or other healthcare provider that has low charges should be more attractive in the marketplace. However, charge levels are not always that visible to patients and sometimes even to third-party payers. In the next section we discuss some general pricing strategies, including market pricing, in which a healthcare provider will attempt to position itself within a relatively normative range of charges consistent with its marketplace.

Healthcare Pricing Strategies

Increased charge structures relative to cost shifting are a definite challenge if charge-based reimbursement is utilized. The challenges extend to both overall charge-based payments and localized charge-based payment for individual drugs, items, and specialized services.

There are four concepts or methodologies that are generally used for healthcare pricing:

■ Strategic pricing
■ Transparent pricing

- Geographic pricing
- Market pricing

Strategic pricing is a process in which the healthcare provider attempts to arrange its prices in a manner that will optimize reimbursement. Depending on the type of healthcare provider, this can become a very complex financial analytical process. Healthcare providers of all types are under a variety of payment systems. For a given service or item, one payer may pay more than another payer. With a different service or item, the payment levels may be reversed. So, at a detailed item level, payments may vary, and the provider will probably move its charges up to be as high as any payer will pay. Let us join the Acme Medical Clinic as the physicians ponder how to set their charges, that is, the clinic fee schedule.

Case Study 3.8: Setting Clinic Charges

The physicians at the Acme Medical Clinic have retained a consultant to review and adjust their schedule of charges on an annual basis. The consultant has analyzed the main payers for the clinic and then set the clinic charges to be as high as the highest-paying fee schedule amount for each individual service on the clinic fee schedule. Over time, this has caused the clinic's charges to become relatively high, but at least reimbursement has been optimized.

We return to this case study as we further discuss the different pricing strategies. Similar processes can be performed by other types of healthcare providers.

Case Study 3.9: Setting Hospital Charges

The Apex Medical Center has retained a consultant to review its charges. There are about 25,000 line-item charges in AMC's chargemaster. The consultant has performed extensive financial analyses relative to the mix of third-party payers that provide payment to Apex. The consultant's recommendations involve increasing certain charges more than others. However, over the years, the charge structure at Apex has risen significantly.

In both of these case studies, the goal has been to optimize* reimbursement, and this process of strategic pricing has generated ever-higher charges. Part of the reason for these increases is cost shifting, although cost shifting to self-pay or uninsured patients can generate significant consternation on the part of patients.

Transparent pricing is a relatively new concept that has arisen as patients have become concerned about the charges made by healthcare providers. The general idea is that the pricing for healthcare services should be readily available and understandable to patients. Having visible charge structures may or may not have much meaning for patients. For a clinic, the charge structure for office visits may be of some usefulness. If the charge structures are available, a patient might compare office visit charges for other clinics and then choose the less expensive. For hospitals, making charges available may not provide much meaningful information to a patient due to the level of detail and variability in structuring charges. In the next section, we discuss hospital chargemasters, in which there are thousands, if not tens of thousands, of line items that represent the hospital's charges.

---

* Due to compliance concerns, the word *optimize* is used instead of *maximize*.

Case Study 3.10: Comparing Hospital Charges

Sam needs to have an elective outpatient procedure performed. While Sam is an enrollee under a managed care plan, he is determined to use a hospital that has reasonable charges or the lowest charges if possible. He has contacted each of the three hospitals in his area and asked about the charges for the procedure. In each case, the hospitals could or would only give some generalized idea of the possible range of charges. Sam has now obtained the chargemasters from each of the three hospitals to compare the charges for the procedure.

While the charge structures for healthcare providers can be readily available, that is, transparent, the usefulness of such information to patients or even third-party payers may be quite limited. For Case Study 3.10, Sam will probably find the hospitals' chargemaster unintelligible relative to his specific procedure. The reason for the difficulty in deciphering a hospital chargemaster is that charge structures are developed under sometimes very different approaches.

Case Study 3.11: Surgery Charges for Different Hospitals

From Case Study 3.10, Sam has been studying the chargemasters from the three hospitals. He has narrowed down the charges for the operating rooms. However, each of the three chargemasters is set up quite differently:

1. In the first hospital, there are simply seven different levels of operating room charges.
2. In the second hospital, there appears to be three different hourly charges for use of the operating rooms.
3. In the third hospital, there appears to be three different base charges plus 15-minute increment charges for each of the three levels.

Also, Sam has been unable to find anything specific to his planned surgery.

Because the charge structures are all different for the three hospitals in Case Study 3.11, there is no real way to compare possible charges for the surgery that Sam needs. Also, the use of an operating room is but one of many charges that will need to be accumulated. For instance, there will be recovery room charges, technical component anesthesia, and presurgery and postsurgery room use.

Geographic and market pricing are similar. For the Acme Medical Clinic in Case Study 3.8, the main concern is market pricing relative to other clinics in Acme's area, that is, its competitors. When the scope of the marketplace becomes broad enough, we move into geographic pricing, for which the charges are compared with similar providers in the region even though the other providers may not be competitors.

For instance, in Case Study 3.8, the physicians at Acme may accept the suggested set of charges, but there may be great sensitivity to office visit charges. These office visits use the Current Procedural Terminology (CPT) code set of what are called E/M codes, which stands for evaluation and management. The physicians at Acme will be very sensitive to their relative position in the marketplace and may well lower the E/M charges to appear competitive.

For larger healthcare providers such as systems of hospitals or large integrated delivery systems, there may be more concern for their relative position geographically. In other words, what are other hospital systems and integrated delivery systems doing relative to their pricing? That is, does a given integrated delivery system have its charge structure so that it is not significantly out of alignment with similar providers within a geographic region? A geographic region could be a state or grouping of states or even nationally.

Note: In the healthcare area, there is great sensitivity relative to price fixing as monitored by the Federal Trade Commission (FTC). Thus, the availability of comparative price structures from other specific healthcare providers may be delimited. Generally, charge structures are statistically amalgamated so that charges are available on some sort of an averaged basis. How these price-fixing concerns address those states where charge structures are public is an interesting question. (See Chapter 6 for further discussion of compliance issues.)

Chargemasters for Hospitals and Integrated Delivery Systems

Charge-based payment for hospitals is common. Charge-based payment is also used for other healthcare providers, such as home health, skilled nursing, and other healthcare entities that are parts of integrated delivery system. Often, integrated delivery systems are developed around hospitals or hospital systems. Thus, hospital billing systems have been developed to address not only hospital services but also physician and clinic services, skilled nursing services, home health services, pharmacy operations, and durable medical equipment (DME) suppliers.

As a part of hospital billing systems, there is a special file called the chargemaster. For a particular hospital billing system, there may be other terminology, such as the service master, charge description master (CDM), or other descriptive terms. Fundamentally, the chargemaster is a listing of all the charges that a hospital makes. The number of charges is routinely in the thousands, sometimes tens of thousands, of line items. If there are different types of healthcare providers being billed through the hospital billing system, then there will be even more line items. For example, the hospital may have home health services or employ physicians and have clinics of various types.

When services are provided at the hospital, the charges are accumulated using the chargemaster to generate the overall itemization of services, supplies, pharmacy items, and so on. For instance, a patient may present to the hospital for a surgical procedure. Charges will be accumulated for such general categories as the operating room, recovery room, anesthesia, pharmacy items, surgical supplies, and the like. Even for a relatively straightforward outpatient surgical procedure, there can be dozens, sometimes hundreds, of different charges.

As illustrated in Case Study 3.11, different approaches are taken to establishing the chargemaster. Sometimes, there is great detail in charges, while in other instances various charges may be combined or bundled into very general categories.

Case Study 3.12: Specialty Orthopedic Hospital

A group of orthopedic surgeons developed an ambulatory surgical center (ASC) for certain orthopedic surgeries. To gain better reimbursement and provide more advanced services, the ASC has been converted into a specialty orthopedic hospital. However, there are only 52 different orthopedic surgery services provided. There is no emergency department, although there is a laboratory and a pharmacy. The decision has been made to have a very simple chargemaster. There will be one single bundled charge for each of the 52 surgeries that are performed.

The chargemaster approach used in Case Study 3.12 is very simple. Great care will be needed to make certain that the single charge for each procedure captures all the costs for facilities, equipment, supplies, implants, laboratory tests, and pharmacy items. How will this simple approach affect payment? Keep in mind that the physician professional charges, anesthesia professional charges, and the like will be made separately outside the hospital bill as such. Also, claims will be filed as usual with procedure and diagnosis coding as required by the given payment system.

Hospital chargemasters are also an issue for other types of payment systems, including cost-based systems and different prospective payment systems (PPS). For hospital PPSs such as MS-DRGs and APCs, the chargemaster along with the cost report generate the all-important cost-to-charge ratios (CCRs).* It is the CCRs that are used to convert charges on the claims into the costs for services, which are then used to perform the statistical calculations to determine the relative weights and finally the associated payments.

For cost-based payment systems, the chargemaster is still used to develop charges for services; the CCRs are used to establish costs, and then comparisons are made to the cost report itself to determine overall proper cost-based payments.

Because hospital chargemasters are used in a wide variety of different payment systems, there are many rules and directives that apply to the chargemaster, particularly from the Medicare program. In addition, there may be some very significant constraints from managed care contracts. Let us return to Case Study 3.4. In this case study, pharmaceutical items must be priced, that is, charged, at 10 percent above the AWP. Thus, the chargemaster coordinator at Apex will set up the pharmacy section so that all the pharmacy items appear with the appropriate charges for this contract. Also, the pharmacy items will need to be separated into inpatient and outpatient items through what are called *revenue codes*. To achieve proper billing, the chargemaster may need adjustment, and the billing system logic may also need to be altered.

Note: Revenue codes are four-digit codes, most of which have a leading zero. These codes are promulgated and maintained by the National Uniform Billing Committee or NUBC.† These codes are used on the chargemaster to categorize the various line items.

Revenue codes constitute a standard code set that is used on the UB-04 claim or the equivalent 837-I electronic format. The revenue code set is an interesting code set that has been developed over the years to meet various billing needs. If you take the time to review this entire code set, you will probably note some seeming inconsistencies because the series of codes has been developed as needed. The official guidance can be found in the NUBC's *Official UB-04 Data Specifications Manual,* which is published each year on July 1 by the American Hospital Association (AHA).

Let us look at one revenue code sequence, 027X. The "X" is used as a placeholder for different fourth digits. Not all of the possible fourth digits are always used in a given sequence. In practice, these codes are often referenced as three-digit codes, such as 272 for sterile supplies:

> 027X: Medical/surgical supplies and devices
> 0270: General classification
> 0271: Nonsterile supply
> 0272: Sterile supply
> 0273: Take-home supplies
> 0274: Prosthetic/orthotic devices
> 0275: Pacemaker
> 0276: Intraocular lenses (IOLs)
> 0277: Oxygen: take home
> 0278: Other implants
> 0279: Other supplies/devices

---

* See *Prospective Payment Systems* for a discussion of establishing payments for APCs and MS-DRGs.
† For more information, go to http://www.nubc.org.

The 027X sequence also has an extension sequent, 062X, that addresses supplies incident to radiology, supplies incident to other diagnostic services, surgical dressings, and Food and Drug Administration (FDA) investigational devices.

Reading through the 027X sequence seems quite reasonable. However, for payment systems that are in any way charge based or influenced in some manner by charges, the treatment of these supply/devices revenue codes becomes important. Let us briefly visit the Maximus Insurance Company.

Case Study 3.13: Variable Payment for Supply Items

The Maximus Insurance Company has established a number of managed care contracts with hospitals and hospital systems. In the supply and device area, the following formulas are generally used:

0270: Maximus does not recognize this revenue code for reimbursement.
0271: Payment is 75 percent of charges for nonsterile supplies.
0272: Payment is 85 percent of charges for sterile supplies.
0273: Take-home supplies are not reimbursed.
0274: Prosthetic/orthotic devices are paid at cost plus 10 percent.
0275: Pacemakers are paid at cost plus 10 percent.
0276: IOLs, including vision-correcting IOLs, are paid on a separate fee schedule.
0277: Take-home oxygen is not reimbursed.
0278: Other implants are paid at 90 percent of charges.
0279: Maximus does not recognize this revenue code.

In Case Study 3.13, there are different payment levels and even different approaches for payment of various supplies and devices. For both Maximus and the healthcare provider filing claims, it is important that items be correctly classified so that the payment process is correct or at least in accordance with the managed care contract. For instance, other implants (i.e., revenue code 0278) are paid at a higher percentage than sterile supplies, although the implants are sterile. So, how does a hospital know what goes into the *other implants* category?

Note: In Case Study 3.13, Maximus does not recognize revenue code 0270. Other third-party payers may well recognize this revenue code. Thus, the chargemaster will need to accommodate this difference or possibly just eliminate revenue code 0270 and then use the more detailed revenue codes for all supply items.

A definition of *other implants* is provided in the UB-04 manual on page 116, Version 6.0, July 2011. Namely:

> That which is implanted, such as a piece of tissue, a tooth, a pellet of medicine, or a tube or needle containing a radioactive substance, a graft, or an insert. Also included are liquid and solid plastic materials used to augment tissues or to fill in areas traumatically or surgically removed. An object or material partially or totally inserted or grafted into the body for prosthetic, therapeutic, diagnostic purposes.

The UB-04 manual goes on to give examples, such as stents, artificial joints, shunts, grafts, pins, plates, screws, anchors, and radioactive seeds. Thus, there is reasonable guidance regarding what should go into this category; however, there can still be some significant questions that do arise. Note that when categorization decisions are made, there can be payment implications and thus compliance issues as well.

Interestingly, there are other challenges with supply items as listed or, as we shall see, not listed in a hospital's chargemaster. One of these is with what are termed *routine supply* items or sometimes *nonancillary supply* items. Let us examine a simple case study before we discuss this concept.

Case Study 3.14: Routine Supply Items

The Apex Medical Center has more than a dozen percentage-of-charges contracts with different payers. As a result, Apex has become very fastidious about separately charging for even inexpensive supply items such as cotton balls, tongue depressors, steri-strips, and a host of other items. There is often a default charge of $1.00 for these items, and staff are supposed to document the number and type of inexpensive supplies used.

Is Apex doing anything inappropriate in Case Study 3.14? Technically, there is nothing wrong with doing this for private payers who do not exclude these items in their contracts. Granted, a quick financial analysis would probably show that there is more cost to tracking, reporting, and billing these items than can possibly be obtained in payment.

However, there is a problem with the Medicare program. Under the Medicare program for these routine supply items, separate charging is not allowed. The payment for these routine supply items is supposed to come from payment for the associated services. Only ancillary or nonroutine supply items qualify for separate charging (i.e., separate line items in the chargemaster.)

Note: This is basically the same concept as discussed in Chapter 2 with routine costs and ancillary costs. Routine costs are supposed to be a part of the room or other service. Only ancillary costs are allowed separately.

Thus, chargemaster coordinators* at hospitals and integrated delivery systems will normally remove these items from the chargemaster and thus not charge anyone for these routine supply items. Clearly, knowing exactly which supply items are routine is of utmost importance to charge correctly for Medicare and thus other payers as well.

The concept of ancillary and routine can arise in unexpected ways (see Case Study 3.15).

Case Study 3.15: Charging for Unusual Nursing Services

The nursing staff for the medical/surgical floors at the Apex Medical Center are concerned that they are not being truly recognized for all of their services. In some instances, they do have to perform duties above and beyond the call of routine nursing services. Assisting physicians with bedside procedures and performing duties for special needs patients are examples. The nurses want to be able to charge extra for these special services.

Under the Medicare program for both costs and charges, the key word is *routine*. Routine nursing services are part of the medical/surgical room charges; that is, they are bundled. There are mechanisms for adding charges or actually establishing higher room charges in special cases. The issue is a compliance challenge in differentiating between routine services and nonroutine or ancillary services that are separately chargeable and represent separate costs.

Let us consider one additional revenue code sequence before we discuss setting charges and then the public scrutiny of charges. Here is the revenue code sequence for pharmacy:

025X: Pharmacy
0250: General classification

---

* Chargemaster coordinators are hospital personnel who develop and maintain the chargemaster.

0251: Generic drugs
0252: Nongeneric drugs
0253: Take-home drugs
0254: Drugs incident to other diagnostic services
0255: Drugs incident to radiology
0256: Experimental drugs
0257: Nonprescription
0258: Intravenous solutions
0259: Other pharmacy

As with supplies, there is an extension revenue code sequence, 063X, for drugs such as self-administrable drugs (revenue code 0637) and drugs that require detailed coding using level II Healthcare Common Procedure Coding System (HCPCS) or national drug codes (NDCs) (revenue code 0636). Revenue code 0250 is used extensively by hospitals for inpatient services. As a general rule, for inpatient pharmacy items the hospital simply makes a charge without any sort of code. However, on the outpatient side, drugs must often be specifically identified with some sort of code. Inexpensive drugs are often not paid separately; instead, payment is bundled into associated services. Of course, what constitutes an inexpensive drug must be defined either for statutory programs or through a managed care contract with private third-party payers.

There are additional concerns with drugs, most of which involve coverage. Take-home drugs are often not covered. The Medicare program does not cover self-administrable drugs (i.e., pills, ointments, salves, suppositories, drops, etc.). Interestingly, intravenous solutions (see revenue code 0258) are listed under the pharmacy revenue code sequence. In some cases, intravenous solutions are considered as routine supply items; thus, according to Medicare, they are not separately billable. In other cases, intravenous solutions may be dispensed from the pharmacy for individual patients and thus are separately billable.

Intravenous solutions are used to administer intravenous drugs either as infusions or as intravenous pushes. Interestingly, in terms of hospital charges, intravenous solutions can become quite contentious. Setting aside for a moment the concept of whether these items are routine (i.e., not separately chargeable) or nonroutine (i.e., separately chargeable), there can be significant consternation relative to how these items are priced.

Case Study 3.16: Intravenous Solution Pricing

Sarah recently had some problems with fainting. It was nothing that serious, but she did go to the emergency department at Apex, where they treated her. Also, she stayed in observation for a day and a half. During her stay, she received several medications through an intravenous access. While Medicare and her supplemental policy covered everything, she received the itemized statement and noticed that there were five bags of intravenous solution listed with a charge of nearly $600.00. Sarah asked her nephew to check on the Internet to see how much these intravenous solutions cost. A quick search showed costs that could be well below $10.00.

For hospitals, which purchase great quantities of intravenous solutions, the costs can be decreased even further. So, why does Apex have such a high charge? There can be a number of reasons. There may be other services bundled (e.g., the intravenous insertion kit and tubing), but the most likely is that over many years the price has simply been increased. This case study is a good example of why transparent pricing has become important relative to patient perceptions.

Now, back to revenue code sequence 025X. Given this brief summary of revenue code sequence 025X, how does this relate to charges and payments? The simple answer is that there are quite variable approaches to establishing charges and the way in which payments are or can be made. An added element with pharmacy items is that there is readily available information concerning the prices for pharmacy items on a national basis. The two most common are:

- Average wholesale price (AWP)
- Average sales price (ASP)

For a given hospital or other healthcare provider, the actual cost of a particular drug may or may not be the AWP or ASP. If a hospital uses a large volume of a pharmacy item, then it may be able to negotiate a better price. Nonetheless, having this type of information affects the way in which payments can be made, which then affects the way that charges may or may not be influenced.

Case Study 3.17: Contractual Difference for Drug Reimbursement

Sylvia, the chargemaster coordinator at the Apex Medical Center, is in a quandary. There is one payer contract that specifies that pharmacy items will be paid at ASP plus 20 percent, but the charge made must be the ASP plus the 20-percent level. Another payer contract indicates that payment will be ASP plus 25 percent, but the actual charge must be the ASP for the drug, and the 25 percent will be added on by the third-party payer. Sylvia is trying to find a way that the chargemaster can be established to meet these differing requirements.

This case study is similar to Case Study 3.4. Meeting variable demands for both statutory programs and a multitude of contractually based payment processes is often a significant challenge. The chargemaster must have special capabilities for applying revenue codes, procedure codes, and even pricing in some circumstances. Keep in mind that the chargemaster is an integral part of the overall billing system. In some cases, providers will even use a separate back-end system that is interfaced to the billing system to modify claims before they are submitted for adjudication and payment.

Charge Compression

To understand the concept and challenge of *charge compression*, we must examine CCRs. Both charges and costs are an integral part of many healthcare payment systems. There may be direct cost-based reimbursement or charge-based reimbursement, but various PPSs also depend, to some extent, on both charges and costs. This dependence arises in the form of the *cost-to-charge ratios* or CCRs. Note that this use of costs and charges affects both statutory programs such as Medicare and Medicaid and contractual payment systems that piggyback in any way on prospective payment processes.

The concept of CCRs is fairly simple: divide the costs by the charges. Well, it is not quite that simple. Both the charges and the costs must be appropriately categorized and then compared to obtain different CCRs for services provided and items dispensed for categories of services and items. In Chapter 2, we discussed the Medicare cost report, and we have just discussed the chargemaster. As long as all the directives for the cost report and categorization of charges are followed, different CCRs can be calculated. Table 3.1 presents some CCRs for the fictitious Apex Medical Center.

This is just a representative sampling. There will also be general hospital CCRs for both inpatient and outpatient services. As you study these CCRs, you should note some interesting characteristics. First, there is a great deal of variation between different CCRs. If the charge structure at

Apex was developed so that charges were uniformly based on costs, would that not produce CCRs that are generally the same? Second, there are two CCRs (i.e., recovery room and ED) that are greater than one. This means that the costs are greater than the charges. How could this possibly happen? The general answer to this question lies in the complexity of the cost-reporting process and how charges, and thus costs, are categorized.

Our intent is simply to illustrate that cost reporting, establishing charge schedules and the calculation of CCRs, is quite complex for hospitals and integrated delivery systems. At the same time, these CCRs are important to gain proper reimbursement under various payment systems, especially for hospitals, nursing facilities, home health agencies, and similar healthcare providers. Physicians and clinics are even being brought into the CCR arena as hospitals employ more physicians and establish provider-based clinics.

Now, we have all of the elements that are needed to discuss charge compression. We illustrate this concept with supply items, although this process occurs in other areas as well (e.g., pharmacy items). Let us rejoin Sylvia, the chargemaster coordinator at Apex. The formula for marking up supply items is being reviewed. A consensus is reached that the algorithm in Table 3.2 be used to establish charges for supply items (i.e., items in revenue code sequence 027X).

Table 3.1   Sample Cost-to-Charge Ratios

Service Department	CCR
Operating room	0.65374
Recovery room	1.10045
Delivery and labor room	0.92834
Ultrasound	0.55641
Laboratory	0.66730
Intravenous therapy	0.88452
Respiratory therapy	0.45885
Physical therapy	0.87043
Observation	0.34650
Emergency room	1.05478

Table 3.2   Supply Item Markup Formula

Tier 1	Items that cost less than $20.00, multiply by 3.50
Tier 2	Items that cost between $21.00 and $75.00, multiply by 3.00
Tier 3	Items that cost between $76.00 and $200.00, multiply by 2.50
Tier 4	Items that cost between $201.00 and $1,000.00, multiply by 2.00
Tier 5	Items that cost between $1,001.00 and $2,500.00 multiply by 1.50
Tier 6	Items that cost above $2,501.00, multiply by 1.20

As this tiered approach shows, inexpensive supply items are priced at 3.50 times their (acquisition) cost. Expensive items such as stents, pacemakers, and the like are marked up only by 20 percent; that is, multiply the acquisition cost by 1.20. Now, all of these items will be under revenue code sequence 027X, with some in the extension to 027X, that is, 062X. If a single CCR is developed for 027X, then this tiered approach will skew the CCRs that are present for each of the tiers.

While overly simplistic, here are the CCRs for each of the tiers:

$$\text{Tier 1: } 1/3.50 = 0.2857$$

$$\text{Tier 2: } 1/3.00 = 0.3333$$

$$\text{Tier 3: } 1/2.50 = 0.4000$$

$$\text{Tier 4: } 1/2.00 = 0.5000$$

$$\text{Tier 5: } 1/1.50 = 0.6667$$

$$\text{Tier 6: } 1/1.20 = 0.8333$$

We can only guesstimate what the overall CCR will be. We would need volumes for various supply items to make an actual calculation. However, the CCR will be someplace in the middle of this range. Let us use 0.4500 to illustrate the concept of charge compression.

Case Study 3.18: Low Reimbursement for Drug-Eluting Stents

Apex is having difficulty being properly reimbursed for expensive drug-eluting coronary stents. Relatively low payment is occurring for Medicare for both inpatients and outpatients, and now various private payers are also lowering their reimbursement for these stents following the Medicare payment levels.

What is happening in Case Study 3.18 is that the CCR of 0.4500 for supply items is being used to calculate what the payers think the cost of the stents is to Apex. Here is a simple example:

$$\text{Cost to Apex for Drug-Eluting Stent} = \$5,000.00$$

$$\text{Markup Cost by 1.20: } 1.20 * \$5,000.00 = \$6,000.00$$

$$\text{Cost-to-Charge Ratio} = 0.4500$$

$$\text{Cost Calculated by Payer from Claim: } 0.4500 * \$6,000.00 = \$2,700.00$$

From this example, you should see that the payers think the cost of the stent is $2,700.00, when in actuality the cost is $5,000.00. If this process is repeated by hospitals all across the country, then payers will generally be underpaying (i.e., paying below cost) for these stents and a host of other expensive implantable medical devices.

To address this charge compression issue, the Centers for Medicare and Medicaid Services (CMS) have changed the cost-reporting process to identify expensive implantable devices (e.g., revenue code 0278) separately and then calculate a more appropriate CCR for these items.* The next case study extends Case Study 2.4.

> **Case Study 3.19: Proper Pricing of Pacemakers**
>
> The Apex Medical Center is performing a rapidly increasing number of cardiac implants, including pacemakers. These devices are quite expensive as technology rapidly advances. One such device costs $12,000.00. Apex has been advised that the charge for this device should be priced at least using the cost divided by the CCR developed through the Medicare cost report. For Apex, the proper CCR is 0.40. This means that the charge will need to be $12,000.00/0.40 = $30,000.00.

The $30,000.00 charge seems, and probably is, outrageous. However, when Medicare receives this charge and then converts it back into the cost, the proper amount of $12,000.00 will be calculated (i.e., 0.40 * $30,000.00 = $12,000.00). The overall solution to this situation is to avoid the charge compression that has produced the low CCR. The changes to the Medicare cost-reporting process mentioned should help with this situation.

Medicare Charging Rule

Toward the beginning of this chapter, the so-called Medicare charging rule was mentioned. Two citations were provided in a footnote:

■ 42 CFR (*Code of Federal Regulations*) §1001.701
■ The CMS *Provider Reimbursement Manual* (Publication 15-1) §2203

In its simplest form, this rule states that hospitals are not to charge Medicare patients more than they charge other patients. If discounts are being routinely provided to non-Medicare patients, then inappropriate payments by Medicare might occur. This is certainly an oversimplification. This will become evident as we discuss some examples. The Medicare charging rule involves both the charge structures as found in the chargemaster and the cost report that must be filed for various types of healthcare providers who participate[†] in the Medicare program.

While a complete discussion of the Medicare charging rule is beyond the scope of this book, we will look at the basics. No matter how this rule is interpreted, conceptually this rule has a significant impact on how hospitals and other healthcare providers establish their charge structures within the chargemaster.

Note: There has been a long-standing interpretation from CMS that does not allow CMS to dictate how hospitals and associated healthcare providers can charge for services.[‡] Thus, hospitals can have high charges, low charges, or something in-between. What CMS can do is to require consistency in setting charges, whether high, low, or in-between.

---

* For instance, see page 24104 of the May 22, 2009, *Federal Register* (74 FR 24104).
† The word *participate* is used in the general sense. There is a more formal use of this word for physicians who formally participate in the Medicare program and agree to accept the payments made by Medicare.
‡ For instance, see 70 FR 68662.

Here are two excerpts from CFR §1001.701:

> Submitted, or caused to be submitted, bills or requests for payments under Medicare or any of the State health care programs containing charges or costs for items or services furnished that are *substantially in excess of such individual's or entity's usual charges or costs* for such items or services; [emphasis added]

> Submitting, or causing to be submitted, bills or requests for payment that contain charges or costs substantially in excess of usual charges or costs when such charges or costs are due to *unusual circumstances or medical complications requiring additional time, effort, expense or other good cause* [emphasis added]

This is the OIG (Office of the Inspector General) section of the CFR. At issue is the OIG's ability to exclude a provider or supplier from the Medicare program. The first statement indicates that the providers or suppliers must not charge in excess of their usual charges. The second statement provides for exceptions to the first statement. In other words, charges can be higher than usual if there is some good reason.

All of these terms and phrases must be carefully defined to apply these rules. Even for the OIG, this area has proven very difficult. This is mainly due to the extreme variability of how hospitals establish their chargemasters (e.g., see Case Study 3.10). This variability includes very different ways to establish markups. The OIG did issue a very interesting *Federal Register* entry on September 15, 2003 (68 FR 53939). While the OIG *proposed* some interpretations, there was never any final rule issued. For instance, the OIG proposed that if a hospital receives discounted payments, then these payments would be imputed as usual charges. Let us visit the Apex Medical Center to see what would happen if this OIG interpretation were to become reality.

Case Study 3.20: Percentage-of-Charge Payment Contract

The largest private payer contract that Apex has is a contract whereby 80 percent of Apex's charges are paid by the payer for services provided both inpatient and outpatient.

The basic facts in Case Study 3.20 are very representative of percentage-of-charges payment contracts. This is a fairly standard contract that pays 80 percent of charges. However, the OIG proposed interpretation would mean that the 80-percent payment would be construed actually to become the de facto charges. In the meantime, Medicare beneficiaries would be charged at the full charges. Thus, the charges to the Medicare beneficiaries would be more than the (imputed) charges made to this private payer. In theory, this would violate the Medicare charging rule.

Again, this discussion is oversimplified. Volume of charges must also be considered. The basic idea is that if the volume of lower charges is not too high, then the Medicare charging rule is not violated. Again, let us join Apex.

Case Study 3.21: Preferential Laboratory Fee Schedule

The Apex Medical Center has a single set of charges for various laboratory tests. To have the community physicians use the hospital's laboratory, a proposal has been made to develop a discounted, preferential fee schedule for community physicians.

For Case Study 3.21, the issue is that Medicare patients would be charged the full fees for laboratory tests, while other patients would be charged less. Of course, because laboratory services, for

Medicare, are paid on a fee schedule basis, there would be no increased payment from Medicare even if there were a preferential fee schedule.* Here is another example in which there may be a need to establish lower, preferential charges.

Case Study 3.22: Sports Therapy Preferential Charges

The Apex Medical Center has several satellite physician therapy clinics. There is an increasing demand for self-pay services for special sports training provided by physical therapists. However, Apex's charges for physical therapy have become quite high over the years to gain the highest possible payment. To attract these self-pay customers, a proposal has been made to develop a lower, preferential set of charges.

Most likely Apex will go ahead and establish the preferential charge schedule. It could also simply provide a steep discount; that is, self-pay patients would only have to pay, say, 60 percent of the usual charges. Based on cursory discussion of the Medicare charging rule, do you think this preferential set of charges could be a problem? Technically, the answer is yes, but the volume would probably be low enough so that the rule is not violated.

There is yet another aspect to the Medicare charging rule, and this is found in the Medicare *Provider Integrity Manual* (PIM) at §2203.

> To assure that Medicare's share of the provider's costs equitably reflects the costs of services received by Medicare beneficiaries, the intermediary, in determining *reasonable cost reimbursement,* evaluates the charging practice of the provider to ascertain whether it results in an equitable basis for apportioning costs. So that its charges may be allowable for use in apportioning costs under the program, *each facility should have an established charge structure which is applied uniformly to each patient as services are furnished to the patient and which is reasonably and consistently related to the cost of providing the services.* While the Medicare program cannot dictate to a provider what its charges or charge structure may be, the program may determine whether or not the charges are allowable for use in apportioning costs under the program. [emphasis added]

This language can be interpreted in different ways. However, the general directive indicates that charges are supposed to be uniformly based on costs.

While we have discussed a number of concepts, there is a very basic question. If charges are based on costs, then the hospital or related healthcare provider must know their costs. This sounds very simple. If a healthcare provider has invested in cost accounting, then there is a good chance that the costs for services can be accurately determined. If we are dealing with a drug, supply items, or device, then the acquisition costs will be known. While some hospitals and other larger healthcare providers may have cost accounting, many, if not most, smaller hospitals and healthcare providers do not have cost accounting. Thus, the costs for various services are simply not accurately known.

Case Study 3.23: Setting a Charge for a New Procedure

Sylvia, the chargemaster coordinator at the Apex Medical Center, has a request to place a charge in the chargemaster for a new procedure. She has spoken with the service area, and a charge of $560.00 has been suggested. This is a guesstimated charge based on roughly similar services. Sylvia decided to contact another hospital on the other side of the state to see if it performed this service and what it charged. She was surprised to find that its charge was $1,800.00.

---

* This assumes that the preferential fee schedule does not go lower than the payments from the Medicare Laboratory Fee Schedule (MLFS).

In Chapter 6, we will look at this case study again from a purely compliance perspective, which involves the concept of price fixing. For our purposes, do you think Sylvia will be influenced to raise the charge above the guesstimated $560.00? Will the charge chosen correlate to the Medicare CCR as developed through the cost report? Will this charge appear as reasonable from a patient's perspective? While the answers to these questions are subjective, setting charges for healthcare services is less than a precise process.

Let us join Sylvia, the chargemaster coordinator at the fictitious Apex Medical Center. For this case study, assume that the CCR for these devices is 0.40 as derived from the Medicare cost report.

Case Study 3.24: Pricing Drug-Eluting Stents

A new drug-eluting stent is starting to be used for coronary (and vascular in the future) catheterizations. The acquisition cost for the stent is $2,800.00. Because the CCR for Apex is 0.40, for Medicare patients the charge is $2,800.00/0.40, which equals $7,000.00. For self-pay patients, the top tier in a graduated pricing scheme is to multiply the $2,800.00 by 1.50, which equals $4,200.00. Of course, there is a managed care contract that pays 100 percent of the cost for these stents, but according to the contract, the hospital can only mark up the charge to 10 percent above the acquisition cost. Thus, a price of $2,800.00 times 1.10 or $3,080.00 is used for this payer contract.

Among the questions raised in this case study, there are two that should be mentioned. First, there should be an immediate concern regarding why the Medicare beneficiaries are being charged more than certain other patients. Second, the $7,000.00 charge for Medicare seems quite high. The first concern involves the Medicare charging rule. Generally, Medicare patients should not be charged more than other patients. The second concern involves a seemingly high charge. This high charge results from the overall charge structure at Apex. In this case, the CCR of 0.40 means that Apex's charge structure is relatively high because this CCR represents a 2.50 multiplying factor when costs are marked up to charges. Because CMS will take the $7,000.00 and then convert it back into costs by multiplying by 0.40, that is, 0.40 * $7,000.00 = $2,800.00, Apex has little choice but to charge this amount.

In some cases, hospitals may use only a single set of charges for everyone and thus use the seemingly high Medicare charge. This approach will tend to engender public comment and consternation.

Healthcare Provider Charges and Public Scrutiny

Transparent pricing is one of the later developments in the whole area of setting charges for healthcare services and products. Individuals who have health insurance are often oblivious to the charges because their insurance coverage has already negotiated some sort of a discounted arrangement by limiting allowed charges. However, for those who are uninsured or underinsured, the charges for even seemingly minor encounters can seem daunting.

The availability of charges to the public, in many cases, is not particularly illuminating. Certainly, knowing what a particular physician or clinic charges for a routine visit, whatever constitutes a routine visit, can be useful. Looking at a hospital's chargemaster with thousands of line items will make little sense to patients. When patients are shopping for healthcare services, they will be much more interested in the total charge for a particular procedure or tests. While some healthcare providers do provide charges for packages of services, this is not yet the norm.

Case Study 3.25: Packaging Pricing at the Apex Medical Center

For a number of different surgical services, the Apex Medical Center has been receiving more requests from patients for a flat-fee charge arrangement. One of the areas is for cataract surgery.

> Apex has typically developed charges through the chargemaster on a case-by-case basis. Sylvia, the chargemaster coordinator, has formed a small team to develop flat fees for certain surgical services. Computer reports have been generated showing what the typical charges are for the various surgical services that are under consideration. The biggest area of concern is that some cases involve complications that can raise the costs so that the flat-fee charge may not be high enough.

Healthcare providers, as with most business operations, will respond to public demand. Packaged pricing can certainly assist in the public being able to be good shoppers in some sense. However, the range of healthcare providers available to any given individual is generally limited, so that comparative shopping is really just beginning in healthcare.

Summary and Conclusion

The charges made by all types of healthcare providers influence payment systems and overall payment amount to healthcare providers. In some cases, the given charge will directly affect payment. This can occur if the payer pays a given percentage of all the charges made on a claim. In other instances, the charge-based payment is localized to a specific service, item, device, or pharmaceutical drug. Payment in these cases is on a pass-through process in which the cost of the item is paid at some small percentage above cost.

In other cases, the charge structures indirectly influence payment rates. This is particularly true with PPSs and to a lesser extent with fee schedule payment systems. As a general rule, the charge structures for all healthcare providers have become inflated over the years. While there are many factors that drive high healthcare prices, one factor is called *cost shifting*. As various payment systems have been developed over the past two decades, reimbursement to healthcare providers has been curtailed. So, those patients who do not have insurance coverage of some sort end up paying more to make up for the losses incurred from payers using sophisticated payment mechanisms.

Healthcare providers use various approaches for establishing charges. The large providers such as hospitals and integrated delivery systems use what are called chargemasters. While different terms can be used, such as the CDM, the basic idea is that there is a large list of charges for thousands of items, such as supplies, pharmaceuticals, laboratory tests, radiology tests, surgery charges, and room charges, and the list becomes quite lengthy.

The general goals for setting charges include that they:

- Be based on costs (regulatory requirement);
- Be Consistent throughout the chargemaster (regulatory requirement);
- Be in conformance with federal and state statutory requirements;
- Meet any third-party payer contractual obligations;
- Be easy to understand, develop, and maintain;
- Be geographically consistent (geographic pricing);
- Be competitive with similar types of providers (market pricing);
- Be amenable to public scrutiny (transparent pricing); and
- Optimize reimbursement across a broad array of third-party payers and different payment systems (strategic pricing).

This generalized set of goals sets a very high bar for achievement. Particularly with the advent of public scrutiny of charges, that is, transparent pricing, some healthcare providers would like to reduce their charges. One of the delimiting factors is that many healthcare providers have contracts by which they are paid a percentage of what is charged. If there were any wholesale reduction in pricing, there would be an immediate decrease in reimbursement. Thus, particularly hospitals and integrated delivery systems providers may decide to hold down on increasing prices to effect some sort of orderly process of reducing prices.

Case Study 3.26: Reducing Prices at the Apex Medical Center

The Apex Medical Center has a payment contract for 90 percent of charges with a major insurance company in its region. Apex would like to reduce its charges overall by 5 percent. It has contacted the insurance company to see if, with the reduced charges, it can change their contract to a payment rate of 95 percent of charges.

The facts in Case Study 3.26 are somewhat simplified. Apex would probably have several different percentage-of-charges contracts, each of which would have to be considered. Also, some care would be needed to consider the impact on any other payment mechanisms that are used to generate reimbursement for Apex. Generally, hospitals that desire to reduce their charge structures must do so by simply not increasing their charges over the years.

The CCRs result from a combination of the Medicare cost report and charges through the chargemaster. To better understand CCRs, we also briefly discussed revenue codes. These are four-digit codes that are used to categorize services and items that appear in the chargemaster. Revenue codes are one of several standard code sets used on the UB-04 claim form.

We discussed the concept of *charge compression* using supplies as an example. When a tiered pricing formula is used, particularly for supplies and even pharmacy items, an average CCR is developed based on the revenue code sequence. For supplies, this is basically the 027X sequence. The revenue code category contains both inexpensive supplies and very expensive implantable devices, and the markups tend to be quite different. This then generates an averaged CCR for the category that is not representative. For expensive implantable medical devices, a significant markup is needed to develop the charge correctly.

The Medicare program also has requirements concerning hospital pricing. This is referred to as the *Medicare charging rule*. While CMS cannot tell hospitals what to charge, CMS can demand that Medicare beneficiaries are not charged more than other patients. Also, charges are supposed to be uniformly based on costs. While this is an oversimplification of a complex set of regulations, this does provide some general guidance in establishing charges for healthcare services and products.

Charge-based payment is quite common for hospitals and certain other healthcare providers. Conceptually, this is an extremely simple payment system relative to adjudication of claims and thus reduced overhead costs. For instance, if there is a payment formula of 85 percent of charges, then all that has to occur to calculate payment is to multiply the total charge times 85 percent. With a little consideration, you should realize that charge-based payment may be more complicated. There may be different percentage rates of payment for different kinds of services and items along with certain services that are carved out for special payment processes. This discussion is continued in the next chapter, which discusses contractual arrangements. Note that if charges are uniformly based on costs, then charge-based reimbursement is one step removed from cost-based reimbursement.

Chapter 4

Contractual Payment Systems

Introduction

Thus far in this book, we have discussed cost-based and charge-based healthcare payment. Both of these types of payment systems can be contractual. We have already encountered a number of concepts that go beyond either cost-based or charge based. Prospective payment systems (PPSs) and fee schedule payment systems were discussed in two previous books that are part of this healthcare payment series. For our purposes, the term *contractual* is used in a very general sense, basically to distinguish:

- Contractual payment agreements and
- Statutory payment laws and regulations.

Statutory payment systems are established in law with voluminous rules and regulations and continuously evolving guidance. The prime examples are the Medicare program and various state Medicaid programs. These two major programs provide for healthcare payment covering a wide variety and types of services. Thus, a number of different types of payment systems may be incorporated in statutorily established payment systems.

Contractual payment systems generally involve the establishment of a contract between a private third-party payer, such as an insurance company, and a given healthcare provider, such as a physician, clinic, or hospital. Sometimes, you may see the phrase *managed care contract*. We will use the generic acronym MCO, which stands for *managed care organization*. The full range of possible MCOs is quite broad, and we use this concept in its general form. MCOs typically establish contracts so that healthcare providers agree to certain terms, conditions, and payment mechanisms that generally limit payments.

Note: In using the acronym MCO in its broadest form, insurance companies and various types of third-party administrators (TPAs) will be included. Even insurance companies often introduce delimitations on services, such as preauthorization for surgeries. In some cases, the given MCO, using our definition, may have little management of services, while others may have significant management of services and demands related to quality of care. Virtually all MCOs do provide healthcare payment mechanisms, often through contractual arrangements.

Establishing a managed care contract implies that there is some sort of management of healthcare provision along with different payment arrangements. In some cases, the payment arrangements may encourage or discourage the provision of certain services or dispensing of pharmaceuticals or medical devices. In other cases, these contracts address primarily payment mechanisms with little concern for management of services or quality concerns.

Note that the word *negotiated* is used relative to these contracts. Depending on the specific healthcare provider and the given third-party payer, there may be virtually no negotiating. For example, a physician clinic may simply accept a number of contracts without requesting any changes. On the other hand, an integrated health care system may devote considerable resources to analyzing a proposed contract and then negotiating changes to the contract. Note also that many of these contractual arrangements, once established, will automatically renew unless one or both of the parties requests termination or changes well in advance of the renewal date.

Case Study 4.1: Acme Medical Clinic Contracts

A consultant has been called into the Acme Medical Clinic to perform an extended coding, billing, and reimbursement audit. Acme has five family practice physicians, two surgeons, and three nurse practitioners. One of the first requests of the consultant is to review the different managed care contracts that the clinic has in effect.

In Case Study 4.1, what do you suppose the consultant will find? Typically, the clinic will have a dozen or more contractual arrangements. However, even locating the contracts may be difficult. Once located, it may be noted that the contracts have not been reviewed, revised, or renegotiated for years. For larger healthcare providers such as hospitals or integrated delivery systems (IDSs), more resources will be applied to carefully reviewing, negotiating, and maintaining contractual relationships.

In some cases, a healthcare provider may not even have a contract, but the provider will still be paid according to a standard contractual process that is used by the third-party payer. For instance, a physician or hospital may be filing a claim with an insurance company with which the physician or hospital has no relationship. In theory, because there is no relationship, the third-party payer should pay the entire charged amount. However, in practice, the third-party payer may well adjudicate the claim and make payment using a default process that approximates a standard contract used by the third-party payer for particular types of services. Thus, healthcare providers must understand contractual payment processes even if a formal contractual arrangement is not established.

Case Study 4.2: Hospital Remittance Advice

A reimbursement specialist at the Apex Medical Center is reviewing the remittance advice (RA) from a claim that was filed with an unknown insurance company several states away. While some of the charges have been paid in full, certain charges have no payment, with a notation of being packaged. Some services have been denied because they do not meet medical necessity criteria. Including patient copayments, overall, about 70 percent of the charges have been paid.

In Case Study 4.2, there is no contractual relationship. What should the reimbursement specialist do? What payment should Apex receive? Apex should receive full payment on its claim. Most likely, Apex will simply accept the payment made because the realization rate of 70 percent on this claim may be considered reasonable. To pursue additional payment from this insurance company would require significant effort and a full understanding of how the claim was adjudicated, that is, how the overall payment process is set up. As indicated, the entire claim should be paid, but the costs in pursuing full payment may outweigh any additional payments that might be gained. Note that cases of this type can become quite involved because of deductibles, copayments, and secondary coverage.

Another question is subtly embedded in Case Study 4.2: If there is no contractual relationship between the Apex Medical Center and the distant insurance company, what rules and requirements apply for Apex to file a claim? The answer to this question is that there are requirements for all healthcare providers and all entities making payments to healthcare providers. These requirements are found in the HIPAA (Health Insurance Portability and Accountability Act) legislation. In terms of filing claims, standard code sets and standard claim forms are required, as are standard remittance information from the payer. So, in some sense even if there is no formal contract, there are still requirements for claims filing and reporting of payments. See the HIPAA TSC (Transaction Standard/Standard Code Set) discussion in this chapter.

The variety of contractual arrangements is almost overwhelming, and the provisions within the contracts can range from the very simple to highly complex payment arrangements.

Case Study 4.3: Hospital Per Diem Payment

The Apex Medical Center has been approached by an insurance company that wants to establish a per diem (per day) payment process for inpatient services. For patients who are admitted with a medical condition, one payment rate will apply, while for surgical admissions, a different, higher payment rate is to be made.

What do you think about the arrangement proposed in Case Study 4.3? There are a number of rather important assumptions made with this kind of arrangement. First, a critical factor in this kind of arrangement is how long the patient needs to be in the hospital. Also, there is a presumption that more severe surgical procedures will involve longer stays in the hospital so that the surgical costs can be recouped by the longer stay. Thus, the per diem payments (one for medical, one for surgical) will require very careful scrutiny. Models may need to be developed to approximate payment for certain types of cases. Medical admissions for conditions such as pneumonia or knee replacement surgeries as surgical admissions may need to be carefully modeled for average length of stay and then the amount of reimbursement to be gained.

While we will look at some possible contractual features, the list of potential features, even those pertaining to payment, is very long and continues to evolve. Negotiating managed care contracts is a major challenge for healthcare providers. Also, once a contract is in place, great care must be taken to ensure that proper payment under the contract is actually occurring. Both parties to these contracts have contractual benefits and obligations.

Case Study 4.4: Venipuncture Payment

The Apex Medical Center, a small integrated delivery system, has a managed care contract with a large third-party payer in the state. While there are various payment mechanisms in the contract, for outpatient services, including clinics, there is supposed to be a separate payment for venipuncture (CPT [Current Procedural Terminology] 36415) of $8.00. A review of remittance advices shows that payment is sometimes occurring, but on many occasions, there is no separate payment.

The issue identified in Case Study 4.4 is not that unusual. Similar types of apparent payment discrepancies arise all the time. Careful monitoring of payments must be made to identify any aberrations. Now, the question for this case study is: What is happening? The answer to this question may vary significantly. For instance, the claim adjudication system may have been changed so that with certain laboratory tests the venipuncture payment is bundled on an averaged basis into the payment for the laboratory tests, which is most likely on a fee schedule. There may also be a new adjudication requirement that the venipuncture is payable only if a certified phlebotomist performs the venipuncture, and this has to be indicated by a special notation on the claim. There may suddenly be limitations on paying for venipuncture more than once per day per patient or more than eight times per month per patient.

The number of possible circumstances can cover a large range of issues. The important point is to track payments and then contact the third-party payer to see what is happening so that issues can be identified and resolved as appropriate. Note that if tracking is not performed on a timely basis, such issues can become major over months or years of inattention.

Case Study 4.5: Skilled Nursing Services

The Apex Medical Center has a managed care contract with a large third-party payer in its region. The hospital itself does not provide skilled nursing care. There is a step-down unit at the hospital, but this is still an inpatient service. Skilled nursing services are provided at several skilled nursing facilities (SNFs) in the area. With increasing frequency, Apex has inpatients who are ready to be discharged to skilled nursing, but there are no SNF beds available. The patients are kept in the hospital, but there is no provision under the contract for payment for these interim services.

As Case Study 4.5 illustrates, there can be gaps when contracts are established. With the circumstances indicated in this case study, the third-party payer is probably willing to pay for these services, but there is no agreement concerning how payment should be made, the amount of payment, or the process that needs to be used. Here, general contract language should afford the ability of the parties to negotiate and place into effect an interim arrangement for payment.

HIPAA Transaction Standards

The HIPAA legislation* was passed by Congress and signed into law in 1996. While there are a number of different areas addressed by this legislation, two areas of interest for our discussions are:

■ Administrative simplification and
■ Health information privacy.

Health information privacy revolves around the concept of protected health information (PHI). This topic may arise from time to time throughout our discussions. Of greater interest is what is called *administrative simplification*. The intent of administrative simplification is to standardize healthcare transactions and bring electronic data interchange or EDI to healthcare. In terms of a healthcare provider filing claims, there are two key elements:

■ Standard transaction formats
■ Standard code sets to use with the standard transactions

We will use the contracted acronym TSC to refer to the Transactions Standard and Standard Code Sets.

---

* See Public Law 104-191.

In a very real sense, the HIPAA TSC provides a default contract through a set of rules for healthcare providers to file claims. While there are guidelines for filing claims, there certainly are no guidelines regarding how the given third-party payer will or will not pay for a given claim.

There are several different health care claims transaction standards. The two that we reference for the most part are:

1. 837-P and
2. 837-I.

For 837-P, the *P* is for professional; this is the electronic implementation of the 1500 claim form or, for Medicare, the CMS (Centers for Medicare and Medicaid Services) 1500 claim form. The 837-I (the *I* is for institutional) is the electronic implementation of the UB-04 (Universal Billing 2004) or, for Medicare, the CMS-1450.

There are numerous standardized code sets. Three that are often referenced are:

1. CPT-4 published by the American Medical Association,
2. HCPCS or the Healthcare Common Procedure Coding System published by CMS, and
3. *ICD-10* or *International Classification of Diseases, Tenth Revision*, published, in the United States by the American Hospital Association.

There are many other standard code sets. For instance, on the UB-04 claim form, revenue codes must be used. The revenue code set is maintained by the National Uniform Billing Committee (NUBC). As with other standard code sets used on the claim forms, revenue codes are updated annually, and the NUBC provides official guidance on how the code set is to be used.

Conceptually, if a healthcare provider has a standard claim format and a series of standard code sets to use in developing claims, then the same claim can be filed for the same services provided to different patients. While this degree of standardization is certainly the goal of EDI for healthcare, we are many years from achieving this goal. Currently, third-party payers often make demands on healthcare providers to file their claims in unusual ways that do not conform to the official guidelines for the standard code sets. Often, these directives from payers occur because of the way in which the payers' payment systems have been established.

Case Study 4.6: Variable Claims Filing Requirements

An auditor has been reviewing claims filed by the Apex Medical Center for emergency department (ED) services. The auditor has discovered that similar types of services result in very different claims. In point are three different claims to three different payers for essentially the same services, in this case, the repair of a laceration along with an assessment of the patient. In one case, the evaluation and the laceration repair are separately coded. For a different third-party payer, only the laceration repair is reported because the payer insists that the assessment be bundled into the reporting of the laceration repair. The third payer insists that only the evaluation be reported, and that the minor surgery is paid through the payment for the evaluation.

The circumstances in Case Study 4.6 may seem rather awkward. What if Apex included both services on the claim to a payer that has requirements that only one service be reported and then an associated code also appears on the claim? At best, the claim would be returned to the provider for adjustment. At worst, the claim might be adjudicated so that both services were paid, and the payer might later insist that an overpayment had occurred.

Note: Healthcare providers have often taken the stance of having the third-party payer indicate how it, the payer, wants the services coded and billed. Then, the provider will accommodate payer requirements to get paid. This particular approach is contrary to the whole thrust of the HIPPA TSC. However, getting paid quickly becomes a financial reality for healthcare providers.

As we discuss contracts and features often found in managed care contracts, keep in mind that the standardization under the HIPAA TSC is implemented more fully on the healthcare provider side. While there are standard transactions for activities such as remittance information, requirements for standardization in claims adjudication are yet to come. This results from the wide variety of payment mechanisms. Anticipate that in negotiating contracts with MCOs that there will be specific requirements for claims filing that may differ from standard guidelines. Often, coding and billing guidance is not in the contract itself. Companion manuals or guidances from the payer through Internet access are quite common.

Managed Care Organizations

As indicated in the introduction to this chapter, MCOs come in all sizes, shapes, and configurations. Even a general discussion of MCOs is well beyond the scope of this text. To illustrate concepts in our payment system discussions, including capitation in Chapter 5, we consider two of the many different types of organizations that fall under the general rubric of MCO:

- Preferred provider organization (PPO)
- Health maintenance organization (HMO)

A PPO is generally a group of physicians, hospitals, and other healthcare providers that have contracted with an insurance company, TPA, or other healthcare payer to provide services. For instance, a physician group may contract with an insurance company to provide services to covered individuals at a discounted rate. While the physicians may give away some reimbursement because they are a member of the PPO, more patients will come to them. As you might imagine, the actual organization of a PPO can be very loosely knit, with different healthcare providers coming to and going from the PPO. On the other hand, the PPO may be very tightly organized, with the careful selection of providers allowed to join the PPO being strictly limited.

As with other terminology in this area, PPO can be variously interpreted. You may also see *participating provider organization* or *preferred provider option*. A spin-off is the EPO or *exclusive provider organization*. A related concept is the independent practice association or IPA. This is generally a group of physicians, possibly both primary care and specialists, who have banded together to negotiate with insurance companies and other payers to provide services. Generally, discounted rates are provided in return for some sort of preferential status. Note that PPOs generally involve an emphasis on payment arrangements as opposed to management of care. However, in some cases there can be some management, although the emphasis will likely be on the financial side.

Case Study 4.7: Expensive Dermatologist

A PPO has been organized in Anywhere, USA. Almost all the primary care physicians have joined, and most of the specialists have joined. There are several dermatologists in the group. While payment to the physicians is on a discounted fee-for-service arrangement, as a part of the PPO contract with insurers, cost containment is monitored by a select committee of physicians in the PPO. One of the dermatologists uses specially compounded salves and ointments. This compounding is significantly driving up the costs to the insurers. The committee of physicians has indicated that this dermatologist may have to be removed from the PPO, and the dermatologist will lose referrals from within the PPO unless the compounding is stopped.

For Case Study 4.7, do you think there might be some conflict relative to the dermatologist? Note that in this case study, the issue of quality of care is really not addressed. The compounded prescriptions may provide higher quality of care. What has been addressed is a financial concern with the PPO.

HMOs extend the PPO concept and are typically much more interested in quality of care along with delimiting services only to those that are really necessary. HMOs typically have a more formal organization structure than PPOs. HMOs are more likely to have an organized delivery system that involves physicians, hospitals, skilled nursing homes, home health agencies, and so on. Of course, there can be enormous differences in scale and degree of integration for the delivery system. A special form of the HMO concept is the *staff model HMO,* in which the physicians are employed and the other healthcare providers are owned by the HMO.

With a provider network or organized delivery system, HMOs can then negotiate contracts for services to employers, groups, insurance companies, or even individuals. Typically, the HMO will receive some sort of periodic payments, for which the HMO will provide services. While this sounds rather simple, establishing the overall process is far from simple. For instance, there may be occasions when a covered individual must seek services outside the organized delivery system. This could be due to specialized services or the fact that the individual is traveling well outside the geographic range of the HMO providers.

There are three key characteristics for HMOs:

1. Preferred Providers: HMOs limit the services provided to their organized delivery system. Thus, patients are required to go to specified providers. If the patient goes outside the organized delivery system, then special provisions come into play.
2. Utilization Management: Great emphasis is placed on managing care through screening, preauthorizations, medical necessity, and even using primary care physicians as gatekeepers.
3. Cost Containment: HMOs make every effort to hold down costs. By using preferred providers and closely monitoring the care that is being provided along with financial incentives for both the providers and the patients, cost can be contained. Cost containment then means profitability for the HMO based on the periodic payments that are received.

Even the Medicare program uses the HMO approach. This is the Medicare Advantage (MA) program. Within the Medicare approach, there are variations. Basically, a sponsor, ostensibly an HMO, will contract with Medicare to provide Part A and Part B services in return for a fixed payment from the Medicare program. Medicare beneficiaries enrolling with a MA plan will not use the Medicare supplemental insurance, that is, Medigap coverage. Deductibles and copayments may be used, although in altered forms. Note that there are many variables in establishing these programs. Healthcare providers that participate, that is, are part of the preferred provider network or HMO, need to fully understand how claims will be adjudicated and paid. MA is further discussed toward the end of this chapter.

Next, we discuss general contract features primarily from the healthcare providers' perspective.

Terminology and Contract Features

We now discuss, on a generic basis, some of the language, terminology, and features that are contained in these contracts. We generally take the perspective of the healthcare providers. These contracts are generally written by the MCOs and thus tend to slant advantages to the third-party payer.

Note: All proposed contracts should be carefully reviewed for both legal form and then substantive features. Healthcare providers of all types may need to negotiate dozens of contracts. While each contract will have some basic similarities, there can be enormously different types of contracts.

As we discuss these contracts, keep in mind the fundamental steps for adjudicating a healthcare claim. From Chapter 1, we have the following:

a. The patient must be covered.
b. The services rendered and items dispensed must be covered.
c. The services are ordered and provided by qualified medical persons.
d. The services are medically necessary.
e. The services must be appropriately documented.
f. A correct claim is filed on a timely basis.

Definitions

Here are some common terms along with a brief discussion of their meaning and use. Keep in mind that contracts may use the same term with different meanings or different terms with essentially the same meaning.

Allowed Amount. Most third-party payers will not fully consider the charges made by the healthcare provider. Instead, for a given service or item that is being billed, a lower allowed amount will be used for the calculations involving the payment of the claim. In some cases, the allowed amount may be significantly lower than the charged amount. Managed care contracts must be specific regarding what or how the allowed amounts are determined.

Capitated. The concept of capitated or per head payment is discussed in Chapter 5. Certainly, if a healthcare provider is reimbursed based on a capitated arrangement by a third-party payer, there will be a significant contractual relationship.

Claim. This is the mechanism by which a healthcare provider submits an itemization of services that were provided to the patient or enrollee of the MCO. Typically, there is an itemized statement of some sort and then an actual claim on a standardized form in a standardized format. The two most used forms are the 1500 (CMS-1500) and the UB-04 (CMS-1450). Note that electronic transmission is now the norm, so paper-based claims are used only when necessary.

Note: See the NUBC website (http://www.nubc.org) for information concerning the UB-04 (Universal Billing 2004) and the National Uniform Claim Committee (NUCC) website (http://www.nucc.org) for information regarding the 1500 claim form. See also the previous discussion concerning the HIPAA TSC.

Coinsurance. This is a percentage, generally the percentage as applied to the allowed payment. The application of this percentage to the overall payment then becomes the enrollee's responsibility, and the dollar amount becomes the copayment. Care should be taken to determine the relationship between the charged amount and the allowable amount relative to applying the coinsurance percentage. On occasion, there may be different coinsurance percentages based on the specific type of service.

Companion Manuals. These are manuals or directives from third-party payers providing instructions on how to code, bill, and file claims for services provided under a contractual arrangement. Guidance from payers may be quite extensive. In other cases, there may be little guidance. However, the true test is how the claims are adjudicated, that is, how the payer's computer systems are programmed. Note that there may be separate manuals, or there may be a series of directives. This information may not be in printed form. Greater use of the Internet or even secure intranets is becoming more common.

Coordination of Benefits (COB). The COB is the process of coordinating the payment for healthcare services between different payers. There may be a primary payer along with a secondary payer and even a tertiary payer. Coordination can become extremely complex and should be well delineated in any managed care contract.

Copayment. This is the dollar amount that the patient or enrollee must pay relative to services. The copayment is generally calculated by multiplying the coinsurance percentage times the payment that is made for the services. Note that this term can be used in a general sense with a specific dollar amount, while in other instances the copayment is pegged to the payment being made. See Case Study 4.8 for an illustration. There can be great variability in this area.

Case Study 4.8: Copayment for Physician Visit

Stanley has health insurance coverage through his employer. However, when Stanley goes to the doctor, there is a general $20.00 copayment for the visit. In addition, if any other services are provided outside of an evaluation, then there is a 15-percent coinsurance amount. The copayment and coinsurance do not apply to an annual physical examination.

Covered Service. Virtually all third-party payers of any type exclude certain services. Thus, for healthcare providers it is important to work with the patient or managed care enrollee to understand what is or is not covered by the payer. Note that noncoverage can result from different types of situations. For example, there may be certain services that are never covered. Other services, such as experimental services or drugs, may not be covered. One of the big issues is noncoverage due to lack of medical necessity. Healthcare providers must be very careful to understand how medical necessity issues are addressed under a given contract.

Deductible. Typically, this is a dollar amount that must be paid by patients or enrollees before medical services are paid or fully paid by the third-party payer. As with other concepts, this term can be used in variable ways. For instance, there may be no deductible relative to physician office visits, but there will be a deductible for therapeutic services provided at a hospital. Also, deductibles can be relatively modest, involving only a few hundred dollars. In other cases, the deductible may be thousands of dollars.

Emergency Condition. Emergency services generally are treated differently from nonemergent situations. Coverage for emergencies is generally going to be made, and various preauthorization processes will be suspended. Thus, the definition of an emergency condition within a given contract is important. While there can be significant variations, there is a formal definition contained in the EMTALA (Emergency Medical Treatment and Labor Act) law and associated Medicare rules and regulations.*

Enrollee. An individual who has purchased health insurance coverage from a third-party payer or is otherwise covered under the third-party payer plan. Contacts may use this term or generally equivalent terms such as *member* or *covered individual.*

Experimental Service. Experimental services, pharmaceuticals, and devices are generally not covered under various health plans. Care should be taken to have specific definitions in a contract regarding what is experimental or how decisions are made concerning experimental status. In certain circumstances, a given definition or process relative to experimental status can create significant consternation on the part of the healthcare provider, patient, and third-party payer.

Fee for Service. Fee-for-service payment means that as services are provided, the third-party payer makes payments for the services. The more services that are provided, the more the payer pays to the healthcare provider. In some sense, this is the opposite of capitation, for which a fixed payment is made regardless of the number of services that are provided. Because of this generalized payment approach, third-party payers are generally very sensitive to the need to provide services.

Holdback. MCOs, particularly HMOs and PPOs, in determining their payment to healthcare providers may want to hold back some of the payments until the end of the contract year. Then, based on the experience for the year, the holdback payment can be distributed or not. Usually, performance formulas are established in advance so that healthcare providers are incentivized to constrain the amount and cost of healthcare provision.

MCO Reimbursement. This is the amount that the MCO will approve for payment for a given service or item. Taking into account deductibles and copayments, the actual amount that the MCO will pay will probably be less than the approved or allowed amount.

Medically Necessary. This is a subjective judgment on the part of medical professionals regarding whether a specific service is necessary. MCO contracts should carefully specify how medical necessity decisions are made relative to diagnoses or other procedures used by the MCO. Medical necessity can become an area of great contention, so definitions and associated processes for medical necessity determination should be clearly enunciated in any contract.

Noncovered Services. This relates to services, pharmaceuticals, and other items that are not covered by the given third-party payer plan. See the discussion regarding covered services.

Notices. Periodic communications from the MCO to healthcare providers are necessary to keep everyone up to date. There may be formal notices that involve possible changes to the contract itself. More likely, most of the communications will involve changes in coding, billing, and reimbursement processing. In some cases, a healthcare provider that is under contract may need to contact the MCO relative to issues such as contract renewal or requested changes in the contract.

Payer. This refers to the MCO itself or whatever organization is making payment for services. We may generically refer to a third-party payer. Also, reference may be made to *private* third-party payers to distinguish contractual situations from government programs such as Medicare and Medicaid, which may be called *public* third-party payers.

---

* For more information on EMTALA, see 42 CFR §489.20.

Plan. Generally, the plan refers to the insurance or coverage contract between the MCO and the individual enrollee. As with other terminology in this area, this term can be used in different ways. Features such as coverage, medical necessity, and experimental services must appear in the plan itself as well as being included or referenced in the MCO contract with the various healthcare providers.

Preauthorization. This is a process by which the payer or MCO must approve or authorize the provision of a given service prior to the service being provided. In many cases, this process involves contacting the MCO and providing the medical justification for the service. Note that if a service is provided for which preauthorization is required and such preauthorization is not obtained, then there may no payment. Contracts need to state explicitly how this process is to work and what services may require preauthorization.

Qualified Provider. Virtually all MCO contracts as well as government health plans require that a qualified healthcare provider actually perform the services. There can be variations. In some cases, subordinate personnel may perform a service as long as the service is provided under the supervision of a qualified provider. Contracts in this area may vary considerably. For instance, nonphysician practitioners such as NPs, physician assistants (PAs), and clinical nurse specialists (CNSs) may or may not be recognized as qualified healthcare providers for separate payment.

Quality Improvement. Virtually all third-party payers, public and private, are concerned about quality of care. The way in which quality issues are addressed, particularly in relationship to payment processes, is highly variable. MCO contracts tend to include certain reporting and monitoring functions relative to quality assessment.

Secondary Payer. Payers are always concerned about paying for services that might be the responsibility of some other party. This is particularly true with accident cases. If a primary or first payer can be identified (e.g., a liability insurance claim), then the healthcare payer may be secondary, and thus the payer's responsibility is mitigated. Secondary payment is closely associated with COB. An individual may have two policies, one through his or her own employer and then another through a spouse's employer. For Medicare beneficiaries using traditional (i.e., not MA) Medicare, one of the standard Medigap policies is often purchased, which is then the secondary payer.

Subrogation. This is a process whereby one party pays a claimant and then the party who has paid pursues payment from another party. A payer may pay for a healthcare claim and then pursue another party (e.g., another insurance carrier) for payment.

Case Study 4.9: Construction at the Apex Medical Center

Stephen is taking his dog for a walk. There is construction taking place at the Apex Medical Center. Some construction debris is on the sidewalk outside the fence. Unfortunately, Stephen trips, falls, and sustains some injuries. He is treated at Apex's ED. No charges for the services are made; that is, Apex pays for the services. However, Apex will now subrogate to the liability coverage of the construction company to recover the costs of providing and thus paying for the services.

Tertiary Payer. A secondary payer is second in line for payment. A tertiary payer is third in line to make payment. As with the concept of a secondary payer, COB is important. MCO contracts will generally address the processes and procedures involved with determining secondary and tertiary payers.

Total Reimbursement. This is the total amount of reimbursement that a healthcare provider will receive for a given claim made under a managed care contract. Note that this total reimbursement may be paid partially by the third-party payer along with payment from the enrollee along with possible payment from other insurance carriers or healthcare payers.

Urgent Condition. Some managed care contracts may differentiate emergent conditions from urgent conditions relative to coverage without preauthorization. There is no universal definition of an urgent condition. Medicare does have a definition involving twelve hours.* The basic idea is that an urgent condition is one that if not treated within twelve hours could become an emergent condition.

This discussion of terminology is informal and should be considered conceptual in nature. In the actual contracts, there will be more formal, legalistic language. Often, these contracts are filled with what is called legal *boilerplate*. Our purpose is to discuss the concepts surrounding the terminology used in manage care contracts, particularly as they relate to healthcare payment.

We now turn our attention to common features found in managed care contracts.

Reimbursement and Payment Terms

For healthcare providers (i.e., physicians, clinics, hospitals, nursing facilities, etc.), the big questions involve: How much will we be paid for services? How quickly will we be paid? For many providers, this is the heart of the contract (at least for financial purposes). Depending on the contract, this section can be fairly simple, or it can be quite complicated. For instance, an insurance company may offer a contract to a physician to pay for services on a fee-for-service basis and simply pay 20 percent above what Medicare would pay for the services. All of the Medicare rules on coding, billing, and edits would be followed for adjudication purposes.

For a hospital, a simple payment approach is to pay 85 percent of whatever the hospital charges. In this type of contract, the adjudication is straightforward, although rules for properly coding, billing, and claims filing will still be in place. The payment is based on the charge structure. For hospitals, this then involves the hospital's chargemaster.

At the other end of the complexity spectrum are contracts that contain numerous payment mechanisms based on certain types of services. For example, many contracts will carve out certain services and pay for them differently from the main payment approach. This tends to happen more at the institutional level rather than with individual physicians or small clinics. For instance, a hospital may enter into a contract with a healthcare payer that covers hospital inpatient services, hospital outpatient services, hospital clinic services, and the like. The payer may then offer payment through modified Diagnosis Related Groups (DRGs) and Ambulatory Payment Classifications (APCs). However, certain services, such as obstetrics, renal dialysis, chemotherapy, and radiation oncology, may be carved out with special payment mechanisms. Likewise, expensive pharmacy items and implantable medical devices may be paid on a pass-through basis using either costs or charges.

Whatever payment mechanisms are contained in the contract, great care should be given to analyzing the financial impact on the healthcare provider. For simple payment mechanisms, this may not be a daunting task. For instance, with our physician previously mentioned, the 20-percent above Medicare payment may be more than adequate. However, for the hospital mentioned, where

---

* For instance, see 42 CFR §405.400.

there were different payment processes for different types of service, a careful analysis may show that financial impact will be negative and thus not financially feasible.

There are a number of timeliness issues involving payment. From the provider's perspective, the first issue is how quickly the claim for services must be filed. Payers may try to delimit the claims filing period, possibly to 30 days, but certainly 120 days or even a year are more appropriate because of difficulties that may arise in coding, billing, and generation of the claim. Refiling a corrected claim should also be considered. The next question is how quickly the payer will make payment for a clean claim. If a claim is received and then goes through the adjudication process without any edits or problems, then payment should be made expeditiously. Perhaps fifteen or thirty days are reasonable. Third is the issue of appealing a claim that is not fully paid, that is, a claim that does not process through the adjudication process without issues. Again, from a provider's perspective there should be a reasonable time for appeal, such as 180 days or even more.

Provision of Services

Any conditions concerning the provision of healthcare services should be clearly indicated in the contract; issues such as who can or will provide services, including any sort of incident-to services that are performed by subordinate personnel under the supervision of a physician or qualified nonphysician practitioner. While this may involve physicians and associated clinic services, the same concerns may be applicable to other types of healthcare providers. For instance, services provided by a hospital may require some level of supervision by qualified medical personnel. The same concern may occur with home health services relative to the degree of supervision of nursing and home health aide staff.

A significant concern on the part of payers is that services must always be ordered by a physician or other qualified medical persons. Such orders must always be carefully documented so that audits can verify such orders.

In some cases, the actual location of services may also be an issue. Facility concerns are relative to licensing and meeting quality standards. Certain healthcare providers, such as hospitals, will generally be accredited. Other healthcare providers may only be subject to state laws and commercial business rules and regulations. See also credentialing concerns relative to these types of issues. Case Study 4.10 illustrates a possible area of concern for location of services.

Case Study 4.10: Aquatic Therapy at Hotel Swimming Pool

The Apex Medical Center, through the Therapies Department, has started a program of aquatic therapy. Specially trained physical therapists are providing this service at the swimming pool of a hotel that is located two blocks from the hospital.

Whether the type of arrangement described in Case Study 4.10 will meet licensing and accreditation standards is an interesting question.

Payer and Payee Obligations

The rights and obligations under a contract apply to both the provider (payee) and payer. Depending on the services and the payment mechanisms, there can be numerous obligations. For instance, if a hospital is being paid a percentage of its charges, then the payer will be very interested in the charge structure, chargemaster, and any updating of charges or addition of new services or products. A payer will also be interested in accessing medical records for audits to verify that services were provided or that services were medically necessary. What kind of notice should be required if a payer wants to access records?

Another issue that should be addressed in any contract is the way in which disputes will be addressed. We are using the word *disputes* in a very broad sense. However, there should be some sort of provision for arbitration or other means of addressing unforeseen problems and issues that might arise. While the contract may address formal issues such as arbitration, a process for identifying and discussing issues should also be clearly evident on an operational basis. See the discussion of administrative proceedings in this chapter.

Another issue is that of terminating the contract by either the provider or the payer. Contracts are often established so that they automatically renew unless one of the parties gives notice. Such notice must normally be indicated at least within thirty days of the contract renewal date. The terms and conditions for terminating the contract by either the provider or payer must be explicitly spelled out. Also, there may be postcontract obligations on the part of both the payer and the payee. Here is a case study illustrating a possible issue:

Case Study 4.11: Terminated Contract during Episode of Care

Stephen has been seeing a specialist for an ongoing medical condition. He typically visits the specialist once a month for an examination and provision of injections. Unfortunately, the specialist has terminated the contract with Stephen's MCO. At this point, there is no other specialist Stephen can utilize.

The contract with the HMO should contain provisions to address this type of situation. While switching physicians might be an option, if another is available, there should really be a mechanism to complete the course of treatment or afford a reasonable time period to switch physicians.

Another area of concern for healthcare providers is being informed about any changes that are made by the payer relative to coding, billing, and claims-filing requirements. The payer may make internal changes in the adjudication process, which in turn can affect the payment to healthcare providers. Also, changes in adjudication processes may necessitate changes in the claims-filing process. Thus, a payer's obligation is to keep the providers up to date on any requirements or changes in policy relative to adjudication.

Case Study 4.12: Bundling of Low Osmolar Contrast Media Payment

The Maximus Insurance Company has several different contracts that are used with hospitals for both inpatient and outpatient payment. While pharmaceutical items such as low osmolar contrast media (LOCMs) are bundled for inpatient service, for outpatient services, LOCMs have been paid separately using the Level II HCPCS Q-codes. However, the cost of LOCMs has continuously declined over the years, and now Maximus has decided that LOCMs should be bundled into the payment for the associated radiological services.

The fundamental question in Case Study 4.12 is how Maximus should inform the hospitals that are under the contracts that have previously paid for LOCMs separately. Is this a change that should only be implemented on contract renewal? Or, should Maximus issue a bulletin? Or, should Maximus simply make the change in adjudication and then adjust the coding and billing requirements?

Payment Mechanisms

As we have discussed in this book and the preceding books in this series, there are many different kinds of payment systems, some of which depend on the type of healthcare services provided. Within all of these systems, there are various payment mechanisms that can be mixed and matched in a large variety of combinations. For example, an HMO might want to establish a contract with a small IDS. Thus, payment for physicians, clinics, hospital inpatient, hospital outpatient, home health, and skilled nursing services might all need to be included for payment in the contract. Undoubtedly, there will be special exceptions and carve outs relative to payment for specific items and services.

From a financial perspective, for both the healthcare providers and the payer, the payment mechanisms are probably the most important part of these contracts. Providers must be very careful that payments will not only cover costs but also generate some degree of profitability. The payer organization is interested in paying for all necessary services, but only those services that are really necessary, at a reasonable cost in order for the payer to maintain financial integrity.

Both providers and payers must carefully analyze the financial impacts of the payment mechanisms. Financial analysts are a necessity in the world of assessing contracts and checking for the impact of adjudication processes. Care should be taken to include coding personnel, billing personnel, and those involved in the actual care. Also, if quality of care and utilization review are part of the given contract, then these issues must be assessed at the financial level.

Credentialing Processes

Credentialing of healthcare providers entails two different concepts. These two issues do overlap:

1. Clinical qualifications for the provision of healthcare services
2. Billing and enrollment privileges for the healthcare provider

Our main focus is on billing privileges and any conditions that might be required to file claims. MCO contracts may not contain specific requirements in this area, and there is a great deal of dependence on who is seeking billing privileges. For instance, if a payer is contracting with a hospital, then credentialing may mainly involve determining that the hospital is duly licensed at the state level and accredited by a hospital accrediting entity, and that other business-related documents are all in place.

If a clinic is trying to gain billing privileges for an NP, issues may arise. Some healthcare payers may be reluctant to grant billing privileges, although the same payer may readily grant billing privileges to PAs. Even if billing privileges are granted for NPs, there may be a laundry list of requirements, including licenses, collaborative agreements, academic transcripts, diplomas, and the like.

Healthcare providers entering into contracts need to assess carefully any possible challenges with the credentialing process, particularly on the billing side. The requirements to gain billing privileges may reside in companion manuals and may even be listed by the payer on a website with various requirements involving coding, billing, and reimbursement. See Chapter 6 for additional discussion of this issue.

Medical Necessity and Coverage Issues

Whether healthcare services provided are really needed or medically necessary is one of the biggest issues for all payers and types of payment systems. Medical necessity even extends to capitated payment systems, which are discussed in Chapter 5. The simple fact is that medical necessity is a subjective process generally relying on the expertise of physicians and other healthcare providers. While a contract cannot really define medical necessity, certainly the process that is used to determine medical necessity can be spelled out. Typically, a clinical reviewer such as a physician, nonphysician practitioner, or nurse will review a case to determine if the services were medically necessary. There should be some sort of an appeal process relative to medical necessity denials. Also, urgent and emergent care should be exempt from undue medical necessity challenges.

Other coverage issues may be addressed through the use of preauthorizations. While this process may concentrate on surgical procedures, there may be other instances in which preauthorizations must be obtained. Again, the contract can cover this issue from a procedural perspective, that is, the process for gaining preauthorization approval. There should also be an appeals process that can be pursued in a timely fashion. Case Study 4.13 gives a little glimpse into how medical necessity and preauthorization can become complicated.

> **Case Study 4.13: Hydration Preceding Cardiac Catheterization**
>
> Stanley's cardiologist has ordered a cardiac catheterization to check for any coronary blockages. Stanley also has been seeing a nephrologist. While the cardiac catheterization would normally be provided on an outpatient basis, the nephrologist wants Stanley to be admitted to the hospital and hydrated overnight with medications that will reduce the toxicity of the LOCMs that will be used during the cardiac catheterization.

There are really two issues in Case Study 4.12. First, there is the question of admitting Stanley to the hospital. A payer may argue that performing this service on an inpatient basis is not necessary and thus not covered. Second, is this hydration and medication administration really needed? This may be a protocol that is not generally accepted by the payer. The payer may come back and indicate that the procedure will be paid only on an outpatient basis, and that the intravenous medication is not medically necessary.

Some additional examples are discussed in the next section.

Administrative Proceedings

MCO contracts involving the payment, and possibly management, for medical services can never cover every possible situation that might arise. Even though the contract itself may refer to various companion manuals or other informational resources, there are still distinct possibilities that conflicts or disagreements will arise.

> **Case Study 4.14: Special Medication Regimen**
>
> A gastroenterologist has an MCO contract for services. This physician has found that for certain illnesses a special combination of drugs is particularly effective. The drugs are quite expensive, and the physician is using a drug combination that does not conform to pharmacy label instructions. The MCO is claiming that the use of this particular drug combination is experimental and is thus not covered.

Case Study 4.15 is an extension of Case Study 4.7.

Case Study 4.15: Compounded Dermatology Prescriptions

A dermatologist in Anywhere, USA, has an MCO contract for a large number of patients. The contract covers most pharmaceutical items. However, the dermatologist prefers to prescribe certain ointments and salves that must be compounded by a pharmacist. The MCO is balking at paying the extra cost and has contacted the dermatologist to make certain that only off-the-shelf ointments and salves are prescribed.

Case Study 4.16: Hospital Inpatient Stay Changed to Observation

The Apex Medical Center has a number of different MCO contracts. An issue that frequently arises is that a patient may be admitted as an inpatient and remain in the hospital for up to four days. A proper claim is filed in a timely fashion, and then the MCO responds by indicating that the case should have been an observation case and makes payment at a much lower rate.

Presumably, for Case Study 4.16, the payment mechanism for the inpatient services is vastly different from the payment process for the outpatient services. Based on the information in this case study, apparently the MCO is concerned primarily about reducing the payment to Apex. This case study illustrates the need to establish agreed-on criteria for the type, level, and location of services.

Case Study 4.17: Location of Service

Sarah needs to have elective surgery. This surgery can be performed at the local ambulatory surgical center (ASC), at the Apex Medical Center as an outpatient, or at the hospital as an inpatient.

The decision regarding where Sarah's surgery should be performed is really a medical decision that will or should be made by the surgeon. However, an MCO will certainly be interested in which location is chosen and why that location was selected. Most likely, the overall payment is the lowest for the ASC, a little more expensive for hospital outpatient services, and probably much more expensive on an inpatient basis. There will probably be different payment mechanisms for the various locations.

Access to Records and Audits

Typically, healthcare payers establishing a contract with healthcare providers will include provisions so that medical records can be reviewed. This may be in addition to requests on the part of the payer to receive copies of specific records related to an individual case. Payers will also want the ability to audit records to determine medical necessity, proper documentation, orders in place for the service, proper coding, and the like. Note that access to records may go beyond medical or clinical records. Itemized statements and claims are generally included in the right to access records.

Because of the wide variety of payment systems, financial information may also be requested in various forms. For instance, if a hospital is being paid on percentage-of-charges basis, then the payer will certainly want to have access to the hospital's chargemaster and associated charge structure information at least on a periodic auditing basis.

Note that most of the information that would be requested by a payer falls under the ambit of PHI and thus under the HIPAA privacy rule. The contract should address any privacy issues related to access to records.

Negotiating and Analyzing MCO Contracts

We have been discussing a number of features and issues surrounding contractual arrangements for paying for healthcare services. Virtually all healthcare providers will have multiple contracts, some of which are quite different. We now look at a very general process that can be used to approach the negotiation and maintenance of managed care contracts. Keep in mind that some contracts that we term *managed* really have few management features, while others have significant management of healthcare services.

Here are the main activities:

- Precontract data gathering
- Contract and relationship analysis
- Financial modeling and analysis
- Compliance analysis
- Operational monitoring
- Renewal and termination

Contracts are between the healthcare payer and the healthcare provider. You can take either perspective. Because these contracts tend to be written by the healthcare payer, we will take the provider perspective because, if anything, the contracts will be slanted to benefit the payer.

Precontract Data Gathering

Both parties really need to know about each other. From the providers' (e.g., physicians, hospitals, etc.) perspective, information about the insurance company or MCO is essential. For instance, the market share, geographic service area, stability, solvency, reputation, and other healthcare providers under contract should all be determined. Any competitive situations with other similar providers under the contract will be of interest. If possible, patient satisfaction with the payer should be investigated. Ownership is another issue. Is this payer part of a larger group or corporation? Also, with what employers and other organizations does this payer have relationships? What kind of turnover is there with other healthcare providers?

Answers to these questions will give the provider some idea regarding what may or may not be in the contract itself. If the patient population views the payer unfavorably, then this may be a payer to avoid unless there are specific circumstances that suggest otherwise.

Contract and Relationship Analysis

The contract itself should be carefully reviewed for terms and conditions, some of which we discussed previously in this chapter. Also, coding, billing, and claims-filing conditions should be reviewed. These contractual guidelines may not be in the contract itself but may be referenced in the contract. Often, there are companion manuals or guidance provided through other means (e.g., payer website). Claims-filing requirements can include such things as how long the provider has to file a claim (e.g., 120 days), how quickly the payer will pay a clean claim (e.g., 30 days), or how long a provider has to appeal a payment denial (e.g., lack of medical necessity).

The terms and conditions provided in the contract should be reviewed. Always look at the definitions because the definitions may be overly broad or too narrowly defined. Issues such as medically necessary services or noncovered services should be well defined. Generally, covered services should be listed with some specificity. Also, the healthcare provider may or sometimes may not be prepared to provide some services relative to the facility involved or the skill or expertise of the individuals providing services. Medical necessity is a major issue when providing healthcare services. While it is difficult to define medical necessity, at least the process used to determine medical necessity for given situations should be delineated in the contract.

Standard-of-care issues can also be of concern. The rather nebulous phrase *community standard of care* may appear. What, exactly, does this mean? Obviously, the use of undefined and sometimes nebulous terms and concepts can lead to disagreements and conflicts.

Note: Due consideration should be given to having legal counsel review contracts.

Financial Analysis and Modeling

Performing financial analyses of the provisions in a contract, particularly the assessment of the payment mechanisms and their impact on reimbursement to providers, vary significantly. For instance, a three-physician family practice clinic in a smaller community may only make a cursory assessment of what a given contract will pay. In some cases, the contracts are simply signed and put into a drawer. At a hospital, the proposed contracts, at least from major third-party payers, may be financially assessed on a quick review basis. At an IDS, there may be financial analysts who will really dig into the contracts and develop models based on the case mix of services provided by the IDS.

Financial modeling is not the only consideration for contracts, but great care must be taken to reasonably ensure that the given healthcare provider will not lose money under the contract.

Case Study 4.18: Payment Averaging

A consultant has recently been analyzing cases at the Apex Medical Center. The consultant has found that Apex is being substantially underpaid for cardiac and vascular catheterization services from one of its largest third-party payers. The financial analysts at the hospital are contacted. This underpayment is fully recognized, but the loss is more than made up by generous payments for inpatient services.

Whether the circumstances in Case Study 4.17 are reasonable is an interesting question. Is it possible that the underpayments, although offset by other, more generous payments, could create some problems from other third-party payers? Could problems occur down the road when the payer wants to lower the inpatient payments and not increase the payments for the catheterization services?

Operational Monitoring

As with levels of financial analysis, the operational monitoring of contracts is certainly important. However, for a small operation such as the three-physician clinic, any sort of operational monitoring of how the contract is working and whether payments are correct will probably receive only basic review. Moving up to the hospital and system levels, the resources dedicated to contract monitoring will increase significantly. Most likely, specialized software will be used to track and assess how well a given contract is working. Certainly, the financial reimbursement will be carefully tracked along with identifying any problems that are generating a realization rate that is less than that anticipated.

Renewal and Termination

For small healthcare providers, MCO contracts are often signed, placed in a drawer, and then allowed to renew automatically without much further consideration. At the hospital and system levels, more attention is devoted to renewing contracts with due consideration to making adjustments, negotiating changes in the contract, or different payment mechanisms. In some cases, healthcare providers do find it necessary to terminate contracts that create unfavorable results.

The financial analysis, operational monitoring, and then consideration for renewal or negotiating changes all require specialized personnel who can perform these types of services. In other words, the healthcare provider must decide what kind of personnel will be devoted to developing and maintaining these contractual relationships. As indicated in our brief discussion of these topics, the infrastructure to support contracts will vary significantly based on the size of the healthcare provider. The range seems to go from virtually no personnel assigned on up to departments of specialized technicians and analysts who study and assess contracts on a regular basis.

Medicare Advantage Plans

As mentioned in this chapter, even the Medicare program uses an HMO or PPO approach. Medicare's approach is called Medicare Advantage (MA). These MA programs are referred to as Part C. Part A is generally for hospitals and institutional providers; Part B is for physicians, clinics, and other suppliers. Part D is the Medicare drug program.

Note: Be careful when using these different *parts* of the Medicare program. Exactly how these different parts fit together, or not, is not always readily apparent, particularly for compliance requirements.

There are several different approaches for MA plans, of which the following three are typical:

- ◼ HMO plans
- ◼ PPO plans
- ◼ Private fee-for-service (PFFS) plans

There are some additional approaches, including special needs plans (SNPs), HMO point-of-service (HMOPOS) plans, and medical savings account (MSA) plans. A full explanation of all these approaches would require considerable discussion. We touch lightly on this topic in the context of our overall discussion of payment systems and contractual arrangements with healthcare providers.

However, the basic process involves several concepts that we have discussed in this chapter. There must be some sort of organized delivery system, which may be referred to as a network of providers.* Regardless of the specific MA plan, healthcare providers of all types may be approached by an MA HMO, MA PPO, or MA insurance company to join a network of providers under the MA plan. This, of course, will involve a contractual agreement that must address all of the issues we have discussed, including how providers will be paid, coverage, coding and billing issues, medical necessity, and so on.

Figure 4.1 shows a simplified diagram distinguishing the open network of traditional or original Medicare compared to the closed network used with an MA plan. The Medicare Advantage

---

* You may see that traditional or original Medicare is an open network of providers.

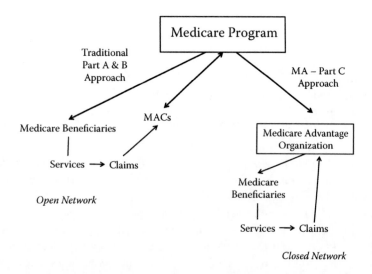

Figure 4.1 Traditional Medicare versus Medicare Advantage.

organization (MAO) provides the organizational structure for the MA plan in which the services are provided by the MAO.

Medicare beneficiaries who decide to enroll in one of the MA plans are still under Medicare. Medicare is still paying, in some sense, for the services provided. The MA plan actually introduces an organizational structure (i.e., the HMO, PPO, or whatever) between the beneficiary and the Medicare program. The intermediate organization is called an MAO. The reason for establishing these MA plans is the possibility of overall savings to the Medicare program. Of course, the MAO itself must also be profitable.

There can be great variability within the MA plans. For Medicare beneficiaries who enroll in an MA plan, there is no need to purchase the Medicare supplemental policies, that is, the Medigap policies. For some MA plans, the monthly premium paid by the enrollees may be less than traditional Medicare, or it may be more. Also, the MA plans may offer increased coverage for items such as vision, hearing, dental, wellness programs, and sometimes the Part D drug coverage.

Case Study 4.19: Establishing an MA Plan

The Maximus Insurance Company in Anywhere, USA, is seriously considering establishing an MA plan of some sort. The intent is to develop this plan on a statewide basis. Maximus already has a fairly extensive network of providers of all types throughout the state. The financial analysts and actuaries at Maximus have been asked to perform a feasibility study on the type of MA plan that would be best and then to identify any problems that may be encountered and to make certain such a move is financially feasible.

The analysts at Maximus have a significant task in studying the feasibility of establishing an MA plan. The analysis must include which type of MA plan, the marketplace, and all of the financial ramifications that might occur. One of the issues that will arise involves an enrollee who seeks services outside the network of the MA plan. For traditional Medicare, that is, the open network, this is not a problem because the Medicare program has statutorily determined how providers of all types are paid. For traditional Medicare, everyone is in the open network.

For an MA program using an HMO or PPO approach, it is now the MAO that must pay for the out-of-network services. Consider Case Study 4.20:

> **Case Study 4.20: Out-of-Network Services under an MA Plan**
>
> Since Stephen retired, he has been traveling well outside his home state. He is under an MA plan that has a network of providers generally within his home state. Unfortunately, Stephen had an accident outside his home state and needed both physician services and a brief hospitalization.

Now, Stephen's MAO will have to pay the out-of-network physicians and hospital. For in-network providers, the MAO has established contracts on payment processes. These payments may be different from what Medicare would ordinarily pay.

What amount should these out-of-network providers be paid? The general answer to this question is that these providers will be paid what traditional Medicare would ordinarily pay. This means that the MAO will need to be able to calculate and pay for services correctly under the myriad Medicare payment systems. Some of these payment processes are not at all straightforward. The MAO will need explicit guidance on how to calculate payment. For instance, if in Case Study 4.20 the hospital were a critical access hospital (CAH), which is cost-based reimbursed, how will the MAO calculate the payment? The basic and oversimplified answer is that the MAO will pay the interim payment rate to the CAH. Of course, the MAO will have to know what the interim payment rate is for the specific CAH.* (See the discussion of CAHs under cost-based reimbursement in Chapter 2.)

Interestingly, the relationship between traditional Medicare and MA plans represents another example of payment system interfacing. In this case, the different payment processes that must interface are all within the Medicare program itself. Payment system interfaces are further discussed in Chapter 7.

Summary and Conclusion

Contractual payment from private third-party payers generally involves a combination of payment mechanisms. There may be some use of fee schedules, some use of prospective payment, cost-based payment in some circumstances, and charge-based payment in other situations. There may also be special payment arrangements, generally carve outs, for specialized, high-volume services such as obstetrics or renal dialysis. The range and type of payment mechanisms are truly astounding.

To discuss and illustrate cases with contractual payment, we have also discussed MCOs in general and then two specific types of MCOs. These are the PPOs and HMOs. We will also see these two types of entities in Chapter 5, in which we discuss capitation. There are many other types of MCOs, with numerous acronyms and varying organizational structuring. Some MCOs pursue the management of care in conjunction with providing payment for healthcare services. Other MCOs almost exclusively provide payment with little concern for managing care.

Healthcare providers of all types frequently enter into contractual arrangements with healthcare payers. We have discussed some, but certainly not all, of the definitions and contractual concerns. These contractual relationships are quite different from the statutory programs, such as

---

* See the Medicare document, "MA Payment Guide for Out of Network Payments" at https://www.cms.gov/MedicareAdvtgSpecRateStats/downloads/oon-payments.pdf.

Medicare and Medicaid. At the same time, private third-party payers that proffer these contracts must address some of the same issues that we find in the statutorily based programs, particularly when payment processes are considered.

Healthcare providers also face the fact that some services will be provided to individuals for whom the provider has no contractual relationship with any sort of third-party payer. While this can occur with self-pay patients, there will be some patients who are enrolled and covered by another payer with whom the provider simply has no relationship. Often, this occurs with patients who may be traveling or patients seeking services outside an approved set of preferred providers. What obligations does a healthcare provider have under these circumstances? Generally, providers will file claims without knowing how their claims will be adjudicated and paid. In cases like this, the default level for developing and filing claims follows the directives under the HIPAA TSC rule, in which standard claim formats and standard code sets are used.

Chapter 5

Capitated Payment Systems

Introduction

Capitated payment is a process whereby the healthcare providers are paid at a fixed rate, typically on a per member per month (PMPM) basis. The given healthcare provider provides whatever services are needed, but the payment remains fixed. From a payer perspective, this form of payment offers the potential of controlling and reducing costs. Using the fee-for-service approach, costs can escalate with a greater volume of services. With capitation, there can be all sorts of services, but the payment will remain fixed.

With a little thought, you will realize that with this payment approach there is a significant shift in risk. With the fee-for-service approach, healthcare payers are constantly concerned about only medically necessary services being provided in order to control overall payments. For instance, physicians using defensive medicine will often have diagnostic tests performed just in case there might be a problem. For that same physician under some form of capitation, there will be some second thoughts about those tests because performing the tests could reduce the profitability to the physician.

Case Study 5.1: Headache in the Emergency Department

Steve has had an off-and-on headache for about three days. He has also had a stuffy nose but no fever. He presents to the Apex Medical Center's emergency department (ED) at about 7:00 pm. The emergency room (ER) physician performs a thorough examination, including lab tests, x-rays, and, just to be sure, a computed tomographic (CT) scan of the head. The final diagnosis is sinusitis, and Steve is provided with a prescription for a strong decongestant.

In Case Study 5.1, if the services are being paid by a payer on a fee-for-service basis, then the payer will immediately question the provision of the CT scan as not being medically necessary. If the hospital is being paid on a capitated basis, then the hospital, along with the physicians, will be concerned about whether the CT scan is needed because the cost of the CT scan will reduce the net profitability to the hospital and, potentially, to the physician.

At a more global level, capitation can also promote wellness programs. On a long-term basis with fixed payments, if the covered population can be kept healthier, then fewer medical services will be required. Also, careful coordination among the various providers under the capitated payment will be encouraged to reduce costs by reducing unnecessary healthcare services.

Capitation: Key Features

Capitation represents a paradigm shift from any of the more common healthcare payment systems. Most payment systems are based on what is termed *fee-for-service* payment. Simply stated, this means that the healthcare provider is paid by a third-party payer as services are provided. More services directly result in more payment. This is why payers will pay only for medically necessary services. Some payers do, indeed, manage the care that is needed for their insured or covered members. If the amount of care being provided can, in some way, be delimited, then the third-party payer will pay less overall.

The word *capitation* comes from the concept of *per capita*, which is Latin for "per head." Under this type of payment system, the healthcare provider is paid a flat amount for services to be provided to a specific group of patients over a given period of time. Often, this is done on a monthly basis. The healthcare provider is paid on a PMPM basis. The number of covered individuals may vary on a monthly basis; thus, the monthly payment may also vary.

So what is the difference with this type of payment system? There is a major change in what is called the *locus of risk*. In others words, who is at risk if there a significant medical service required? Under the fee-for-service arrangement, it is the third-party payer or insurance company that is at risk. Under capitation, it is the healthcare provider that is taking on the risk. Consider Case Study 5.2:

Case Study 5.2: Capitated Contract for the Acme Medical Clinic

There are seven family practice physicians at the Acme Medical Clinic. The clinic has been approached by a larger local employer. The employer wants the physicians at the clinic to handle all primary care services for its employees. Any specialty services and hospital services will be paid outside this particular contract. Each employee or family member at the company will be covered, and the company is offering to pay $30.00 per month per head. The average monthly census is estimated at 900 members.

Should Acme accept this offer? There will be a steady flow of $27,000.00 per month to the clinic.

From the clinic's, that is, the physicians', perspective, there is a giant unknown. The issue is how often any of these 900 individuals will possibly come to the clinic to receive primary care services. In general, physicians do not have statistical or actuarial information concerning the incidence of services for given populations of patients. This kind of information has been developed for decades by insurance companies and other third-party payers. Also, exactly what is included in primary care? For instance, if a patient needs to have a small lesion on the arm removed, is this part of primary care, or should this patient be referred to a specialist, possibly a dermatologist?

The physicians need to know not only the incidence of patient encounters but also the typical level and type of care for these encounters. If there is reasonable statistical data, then the potential risks and associated profit or losses for this patient group can be assessed. Encounters typically fall into two categories:

■ Routine or preventive
■ Unanticipated or reactive

Routine services involve physical examinations, vaccinations, and other preventive medicine services. If our physicians at the Apex Medical Center enter into a contract, then certainly the routine or preventive services will need to be carefully delineated, most likely based on the age of covered members. For instance, these routine services could include an annual physical examination for adult members ages 45–65 or vaccinations for children from age 2 to age 18. If these services are well defined, then the clinic can project possible costs for services based on the age of the covered members.

Note: Most capitation arrangements are predicated on the PMPM concept. The size of the group of covered members may, and probably will, change from month to month. Thus, composition of the members will also sometimes change significantly. This change in membership then changes the risk for the number and type of services.

Case Study 5.2 represents a very small-scale situation, in this case a single family practice clinic. In practice, capitation is typically pursued on a much larger scale and involves a wide range of services and different providers. Nonetheless, the basic issue of transfer of risk to healthcare providers and the fact that healthcare providers do not typically have the necessary statistical and actuarial data even to begin proper risk assessment remain in place.

To develop capitated payment for healthcare services, there must be some sort of organization that has the ability to develop a capitated plan and then contract with provider groups to develop and implement such a payment process. The impetus for establishing capitated payment is that the payer can accurately predict, at least for a given period of time, its costs for providing healthcare to its membership. For instance, a larger employer in a community may want to provide health care for its employees and families. Let us join the Wile Fabrication Company, the largest employer in Anywhere, USA.

Case Study 5.3: Employer Reducing Healthcare Payments

The Wile Fabrication Company is the largest employer in Anywhere, USA. There are now well over 1,000 employees, and steady growth continues as Wile expands its product lines. Health insurance premiums have grown to the point that Wile has to consider some alternative, or the health insurance may have to be significantly curtailed. Wile has been working with an outside consulting firm that is suggesting establishing a capitated arrangement with the healthcare providers in and around Anywhere, USA. Wile is fortunate in that virtually all of its employees live in Anywhere, USA, or at least within fifty miles of Anywhere, USA.

The question then becomes, what will Wile need to do to set up a capitated arrangement? With a little thought, you will realize that there is a great deal of work to establish some sort of capitated arrangement. For instance, the actual services to be included must be identified. In this case, this would involve primary care physician (PCP) services, specialty physician services, hospital inpatient services, and hospital outpatient services. Other services might have to be considered, such as skilled nursing, home health, and the like. After the services have been identified, then the actual healthcare providers must be identified. Also, the actual arrangements and PMPM payments would have to be determined. Then, the whole capitated approach would have to be marketed to the healthcare providers.

For Anywhere, USA, the Apex Medical Center is the only hospital within forty-five miles. There are two family practice clinics, a multispecialty clinic, and several other smaller specialty physician groups. Obviously, the hospital would have to be included. But, what about the various physicians and physician groups? Are they all going to be included, or are only selected physicians going to be included? For instance, can more than one primary care group be included?

This discussion leads very quickly to the concept of a preferred provider organization or PPO, which was discussed in Chapter 4. PPOs can exist for different reasons and to different levels of formality. A PPO is simply a grouping of healthcare providers that has special service and payment arrangements for a given population of individuals. Typically, the covered individuals have incentives to use the preferred providers in that healthcare coverage may pay for all the services from members of the PPO, but only a limited portion for providers outside the network. Ordinarily, the healthcare providers in the PPO are not employed or owned by another organization. While the PPO approach is often used with standard fee-for-service payment arrangements (e.g., an insurance company), the PPO concept is one of the typical ways to implement capitated payment arrangements.

Note that we have given two examples, one at a clinic level and the other at an employer level, relative to capitation. This same concept can be extended to regions and even states. For instance, a state Medicaid program could, at least in theory, establish a capitated payment system. The same fundamental issues would be present as with our employer case study. Questions like which healthcare providers are involved, which patient populations are associated with which providers, how services are to be divided between different providers, how payments are to be made, what happens if there are losses on the part of a given provider, and the list certainly continues. Establishing a capitated arrangement at any level requires a great deal of work.

Before we start addressing risk management, reinsurance, and excess coverage concepts, we consider a case study that illustrates how capitated arrangements change the whole landscape for providers.

Case Study 5.4: Dermatologist Specialists under Capitation

There is now a capitated payment system in place in Anywhere, USA. A large PCP group along with several specialty physician groups are under this payment arrangement. There is a three-physician dermatology group in this arrangement, and now some conflicts are arising. Previously under the fee-for-service payment systems, the dermatologists encouraged referrals from the PCPs. Now, the dermatologists are claiming that the PCPs are inappropriately referring routine cases that the PCPs can readily address.

Case Study 5.4 illustrates the paradigm change that occurs with capitation versus fee-for-service payment. Prior to the capitated arrangement, the specialists were more than happy to accept referrals from PCPs. The process was that more referrals engendered more services and then more reimbursement from the increased volume of services. With fee-for-service payment, the dermatologists complained that the PCPs did not refer all appropriate cases. Now under capitation, the PCPs are referring almost anything associated with dermatology so that the PCPs can reduce their costs and increase profitability under the level payments made through capitation.

Case Study 5.5: Access to Specialty Care

Stephanie has health coverage through her husband's employer. The company has recently moved to a capitated payment arrangement and is using preferred providers. Stephanie had to change PCPs. Stephanie has had some gastrointestinal issues. She has been to the PCP several times and has been given a diagnosis of irritable bowel syndrome. She has been instructed to alter her diet, and in time, the prognosis is that the condition will resolve itself. Stephanie disagrees and has requested that she see a specialist. As a part of the capitated payment plan, access to specialists is strictly limited to a referral from the PCP.

While the clinical facts in Case Study 5.5 can certainly be discussed at length, the fact that a capitated payment arrangement is being used could certainly influence the delimitation for seeing a specialist. If this were a fee-for-service arrangement, then the PCP would probably have little compunction in referring Stephanie to a specialist. Because of the capitated arrangement, attempts will certainly be made to reduce the amount and level of service to enhance cost reduction.

Risk Management through Insurance

Everyone is subject to risks of various types. If you buy a home, you then have the risk of the home being destroyed by a tornado,* or an individual may injure him- or herself on your property so there is a liability risk. Risk management is a discipline that addresses risk and what steps to take to reduce risk. Probably the most common approach to risk is to transfer the risk, whatever it is, to insurance. For your home, you typically purchase homeowners' insurance, which includes things like property coverage, liability coverage, medical payments, and the like. Thus, if incidents occur that are covered by the insurance policy, the insurance company will address the incidents up to the limits of coverage. This means the risk, at the financial level anyway, are transferred to the insurance company.

Returning to our physicians at the Acme Medical Clinic in Case Study 5.1, what is really needed is some sort of insurance that will pay if there are unusual events that cause significant services to be provided by the physicians, which then cause a net loss to the physicians under the capitation contract. For instance, the physician might want an insurance policy so that if in a given month there is a loss greater than $10,000.00, then the insurance policy will pay for all the costs above the $10,000.00 threshold. In this case, the clinic is, in some sense, self-insured for the first $10,000.00 in a given month, and the insurance company pays anything above the $10,000.00.

This type of insurance is generally referred to as excess coverage or sometimes reinsurance. Excess coverage can be divided into:

- Specific excess insurance and
- Aggregate excess insurance.

Using our Acme Medical Clinic example, the physicians may be worried about unusually expensive individual cases. For instance, for a given individual over the period of a year, if the cost of care exceeds a given threshold, then insurance coverage will kick into place. More likely, the physicians' concerns will be at an aggregated level. There may some patients who are more costly than others are, but these may be offset by individuals who do not use any medical services. However, if there is some unusual rush for medical services, the physicians at the clinic may not only be overwhelmed in providing services but also their cost may vastly exceed the capitated payments. Thus, some sort of insurance is needed to pay for cost overruns during the period of a year. For instance, if there is an aggregate loss (costs greater than payments) of more than $25,000.00 in a year, then the excess coverage will pay for all the losses that are greater than, say, $15,000.00.

Note: When you start analyzing such concepts, you will quickly realize that there are some significant subtleties. For instance, what exactly is the definition of a *loss*? Simplistically, a loss would occur if the costs are greater than the payments. But, what is included in the costs? For instance, does this include the physicians' salaries?

---

* Depending on where you live, you can change "tornado" to hurricane, earthquake, tsunami, flood, and so on.

You may also see the term *reinsurance*. This term is generally used when there is some sort of insurance policy in addition to a base policy of some sort. For our purposes, excess coverage and reinsurance are essentially the same concept as applied to the concept of capitated payment systems.

Self-insurance occurs when an organization or entity decides to assume the given risk. Generally, some sort of financial pool of money is set aside to address the risk. For capitated payment systems, the concept of a risk pool is typically utilized. For instance, the physicians from Case Study 5.1 may decide that a certain portion of the PMPM payment should go into a risk pool just in case there are any cost overruns. If at the end of a year the risk pool has grown to an appropriate size, actuarially, then a portion of the risk pool can be distributed back to the physicians. As a further risk management tool, the risk pool itself can be reinsured or some sort of excess coverage can be put into place.

Note: Insurance companies and associated issues are regulated at the state level. Thus, when establishing the rather intricate organizational structures and associated legal agreements, be certain to check for state-level insurance requirements.

Models for Capitation

There are many different approaches to capitated payment arrangements. Because our focus is on capitation as a payment system, we will not try to categorize all the different approaches, many of which become involved in different managed care structures. In Case Studies 5.1 and 5.2, we started the logical discussion of establishing simple capitated arrangements. This discussion naturally led to the concept of a PPO capitation arrangement. The healthcare providers involved became part of a network or group of providers treated as preferred providers under the capitation arrangement. These preferred providers received capitated payments and provided services to the members of the capitated plan.

In Figure 5.1, we bring together a number of the concepts that we have discussed involving establishing capitated payment arrangements. As seen in the figure, an employer is purchasing certain healthcare through a health plan. The services considered in this illustration include:

- PCPs
- Hospital services, inpatient and outpatient
- Specialty physicians

The PCPs and hospital are 100-percent capitated for this particular case. The specialty physicians have remained fee for service. There is reinsurance or excess coverage for the hospital services and primary care services. There are separate risk pools for the hospital and the PCPs. Note that there is also a risk pool relative to the hospital, PCPs, and specialists. Note that the specialists, even though using fee-for-service payment, participate in the risk pool settlement. The participation of the specialists helps to ensure that there is a smooth interface between the PCPs and the specialists. See Case Study 5.4 for an illustration of the types of interface problems that can occur.

Of course, there are other services that must be addressed, and there will also be situations in which covered members will receive services outside this particular health plan, that is, outside the network. These two issues are simply included in the figure for completeness.

Figure 5.1 shows, at a conceptual level, that capitated arrangements can, and do, become complicated. You should be able to discern that a great deal of work must be accomplished in setting

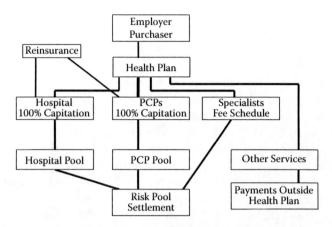

Figure 5.1 Simple capitated payment arrangement.

up these arrangements. There are also numerous legal documents and agreements that must be reached by the various parties.

We consider another possible model for developing capitated payment. In the cases discussed, the healthcare providers were independent from the organization (e.g., health plan, employer, insurance company) that was actually sponsoring the capitated plan. Another approach is to have a sponsoring organization that already has providers, particularly employed physicians. Such an organization could also own hospitals and other institutional healthcare providers. This way, the organization could offer capitated payments to an employer or other group that desired to obtain various health services.

One form of this approach is called the staff model health maintenance organization (HMO) mentioned in Chapter 4. This is a specific form of the more general concept of a managed care organization (MCO). As usual, be careful with terminology because there are no universally accepted definitions of these concepts. Always look at the details of a given situation. Our focus is on the payment aspects of these types of arrangements.

A staff model HMO has the advantage that multiple capitation arrangements can easily be made because the entire infrastructure of providers is already in place. The HMO will need to have the proper actuarial data for the given group of members to know what kind of pricing is appropriate. For employers, this type of approach may be quite attractive if the pricing (i.e., the PMPM payment) is competitive with traditional health and accident insurance coverage. All of the issues, such as coverage, medical necessity, quality of care, accessibility, and the like, are still very much a part of the mix. Consider Case Study 5.6:

Case Study 5.6: Capitated Health Coverage

Road Corporation is a growing company with about 650 employees. Health and accident insurance coverage is rapidly becoming unaffordable, particularly as the company is expanding with minimal capitalization. Most of the employees are located within about 200 miles of the corporate headquarters. Road has been approached by an HMO that owns six hospitals and numerous physician clinics in the general area. The HMO is offering what appears to be a very competitive capitation arrangement that involves a PMPM payment for each employee and family member.

The basic facts in Case Study 5.6 should be attractive to the Road Corporation as long as the PMPM payments are reasonable relative to current health premiums. Of course, there are many questions. Just as with traditional health and accident insurance, there will be questions about coverage, accessibility to specialists, coverage outside the HMO's service area, preauthorizations, emergency and urgent coverage, and the like. There will also be questions about new treatments, new drugs, and possibly new medical devices.

Most of these questions are not dissimilar to questions concerning traditional health and accident coverage. However, because the payment process for the healthcare providers is on a limited, capitated basis, there will be significant pressure to delimit the delivery of services to maintain financial viability for the healthcare providers. The paradigm change that capitation represents may not always be immediately evident to those who may come under a capitated plan. Different imperatives and priorities suddenly come into play with this type of healthcare payment system.

Consider Figure 5.2, in which the PMPM payment is distributed across several types of healthcare providers. If we know the incidence of services for the covered population, then we can start calculating the overall costs and compare the costs against the PMPM payment that is offered. For most healthcare providers, the actuarial data for incidence of services for a given population is not known, and thus entering into capitated contracts can be unsettling.

All of the amounts in Figure 5.2 are fictitious and are for educational purposes only. If we assume that there are 10,000 covered members each month, then we can start making some calculations:

Administrative overhead	120,000 Members per Year * $10.00 per Member = $1,200,000.00
Primary care visits	40,000 Visits per Year * $35.00 per Visit = $1,400,000.00
Specialist services	8,000 Visits per Year * $150.00 per Visit = $1,200,000.00
Hospital outpatient	20,000 Visits per Year * $200.00 per Visit = $4,000,000.00
Hospital inpatient stays	5,000 Days per Year * $1,000.00 per Day= $5,000,000.00
Ancillary services	40,000 Visits per Year * $30.00 per Visit = $1,200,000.00

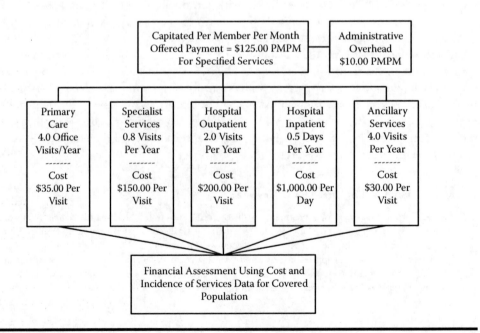

Figure 5.2   PMPM capitated payment breakdown.

The total of all the costs is $14,000,000.00. So, what is the cost PMPM? There are 10,000 members per month on average, so 12 * 10,000 = 120,000. Dividing $14,000,000.00 by 120,000 gives us $116.67 (rounded) per month. From Figure 5.2, the amount of the PMPM payment is $125.00. While there is still a significant amount of information that is needed, on the surface the $125.00 payment is greater that the projected costs by $125.00 − $116.67 = $8.33 (rounded) PMPM. Multiplying this over an entire year, the profit is projected to be 120,000 * $8.33 = $999,600.00.*

Obviously, this model is grossly oversimplified. If all of the data in the model is actuarially correct, then there will be profit. However, what if 10 of the members over the course of a year required hospitalization of 25 days on average. Also, assume that the cost for these patients was $2,000.00 a day and not the projected $1,000.00 per day. That would be 250 hospital days at $2,000.00 per day or $500,000.00. The projected profit margin could easily be jeopardized by such adverse events. Again, note that the risk under capitation resides with the healthcare provider.

There are many different types of arrangements that can be made based on the general concept of capitated payment. However, the arrangements are organized, careful financial modeling should be conducted at least to estimate the possible risks involved. Once the risks are known, appropriate steps can be taken to minimize or to transfer the risk to some extent. Risks for capitation are often addressed by risk pools or by transferring risk to special types of insurance policies.

Summary and Conclusion

Capitated healthcare payment simply means that the payment to healthcare providers or group of providers is on a flat-fee basis, generally a PMPM basis. The payment amount is fixed in advance through a contractual arrangement that generally lasts for a year. While this type of payment seems quite straightforward, in comparison to all of the other healthcare payment systems that have been discussed in this book and the three associated books in this series, there is a major change with capitation.

The change is with the location of risk relative to unanticipated utilization of healthcare services. Virtually all other healthcare payment is on a fee-for-service basis. This means that for a given provider, if there is a need for more services, then the provider will be paid for the services actually provided. Services must be medically necessary. Payers will not pay for services that are not really needed. However, the financial risk for the level and type of services rests with the payer. Generally, the payer will be some sort of insurance company or some other organization that has access to proper actuarial data concerning incidence of services for given populations.

With capitated or flat-fee payment, the risk for providing unusual volumes of healthcare services moves to the healthcare provider, that is, the physician, hospital, nursing facility, and so on. While healthcare providers might be willing to entertain capitated payment arrangements, there is one very large piece of information missing. The healthcare providers have no statistical or actuarial data concerning the possible incidence of services or levels of care that might be involved. In other words, the healthcare providers have no idea what sort of risk is involved. The data and actuarial analyses of healthcare risk lie with the insurance companies and other third-party payers who have been paying for services over the decades.

Different models of capitated payment systems have been developed. Two of these general models have been briefly discussed in this chapter. One approach is for the capitated plan to use a group of preferred providers, who then as a group can enter into capitated arrangements

---

* If you calculate this without undue rounding, the profit is $1,000,000.00.

at different levels. The preferred providers, generally part of a PPO, remain independent within their own organizational structures. Another approach is to have the healthcare providers all be employed or owned by an organization. We have considered this approach through what is called a staff model HMO. The basic idea is that the HMO has the healthcare providers (e.g., physicians, hospitals, nursing facilities, etc.) in place, and then the HMO can establish capitated contracts with employers and other groups of individuals. Because there is a fixed, flat-fee payment made for the covered members, if the capitated rates are competitive with fee-for-service arrangements, then capitation becomes competitively attractive.

Because the locus of risk shifts to the healthcare providers, the concept of reinsurance or excess coverage becomes important. These are concepts in which the healthcare providers or the organization establishing the capitated arrangements transfer risk for unusual events or unusual volumes of services to an insurance policy. This risk can also be self-insured to some extent, with the use of risk pools that accumulate money for contingencies such as unusual services.

The most important aspect of capitation is to appreciate fully that there has been a paradigm shift. In this chapter, we used the concept of medical necessity to illustrate this change. With fee-for-service payment, payers will pay only for medically necessary services. Often, the payer will want to preauthorize services whenever possible. The payers are concerned that the providers are simply providing too many services to generate more reimbursement.

Under capitation, the reverse is true. Healthcare providers want to reduce the number and type of services being provided; the fewer the services, the greater is the potential profitability from the per capita payments. Thus, the concern becomes whether all medically necessary services are being provided. For fee for service, only medically necessary services are payable, and under capitation all services that need to be provided (i.e., that are medically necessary) should be provided.*

---

* This discussion should take you back to your high school days in algebra and geometry when you studied necessary sufficient conditions and the concept of *if and only if* logic.

Chapter 6

Claim Adjudication and Compliance

Introduction

Coding, billing, and reimbursement compliance is a major issue for health care payment. While most of the publicity for improper payments is with the statutorily established payment systems such as the Medicare Physician Fee Schedule (MPFS), Ambulatory Payment Classifications (APCs), and Diagnosis Related Groups (DRGs), compliance is also an issue with healthcare payment from private third-party payers. The main difference is that for private third-party payers such as insurance carriers, the compliance issues revolve around contractual compliance. That is, whatever is in the contracts and associated companion manuals provides the framework for determining appropriate payment compliance within the contract itself. With the statutorily established payment systems, criminal prosecutions sometimes occur. With contractual compliance, litigation is generally over payments at the civil level.

Even with a formal contract, there can still be significant challenges between the third-party payer and the healthcare provider. Many contracts have an arbitration process so that the two parties can go through arbitration as opposed to actual legal proceedings. Private third-party payers may also include obligations in their contracts to allow for various audits that can be conducted. For instance, a payer using a percentage-of-charges payment process will be very interested in how a healthcare provider determines and updates its charge structures. A payer that typically has contracts with physicians may be interested in proper evaluation and management (E/M) coding because a fee schedule arrangement is often used, and the physician may be upcoding cases for increased reimbursement.

For hospital inpatient services, there may even be auditing, in a general sense, in real time. The payer may actually have nursing staff visit the hospital to review cases for the payer's enrollees at the time of services. Thus, compliance for private third-party payers is similar to concerns that are found with the statutory programs, such as the Medicare program.

Note: A major issue with coding, billing, and reimbursement compliance has to do with the accuracy, adequacy, and detail of the documentation. Healthcare coding staff often quip that if the service is not documented, then it did not happen. In other words, coding staff will not code something that is not documented. Obviously, services can be provided, but if not documented, then there is no way to substantiate the provision of service or dispensing of an item.

A general question, particularly relative to compliance, is what happens when a healthcare provider files a claim, or at least submits an itemized statement, to a private third-party payer with whom the provider has no contract. In many cases, the healthcare provider may have little knowledge of the payer and how reimbursement will be made. In theory, the full charges should be reimbursed. For that matter, the healthcare provider might be wise to collect payment directly from the patients and then have the patient request payment from his or her carrier. Consider Case Study 6.1:

Case Study 6.1: Out-of-State Patient

On Wednesday morning, the Acme Medical Clinic addressed a patient presenting with two lacerations. The individual was assessed, and the lacerations were repaired. The patient was visiting Anywhere, USA, and had insurance coverage from a regional insurance company several states away. The coding and billing personnel at Acme prepared a typical claim for the evaluation and laceration repairs.

In this case study, Acme had no relationship, let alone a contract, with the insurance company. So, how will Acme prepare the claim? The general answer is that the claim will be prepared according to the standard claim format and standard use of Current Procedural Terminology (CPT) procedure and *ICD-10* (*International Classification of Diseases, Tenth Revision*) diagnosis codes. This statement should remind you of our discussion of the Health Insurance Portability and Accountability Act of 1996 (HIPAA) TSC (Transaction Standard/Standard Code) rule discussed in Chapter 4. The HIPAA TSC rule provides a default set of rules for filing claims with private third-party payers for which there is no contractual arrangement. While the best course of action is to ask for payment directly from the patient and then allow the patient to obtain payment from the patient's insurance, many healthcare providers will go ahead and file a claim on behalf of the patient.

Even though the HIPAA TSC rule provides for a standardized mechanism to file a claim, there is no standardized way in which payment will be made. The payer may have some sort of default payment mechanism that pays for the services at significantly less than the charged amount. There can also be other complications. For instance, in Case Study 6.1, Acme may learn that the repair of the lacerations needed to be approved in advance before a claim is filed. The lacerations that were repaired certainly rise to the level of urgent care but may not be considered as emergent. From the perspective of the patient, these lacerations were probably an emergency. However, Acme may find itself in a position in which the insurance carrier pays nothing, and Acme must then attempt to collect directly from the patient.

We can take Case Study 6.1 and expand this discussion further.

Case Study 6.2: Out-of-State Patient Fall in a Parking Lot

Referring to the basic facts in Case Study 6.1, several weeks after the services were provided, Acme learns that the lacerations that were repaired resulted from a fall in the parking lot of a local store. The patient's attorney has now filed a liability claim with the local store.

In Case Study 6.2, the liability coverage* for the local store will be primary, and now the distant insurance company will be secondary. The coding and billing personnel at Acme will need to follow up with great care to make certain that the clinic charges are paid at least to the level that the insurance company will make. In cases like this, the private payer may well make a payment and then subrogate to the liability company that covers the local store.

We have already encountered some compliance issues in previous chapters. For instance, in Case Study 3.23 in Chapter 3, price fixing was mentioned. Enforcement of allegations of price fixing comes under the aegis of the Federal Trade Commission (FTC). Healthcare providers are certainly not allowed to coordinate the setting of their charges to gain unjust enrichment. Also, the concept of protected health information (PHI) has been mentioned relative to the HIPAA privacy rule.[†] PHI is usually associated with patients' medical records. Interestingly, PHI also includes billing and claims-filing information, so all of the compliance issues surrounding health information privacy also come into play relative to claims filing and reimbursement.

The bottom line is that compliance, even when there is no contractual arrangement, can become quite complex for healthcare providers of all types.

Note: See the book, *Compliance for Coding, Billing and Reimbursement: A Systematic Approach to Developing a Comprehensive Program*, 2nd edition (CRC Press, 2008).

Statutory versus Contractual Compliance

The biggest difference between statutory and contractual compliance is that legal proceedings for the statutory programs may involve criminal prosecutions. For instance, the Medicare and various state Medicaid programs have a host of auditing entities and associated auditing processes. Here is a brief list:

- RACs: recovery audit contractors
- ZPICs: zone program integrity contractors
- CERT: comprehensive error rate testing

In addition, the Medicare administrative contractors (MACs) and the OIG (Office of the Inspector General) along with the DOJ (Department of Justice) perform audits. The OIG publishes a work plan on a fiscal year basis that describes its current audit areas.[‡] For each of the audit areas, a report is issued with findings and recommendations.[§]

Contractual obligation almost always involves civil litigation or arbitration. However, even in contractual situations, if there is a pattern of abuse, then there could be criminal prosecutions. While most of the public reporting concerning fraud and abuse is with the Medicare and Medicaid programs, there is still significant activity with private third-party payers.

With statutory compliance, if there is an overpayment for any reason, then the overpayment amount must be recouped from the healthcare provider. Such recoupments can involve cases

---

* For our purposes, we assume the store has liability coverage, although the store may be self-insured up to a certain level.

[†] See 45 CFR §§160 and 162.

[‡] See the OIG website: http://oig.hhs.gov/reports-and-publications/workplan/index.asp.

[§] See the OIG website: http://oig.hhs.gov/reports-and-publications/oei/subject_index.asp.

in which the healthcare provider has coded, billed, and filed claims correctly. Consider Case Study 6.3:

> **Case Study 6.3: Improper Payment by the Payer**
>
> The Apex Medical Center has been informed that overpayment has been made for certain types of services. Apex properly filed the claims with all of the correct codes, proper authorizations, and proper charges. The problem is that the claims were improperly adjudicated by the third-party payer. Basically, there was a programming error in the adjudication system.

Now, the action that will be taken in Case Study 6.3 will very much depend on whether Apex is dealing with a statutorily established payment system versus a private third-party payer contractual payment process. For instance, if this situation were discovered relative to the Medicare program, the MAC would calculate the total amount of overpayment. In some cases, this calculation could go back several years. Apex would then have to repay the overpayment even though Apex did nothing incorrect. If this situation occurred under a private contract or some sort of managed care contract, then the contract should determine the proper course of action. There may be no repayment, or there may be some repayment required.

Note: In some cases, there can be state laws and even contractual provisions so that if a healthcare provider files a claim that is then adjudicated and paid, after a year has elapsed the claim and associated payment are considered final. Thus, whether there was an underpayment or overpayment, the process is considered final. Obviously, if the claim is appealed by the healthcare provider or if there is fraud involved, then the overall process remains open until resolved. For Medicare, possible fraud can go back for ten years or sometimes more.

Healthcare providers who have managed care contracts are generally fastidious about tracking payments that are generated through the adjudication process used by the payer. Because coding, billing, and claims-filing requirements sometimes change, healthcare providers must be very careful to track reimbursement. The payer may make changes to the adjudication software that processes the claims. Sometimes, these changes are not explicitly stated, and there may not be any sort of notice given to the provider filing claims. Let us visit the Apex Medical Center for an example.

> **Case Study 6.4: Injections Provided during Surgery**
>
> The Apex Medical Center has a percentage-of-charges contract with a local insurance company. The percentage payment is generally 80 percent, although there are other percentages for certain types of services, pharmacy items, and devices. Reimbursement personnel have noted a change in payments for outpatient surgical cases. While injections and infusions generally have been paid separately, there has been a subtle change in that injections and infusions provided with surgical cases are not being paid separately. These charges are simply being dropped relative to the percentage-of-charges calculation.

Changes of the type indicated in Case Study 6.4 can sometimes be difficult to discern. While Apex may monitor the overall realization rate (i.e., overall payment relative to charges) for this third-party payer, because of the variable percentages involved in the contract, picking up the decrease may not be obvious. In this case, reimbursement personnel will need to review a sampling of cases to identify this change in the adjudication of claims.

After this change is identified, then the payer can be contacted to correct what appears as incorrect reimbursement. In cases of this type, it is highly probable that the payer made changes to the adjudication system for other types of contracts, not for the percentage-of-charges contracts.

For instance, the payer may have decided that for contracts using a modified form of APCs that the injections and infusions in connection with outpatient surgical cases should be bundled. This change in adjudication was then incorrectly applied to the percentage-of-charges payments as well.

Contractual compliance works both ways; that is, both the healthcare provider and managed care company or third-party payer have rights and obligations as delineated in the contract. Often, the contracts themselves will provide for the process of resolving disputes that might arise. Arbitration is a common process. Note that even with best intentions on the part of both parties, the dynamic nature of healthcare services will generate issues that were never anticipated. Also, geographic changes in service providers may alter the way in which services can be provided, which in turn can affect a contractual arrangement.

> **Case Study 6.5: Shortage of Skilled Nursing Beds**
>
> Anywhere, USA, has had the good fortune to have five different skilled nursing facilities. As a result, the Apex Medical Center has not entered the marketplace for skilled nursing facility services. In recent months, one of the facilities had a severe fire, and another was closed for financial reasons. Apex has now found itself needing to keep patients at the hospital who are waiting skilled nursing placement. Unfortunately, several of Apex's private payer contracts contain no provisions for paying the hospital for skilled nursing services.

In Case Study 6.5, what Apex is experiencing is that patients who are ready for discharge cannot be discharged because there are no skilled nursing beds available. While the Medicare program has provisions to handle this type of situation,* some of Apex's other contracts have no provisions for billing for such services and certainly no way for the services to be paid. While it would appear that Apex should be able to address this situation easily, sometimes these issues can become quite protracted, with significant amounts of reimbursement left in limbo.

Audits and Reviews

Types of Audits

Various types of audits and reviews abound in healthcare, with particular attention to proper coding, billing, and reimbursement. The need for audits and the types of audits that are conducted depend on the type of payment system that is being utilized. Note also that there are associated issues that may affect payment, such as proper credentialing, supervisory requirements, medical necessity, coverage issues, and the like. Thus, whether for statutory payment systems or for contractual payment systems, compliance concerns are generally addressed by some sort of review or audit. There are numerous approaches and techniques that are used to ensure proper payment. In theory, these audits and reviews should focus on both overpayments and underpayments. However, in reality most of these audits are conducted by third-party payers, so that the primary focus seems to address mainly overpayments.

Note: We use the word *audit* to refer to a formal process and the word *review* to address more informal activities. For instance, when a formal audit is conducted, the universe of cases will be identified, a random sampling of cases will be chosen, and then the audit will be conducted. A report will generally be issued that delineates the findings and any recommendations. A simple review might

---

* For Medicare, the extra days simply go into the hospital stay and are paid under MS-DRGs (Medicare Severity Diagnosis Related Groups).

involve selecting twenty-five cases and taking a quick look to see if everything is in order. These two terms are not completely discrete in that a formal review could easily be constructed as an audit.

First, let us consider the following division for audits:

■ Prepayment audits
■ Postpayment audits

The vast majority of audits and reviews occur after the adjudication process, with payment already made. There are some prepayment audits or review; this prepayment activity takes claims and checks them before payment is made. The concept of prepayment could also be used with hospital inpatient services in which there is a concurrent review of cases while the patient is in the hospital. These reviews would typically be performed by specially trained nursing staff on the hospital inpatient floors. In this case, the word *concurrent* means that the review is performed at the same time the patient is receiving services.

Audits and reviews can be divided into the following categories:

■ Prospective
■ Concurrent
■ Retrospective

This division of activities is based on process (i.e., claim development and adjudication) versus the end result (i.e., claim and payment). With prospective reviews, it is the systematic way in which the claim is developed that is carefully examined. This includes any special adjudication requirements that might exist for a particular payment system or a specific managed care contract. Thus, in a prospective review, the computer system, or sometimes systems, that actually develops the claim is examined. This includes entry of information into the computer system as well as the generation of the claim. With all of the claims-filing requirements for both statutory healthcare payment systems and then the wide variety of contractual payment processes, healthcare providers must make certain that everything is being performed appropriately.

> **Case Study 6.6: Back-End Processing System**
>
> The Apex Medical Center has a billing system that generates the itemized statements and claims for services provided. The main billing system follows all of the standard rules for developing claims following the HIPAA TSC rules. Because there are special edits and varying requirements, a back-end computer has been developed to modify claims to meet any special requirements from Medicare, Medicaid, and a host of contractual arrangements with various managed care contracts.

With the back-end computer system as described in Case Study 6.6, a major part of a prospective audit of the coding, billing, and associated reimbursement process would focus on the back-end system. These computers are often called *scrubbers* because they clean up the claims and itemized statements to meet differing requirements from various third-party payers.

Concurrent reviews address both the systematic process for developing claims and itemized statements along with an examination of the final products, that is, the claims and itemized statements. The use of the word *concurrent* in this context denotes that current claims, that is, claims that go back over the last several months, are examined. Often, these claims may not yet have been paid. If claims are examined that are paid, the claims can still be corrected and refiled. Thus, in a concurrent audit, if errors are found, then the claims that have errors can be corrected and refiled as appropriate.

Retrospective audits and reviews go back in time and generally do not address any of the systematic processes that are used for generating claims and itemized statements. These are the classic audits that have been used for years by governmental entities to address false claims and fraud with statutorily established programs such as Medicare and Medicaid. These audits can go back years, sometimes up to ten years for statutory programs. For managed care contractual payment, the contracts should address how far back the audits and reviews can take place.

You will also see other terminology relative to audits and reviews. Here are some examples:

Focused Reviews. These are generally smaller audits and reviews that are delimited to specific areas. This terminology can be used for both prepayment and postpayment situations. For instance, a hospital may be informed that a private payer is performing a 100-percent focused prepayment review of all physical therapy claims. A physician or clinic may be informed that there is a focused postpayment review of the use of the level 5 office visits (i.e., CPT codes 99215 and 99205).

Probe Audits. These are audits that are conducted on a limited scale to determine possible error rates. A statistically magic number is 30. Thus probe audits are often associated with the number 30, although a different number may be chosen, but there tends to be thirty or more audits. See the concept and process of extrapolation discussion in this chapter.

Educational Audit. In some cases, a third-party payer, including governmental programs, may note that there are some aberrations in claims being filed by a particular healthcare provider. A focused audit may be conducted to determine what sort of problem exists. The payer will then educate the healthcare provider to generate claims that meet the requirements of the given third-party payer.

Audits and reviews in the healthcare area are quite common and, if anything, are increasing in number and scope. This is particularly true with Medicare and Medicaid with the development of the RACs. While payers may provide the impetus for audits and reviews, healthcare providers also have audits and reviews performed to ensure correct coding, billing, and reimbursement. In today's healthcare compliance environment, every healthcare provider should have a compliance plan that includes routine audits and reviews by external auditors and consultants.

Audit Process

The specific audit processes utilized by auditors very much depends on the payment system being utilized to generate payment for healthcare services. However, audits typically involve selecting a set of cases for review. The cases are usually selected from the population of cases on a random basis using statistical software to ensure randomness. Frequently, auditors will use the same software that governmental auditors use, namely, the OIG's RAT-STATS* program. After the sample has been selected, then the audit can be performed.

For healthcare providers to obtain independent, objective reviews, care must be taken to select consulting or auditing firms that can act as independent review organizations or IROs. This simply means that the organization conducting the review will be objective in its assessments and findings.

One of the key elements in conducting an audit is for the auditors to use audit guidelines. If directives for properly coding, billing, and filing claims are not in place, then auditing becomes

---

* RAT-STATS is freely downloadable from the OIG's website at http://oig.hhs.gov/organization/oas/ratstats/ RAT-STATS2007.zip.

problematic because there will not be specific audit guidelines by which to judge the correctness of a claim and the associated payment that was made. Here are some simple case studies that illustrate some of the auditing concerns to ensure proper payment.

Case Study 6.7: Apex Medical Center Auditing Program

Apex has developed a rigorous auditing program across all of its service areas. While internal checks are made routinely by reviewing small samples of claims within the different service areas, there are several external audits conducted by independent consultants. The two areas for external audits are inpatient and outpatient. Typically, there is a DRG audit and an APC audit. These audits extend across all payers because Apex codes all cases according to Medicare directives.

There are numerous payment systems and associated processes for both inpatient and outpatient hospital services. While there can be significantly different directives from various payers, for Apex the base approach is to code everything according to Medicare guidelines. If changes are needed for billing and filing the claims, then these changes can be made. For inpatient services, the cases chosen will be inpatient stays. On the outpatient side, the cases chosen will be based on encounters.

Case Study 6.8: Acme Medical Clinic Auditing Program

There are four family practice physicians, one internal medicine physician, and two surgeons at Acme. The physicians have been working on a written compliance plan. Part of the plan involves internal auditing and using external auditors to some extent. The main concern for the physicians involves their office visits, hospital visits, and then any procedures that are performed at the hospital along with those that are performed at the clinic itself.

The general areas of concern for the physicians at Acme are quite reasonable. Office visits and routine hospital visits use the E/M CPT codes. There are specific guidelines in the CPT manual itself. For Medicare, additional guidelines have been developed. For private third-party payers, there may also be contractual concerns for properly reporting the level of office or hospital visits.

Minor surgical procedures may be performed at the clinic, and the surgeons from Acme will go over to the hospital to perform surgical procedures. All of the physicians are also on call to the emergency department (ED) at the hospital. For surgical procedures at the hospital, both the hospital and the surgeons will be coding for the procedures. Thus, for surgical procedures there is a concern that the coding be the same at the clinic and the hospital.

Case Study 6.9: Correlating Hospital and Physician Coding

The Apex Medical Center has a large group of surgeons who provide services at the hospital. Most of these surgeons have their own staff that does the billing and claims filing. The compliance personnel have selected a sample of 50 surgeries that include most of the surgeons. The CPT coding for the surgeries was compared, and surprisingly, in about 25 percent of the cases, the CPT codes used by the physicians and hospital were not the same.

Case Study 6.9 illustrates an interesting compliance challenge. In the case of Apex, after this situation was discovered, a process was established whereby the hospital shared what hospital coding staff developed with the surgeons' coding staff. For this study, where there were discrepancies, for the most part the surgeons' staff had undercoded the surgeries.

Here is another case study that illustrates questions concerning what exactly to audit relative to a particular type of provider that deals mainly with the Medicare program.

Case Study 6.10: Apogee Home Health Auditing Program

Apogee wants to have an audit conducted for both Medicare and its private payers. The question is what is to be audited. Everything for home health involves a sixty-day period of care, with various nursing and home health aide visits occurring within the sixty-day period.

When moving beyond clinics and hospitals, the auditing process may have to be altered to accommodate the way in which services are provided or the way in which payment systems provide reimbursement. Home health is heavily dominated by Medicare patients in most locales, with some private payers and self-pay patients. Auditing can be performed at the visit or encounter level, that is, selecting nursing or home health aide visits, or auditing can be performed at a case level, which considers all the services provided within the sixty-day care period.

Extrapolation Process

Extrapolation is a statistical process whereby estimation is made that goes outside a given set of data. The opposite process is interpolation, in which data points within the given set of data are estimated. In healthcare auditing, as with other types of auditing, extrapolation is a formal statistical process that must be addressed with great care. Particularly, government auditors will consider a relatively large universe of cases, study a subset of the data, and then extrapolate the results of the subset to the entire universe. If a certain number of errors are discovered with overpayments involved, then extending the results to the entire universe can develop overpayments into the hundreds of thousands of dollars and sometimes in the millions of dollars.

Extrapolation can be used when there are repetitive cases occurring in large numbers. Let us visit the Acme Medical Clinic, where Medicare auditors are conducting an extensive audit.

Case Study 6.11: Clinic Visit Coding Audit

Acme has a wide range of patients, but Medicare beneficiaries make up about 40 percent of its business. Over the past two years, for Medicare patients there have been nearly 30,000 visits, each of which has been coded with a clinic visit level. There are five levels of E/M CPT codes. One set of codes is for new patients (99201–99205), and another set of five codes is for established patients (99211–99215).

For the basic facts from Case Study 6.11, what the Medicare auditors will do is first conduct a probe audit, that is, a small audit, to determine a possible error rate. Once the error rate is determined, then a sample size will be determined that is statistically valid for the entire universe of 30,000. For our purposes, let us assume the sample size is 500. A detailed audit will be conducted of the 500 cases, randomly selected, to find errors, generally overpayments. Let us assume that there were overpayments in 15 percent of the cases, and the average overpayment was $20.00. Now, the extrapolation can take place. Take the error rate of 15 percent and apply it to the whole universe. Thus, 15 percent * 30,000 is 4,500. The average overpayment is $20.00, so the total, extrapolated, overpayment is 4,500 * $20.00 or $90,000.00.

While the brief discussion provided is an oversimplification, the basic concept should be discernible. Healthcare providers that find themselves subject to audits that involve extrapolation will justifiably be nervous about the possible findings. Given the fact that there can be significant amounts that may be recouped or have to be repaid, such studies need careful analysis by the healthcare provider.

Audit Reports

Audit reports are a valuable tool for healthcare organizations. While healthcare providers would like the auditors to find no mistakes and thus be assured of compliance, this is rarely the case. Given the dynamic nature of healthcare services and the ever-changing landscape of rules and regulations, auditors sometimes find themselves in a position with no specific audit guidelines. For coding and billing, there will almost always be errors of some type. A significant part of the value of reviews and audits lies with the recommendations that the auditors make for improving processes, which will in turn better ensure compliance, both statutory and contractual.

Let us return to the Acme Medical Clinic, where the physicians have received an audit report with recommendations.

Case Study 6.12: Audit Report Recommendations

The six physicians at the Acme Medical Clinic are meeting with administrative staff and reviewing an audit report. A comprehensive audit had been conducted on the different levels of clinic visits. The intent of the study was to determine if the coding guidelines in this area had been followed. While there were some cases for which the levels were questionably high, the most significant finding from the audit was that there were significant documentation differences between the physicians. For essentially the same type of visit, one of the physicians was documenting volumes, another physician was very parsimonious with the documentation, and the other physicians seemed to fit between these two extremes. The visit levels for the physician with significant documentation was higher than for the other physicians, while the physician with less documentation had fewer visits, although the actual services were about the same.

Given the general facts presented in Case Study 6.12, what remedial action needs to be taken? Certainly, the physician with relatively little documentation needs to become more verbose and provide more detail. The physician with extensive documentation will probably not be requested to make any changes. Of course, the physician with extensive documentation will probably have a lower productivity rating; that is, this physician will probably be seeing fewer patients.

Healthcare providers should always pay very close attention to the reports and recommendations that are generated from audits and reviews. Because these reports are in writing, if recommendations are ignored and problems are later uncovered, then the failure to address recommendations properly can be an issue.

Note: Because compliance, both statutory and contractual, is a major issue for healthcare payment, healthcare providers often opt to have audits and reviews performed under the auspices of legal counsel.

Audit Dependence on Payment Mechanism

Great variability occurs with audits depending on the type of payment system used. Again, the reference to payment system can be on a macro level, covering services such as inpatient hospital or physician clinic payment. Or, the reference can be on a micro level, addressing a given device or pharmaceutical item. Consider the following case studies:

Case Study 6.13: Chargemaster Review Requirement

The Apex Medical Center has a percentage-of-charges contract with a regional insurance carrier. For both inpatient and outpatient services, the percentage payment is 90 percent. While there are carve-outs and other special payment mechanisms for certain services and items, generally the contract pays the 90 percent. One of the provisions in the contract is that every three years the payer has the right to review the hospital's chargemaster and to assess the way in which charges are established and increased.

The circumstance described in Case Study 6.13 is quite different from the more standard coding and claims review processes used with fee schedule and prospective payment systems. Exactly what the insurance company auditors will review is an interesting question. Hospital chargemasters are discussed in some detail in Chapter 4. Basically, hospitals establish their chargemaster using different approaches. The biggest difference tends to involve the level of detail in separately charging for items. One hospital (e.g., an academic medical center) might decide that supply items with a cost that is less than $500.00 will not be charged separately. Another hospital might decide to bundle all supply items and not charge separately for any of them. Yet another hospital may track and separately bill for supply items that cost less than $10.00.

Case Study 6.14: Price Increase Limitations

A system of three hospitals has a managed care contract with a major insurance company in its area. The contract utilizes a variety of payment mechanisms, some of which involve payment based on charges. The contract has a provision delimiting annual price increases to the consumer price index (CPI) percentage increase for the preceding year. The insurance company auditors want to review the changes in charges for the past two years to ensure compliance with the contract.

Case Study 6.14 involves the chargemasters for the three hospitals. Let us assume that there is a single chargemaster used by all three hospitals in the system. Also, let us assume that the percentage increase in the CPI is 2 percent. Thus, the system cannot increase its pricing by more than 2 percent. But, what does this really mean? The contract should carefully state how the concept of a price increase should be interpreted. For example, should the price increase be calculated relative to each line item times the volume of that line item over the period of a year? Will the contract allow price decreases to offset price increases?

Generally, this type of contract provision involves the actual charges made. However, some charges may go up while others may go down, and there could be variable percentage changes within the chargemaster itself. Another question is whether the volume of certain types of services should be considered relative to pricing changes. Generally, the provision of delimiting the overall percentage of increases is used to prevent a hospital or system, in this case, from making a blanket increase for all charges in the chargemaster. Increases of 5 percent, 10 percent, or even 15 percent are not that uncommon. Whatever the case, the contract itself should spell out very carefully how compliance is attained and how any audits to ensure compliance can be made.

Case Study 6.15: Cost-Based Payment for Selected Items

The Apex Medical Center has a managed care contract in which a number of expensive items, mainly devices and pharmacy items, are paid at cost plus 10 percent. However, Apex must charge these items at cost plus 10 percent for proper adjudication and thus payment.

While the approach in Case Study 6.15 seems quite reasonable, particularly for items such as pacemakers and expensive pharmacy items, Apex may have some difficulty in billing everything correctly. First, the given items must be separately identifiable so that the adjudication of the claims is appropriate. Also, Apex must fastidiously charge for the items at 10 percent above cost. This raises the further question of what cost should be used. Typically, the contract will specify acquisition cost, in which case Apex may need to produce receipts or records of the acquisition costs.

While the arrangement in Case Study 6.15 is conceptually straightforward, maintaining and then auditing for compliance can become a major process. If the charges are set at cost plus 10 percent, then how does this affect payment for the same items for other payers? In instances of this type, Apex may need to have a separate set of charges for this particular contract.

Claim Modification Issues

In Case Study 6.6, the concept of a back-end processing system was presented to alter claims that must conform to specific third-party payer requirements. While this type of situation should not occur, in practice payers may insist on the specific form of the claim and the inclusion or exclusion of certain items, codes, or charges. This is in direct contradiction to the HIPAA TSC rule. Under this rule, for a given service or set of services, every healthcare provider should be able to prepare the same claim using the standard claim format and the standard code sets. It should be up to the payer to adjudicate the claim properly using the payer's specific payment system and the standard claim.

For auditing, these differing billing and claims-filing requirements become a significant challenge. Actually, the same challenge exists for the healthcare provider if the provider wants to file correct claims that generate proper payment under the given payment mechanism. Let us consider a simple case study:

Case Study 6.16: Laceration Repair in the ED

The auditors are at the Apex Medical Center. Among the cases being reviewed are three, almost-identical, cases in which there are three distinctly different third-party payers that have differing billing and claims-filing requirements. Each of the cases is essentially an encounter for a laceration on the arm. Each of the individuals involved presented to the ED, a medical screening examination mandated by the Emergency Medical Treatment and Labor Act (EMTALA) was provided, and the laceration was repaired. However, the claims that were filled were distinctly different.

Claim 1		Claim 2		Claim 3	
99283-25	$100.00	99283	$250.00		
12003	$150.00			12003	$250.00
Total	$250.00	Total	$250.00	Total	$250.00

These claims are for the technical component, hospital outpatient services. For each claim in Case Study 6.16, the total charges are the same. However, the actual claims are quite different. In the first claim, both the E/M level (i.e., 99283) and the surgery (12003) are coded and billed. The "–25" modifier is used to indicate that the 99283 is distinct from the surgery (12003). Coding staff have coded these similar encounters using both the E/M level and the surgery code. This coding follows the standard coding guidelines for such a hospital outpatient encounter.

This case illustrates that the payer for the first claim uses the standard CPT coding approach. The payer for the second claim wants minor surgeries such as laceration repairs bundled into the E/M level. The third payer does the opposite of the second payer; the requirement is to bundle the E/M level into the surgical procedure. For the second and third payers, unless the claims are developed in this fashion, there will be a problem in getting the claim properly adjudicated and paid. All healthcare providers struggle with generating *clean claims*, that is, claims that will sail through the adjudication process without any hitches. If there are problems, then claims may need to be reworked and refiled, which in turn increases the administrative costs for the healthcare provider and delays payment.

A Systematic Approach to Compliance

For healthcare compliance personnel, maintaining a proper compliance stance is an adventure in problem solving. One of the first issues is to determine or discover if there is a problem. As it turns out, this is not always a challenge. At other times, problems can be subtle. Fortunately, in some sense, many compliance issues involving coding, billing, and reimbursement have been identified, and the lists of potential issues continue to grow. For example, the OIG has issued hundreds of pages of compliance guidance to almost all types of healthcare providers. The RACs continue to expand their areas of investigation in identifying overpayments and, to a lesser extent, underpayments.

Whatever the case, healthcare compliance personnel must be expert in the different payment systems and combinations of payment processes that are used by various third-party payers. In addition, there is a need to have a systematic way to approach problem solving to resolve possible compliance issues. Probably the biggest issue is to prioritize limited resources because of too many issues.

Audits of all types can assist in sharpening policies and procedures in providing services and then in documenting those services. Let us visit the Pinnacle Home Health Agency.

Case Study 6.17: OIG Auditor Visit

While quite a surprise, an OIG agent has come to the Pinnacle Home Health Agency. Apparently, there have been some patient complaints about possible incorrect billing. The OIG agent has already chosen 30 cases for review. These cases involve actual nursing visits. Pinnacle provides all of the documentation concerning the nurses' visits. As a check, the OIG agent actually calls the patients to verify that the nurse was at the patient's home on the date and at the time indicated in the documentation.

While Pinnacle generally came through the audit in good shape, there were some cases in which the patients could not remember whether the nurse visited or not. There were two cases in which the patients had died. While no action was taken concerning this probe audit, Pinnacle decided that it needed an affirmative way to prove that the nurse did actually visit the patient.

On the nursing form, a signature line was provided for the patient or the patient's representative to sign, date, and indicate time of the visit. This way, there was an affirmative indication that the visit did take place.

Compliance for healthcare, particularly involving coding, billing, reimbursement, and thus the payment systems being used by different payers, involves problem solving. Because there are a seemingly endless variety of situations that arise, a systematic way to address possible problems can be very useful. Here is a seven-step approach* that emphasizes the full identification of the problem along with development of a solution.

- Problem identification
- Problem analysis
- Solution design: internal
- Solution design: external
- Solution development
- Solution implementation
- Monitoring and remediation

There is no magic in using a systematic approach. Because healthcare provider organizations and the payment systems with which they must deal are complicated and interrelated systems, a key element is the identification of the true problem as opposed to possible symptoms of the problem. The discipline of *root cause analysis* can be useful in such situations. Basically, root cause analysis involves digging more deeply into the given problem or situation until there is some assurance that the situation is fully understood.

Case Study 6.18: Technical Services Diagnosis Codes

During a routine hospital outpatient audit, a number of claims from the technical services area were reviewed. While everything seemed in order, there were diagnosis codes appearing on the claim that were not readily evident in the associated records. The auditor investigated at some length and discovered that when a patient presented for tests, reception personnel were inquiring regarding the patient's diagnoses and conditions. These diagnoses and conditions were placed on the encounter form, and this data was eventually entered into the billing system.

While patients might be an appropriate source for information on diagnoses, when medical necessity justification is a concern, diagnoses need to be stated by a physician or practitioner. The overall record should clearly indicate that the diagnoses are noted by a physician or qualified practitioner.

Healthcare compliance is growing in importance with the movement toward containing overall healthcare expenditures. Both statutory compliance and contractual compliance generate challenges for healthcare providers. Generally, healthcare providers of all types will maintain that if the payers would simply tell the providers how to code and bill in order to be paid, they, the providers, would certainly code and bill in that fashion. Of course, because there are many different payment systems used by hundreds of payers, there may be significantly differing requirements for coding, billing, and filing claims. The goal of coding billing personnel along with compliance personnel is to keep everything straight and in compliance.

---

* See Chapter 4 of *Compliance for Coding, Billing & Reimbursement* for additional information.

Secondary-Payer Issues

Throughout most of the discussions in this four-volume series of books, we have addressed various payment systems and payment mechanisms on what is called a primary-payer premise. The reason for this is that our main objective is to study the different ways in which healthcare services can be paid. In many cases, when an individual receives healthcare services, there will be more than one healthcare payer involved. The natural questions are who pays first, and how much do they pay? The first payer, the primary payer, will pay according to their contractual or legal obligations. The second payer, that is, the secondary payer, will then consider the primary payment and determine if they, the secondary payer, should pay anything, and if payment is to be made, how much payment will be made. While not typical, there could be a third payer, the tertiary payer, that may also become involved.

Given the diversity of payment systems and then payment mechanisms within any given system, the primary and secondary payers may have vastly different approaches for making payments. Is it possible that these payment mechanisms will not fit together smoothly? The answer to this question is a definitive yes.

We actually started our discussion of secondary payers with Case Study 6.2. Here is a simple case study that will continue our discussions:

Case Study 6.19: Hospital Services Paid by Two Insurance Companies

Sally was recently hospitalized at the Apex Medical Center for a surgical procedure. She was in the hospital for five days with no complicating factors. Sally is fortunate in that she has insurance coverage under a group health plan, and she is also covered by her husband's employer's health plan. However, there seems to be some problem in getting everything paid. Her group health plan pays for services using a modified DRG approach, while her husband's coverage uses a per diem payment approach.

Case Study 6.19 illustrates the concept of *coordination of benefits* or COB. Let us fill in some details on a hypothetical basis. Assume the total hospital charges are $11,000.00. Sally's coverage uses a $1,000.00 deductible per hospitalization. Otherwise, using a modified DRG approach, Sally's coverage pays $6,000.00, which, less the deductible, is $5,000.00. Under her husband's policy, payment is made on a surgical per diem approach. In this case, the secondary company would pay $7,500.00 (i.e., $1,500.00 per day), and there is a global $750.00 deductible. Generally, the secondary payer will never pay more than it would if it were the primary payer.

The secondary payer would normally pay $7,500.00 less the $750.00 deductible, or a total of $6,750.00 would be paid if primary. The actual primary payer paid a total of $5,000.00, which leaves $6,000.00 still owing. In theory, the secondary payer would pay this $6,000.00 because it is less than the $6,750.00 that the secondary payer would pay as primary. Wait a minute—there may be some complicating factors. For instance, Apex may have a contract with the primary insurance in which Apex has to accept as payment in full the amount that the insurance would pay. In this case, this is $6,000.00 less the deductible that Sally has to pay. Under these circumstances, the secondary payer would then cover the $1,000.00 deductible that was remaining. However, the secondary coverage also has a deductible of $750.00, which we will assume has not been met, so the secondary payer would pay only $250.00.

Case Study 6.19 and the attendant discussion is a *simple case study*. COB under different insurance policies, and thus different payment systems, can become extraordinarily complex. Because of compliance issues, complexity in this area must be approached with great care.

While the concept of secondary payer is straightforward, in real-life situations circumstances may become ambiguous when determining if there is a secondary-payer situation. Here is a slightly modified version of Case Study 1.2:

Case Study 6.20: Fractured Hip from Slippery Stairs

Sarah, an elderly resident of Anywhere, USA, visited a neighbor across the street and down two houses. On leaving her friend's home, she slipped on the snowy steps and fell. Everything seemed fine. She went ahead and walked home. An hour later, she was in great pain; an ambulance was called, and she was taken to the hospital, where she was admitted for a fractured hip. The ambulance report indicated that she slipped on her steps.

The basic facts in Case Study 6.20 are not unusual. Sarah will receive services and then return home or possibly go to a skilled nursing facility. Her insurance, whether Medicare or private, will pay for the services according to the insurer's payment mechanisms (i.e., coverage, coinsurance, deductible, etc.). There may even be a secondary policy that is involved; particularly for Medicare, there are often supplemental policies. *However*, for this case the proper primary payer has not been correctly identified. Because this accident occurred at Sarah's neighbor's home, the homeowner's policy of Sarah's neighbor is primary. Payment would typically be made through a combination of *medical payments* and then *liability* coverage.

Note: For the Medicare program, this issue of being secondary is a *major concern*. There is a whole program, the Medicare secondary payer* (MSP), devoted to making certain that Medicare is appropriately determined as secondary. In the past several years, a whole new mandatory reporting program has been established.[†]

While there are many much more complicated cases, Medicare as well as other insurance companies have taken steps to automate, as much as possible, the identification and proper cross-over of claims. There are the COBA (Coordination of Benefits Agreement) that can be put into place along with the Medicare coordination of benefits contractor (COBC). In addition, the Medicare program has special monitoring and compliance efforts in this area. Here are several additional case studies that illustrate some of the difficulties encountered in this area.

Case Study 6.21: ED Visit with Injuries in the ED

Sarah is out with her speed walker and is walking by the Apex Medical Center. There is construction taking place; unfortunately, there is some construction debris outside the fence on the sidewalk. Sarah encounters the debris and takes a tumble. Luckily, her speed walker is not damaged. However, she has several lacerations. In the ED, the lacerations are repaired, but in the middle of the procedure Sarah attempts to get up, falls slightly, and sprains her wrist. X-rays are taken, and a splint is applied to the wrist.

Now, whether Sarah is a Medicare beneficiary or has some other coverage, there are really two issues. First, there is the accident with the building debris. What coverage is primary for the laceration repairs? Eventually, it will probably be the construction company's liability insurance. Certainly, Sarah's coverage is not primary. Then, there is the incident in the ED in which Sarah sprained her wrist. What coverage applies here? This is a more difficult question. Chances are very good that the

---

* See CMS publication 100-05, *Medicare Secondary Payer Manual.*
[†] See the CMS website: https://www.cms.gov/MandatoryInsRep/.

hospital will assume liability and not even bill Sarah. Of course, this would have to be coordinated with the hospital's liability coverage. Again, Case Study 6.21 illustrates the fact that secondary-payer considerations can become quite complex, and they can represent significant compliance issues.

Here is another case study that illustrates how difficulties can be encountered when there are differing claim-filing requirements between healthcare payers.

Case Study 6.22: Consultation Services with Medicare Secondary

Stephanie received services at the Acme Medical Clinic, a provider-based clinic operated by the Apex Medical Center. Among other services at the clinic, there was an extended consultation with one of the physicians. The primary payer was billed using only the 1500 claim form with the consultation code. Some payment has been received, and now Medicare is secondary. However, the billing personnel at Acme are in a quandary. First, Medicare does not recognize consultations, so the coding must be changed. Second, for Medicare both a 1500 and a UB-04 are filed (i.e., split billing), so the charges must be adjusted and split between professional and technical components. The billing staff is not certain how to proceed.

Case Study 6.22 illustrates the fact that coding and billing properly for both a primary payer and a secondary payer using different payment systems can create a significant challenge.

Note: The HIPAA TSC is referenced several times in this text. If all healthcare payers used a standard claim format and followed the coding and billing guidance relative to the various standard code sets, then these complications relative to secondary payers could generally be avoided. There will still be some challenges because significantly different payment systems are used by the healthcare payers.

Here is a final case study relative to the overall primary, secondary payer issue.

Case Study 6.23: Divorced Parents, Children under Two Policies

Susan and Stan have divorced. While this is a reasonably amicable situation, it turns out that their children have dual coverage. The children are covered under Susan's policy from work and by Stan's policy from his employer. A significant problem has arisen in that when their children need medical services, the two respective insurance companies each refuse to be primary. Both of the insurers want only to be secondary.

Needless to say, for situations like that described in Case Study 6.23, there can be significant frustration in getting everything in order.

Healthcare Provider Credentialing

In Chapter 4, we briefly discussed credentialing for managed care contracting. The two major aspects for credentialing are:

1. Clinical credentialing
2. Billing privileges

Because credentialing is a significant compliance issue that spans all types of payment systems, a separate discussion is provided in this chapter.

Clinical credentialing addresses establishing the competency of a healthcare provider to provide medical services of various types. This ranges from individual providers such as physicians, nonphysician practitioners (NPPs), and nurses on up to institutional providers such as hospitals, skilled nursing facilities, and the like. From a payer perspective, payment should be made only for services that are provided by qualified individuals and entities. One of the fundamental steps in adjudicating claims is that the services must be provided by a qualified medical person.

At the institutional level, clinical credentialing quickly becomes a licensing and accreditation issue. Most institutional providers are licensed at the state level. Accreditation is normally provided by one of several national accrediting bodies. The specific accrediting body will depend on the type of provider. For instance, for hospitals one of the main accrediting bodies is the Joint Commission.* Physicians and NPPs (e.g., nurse practitioners, physician assistants, and clinical nurse specialists) must provide credentials such as academic degrees and special training along with appropriate licenses from state medical boards.

To enroll with a given third-party payer, healthcare providers of all types must provide not only their clinical credentials, but also information about who they are, what they are, who owns or employs them, adverse legal history, and the like. The most formal of the enrollment processes is with the Medicare program, which has six different CMS-855 forms that are quite lengthy. Private third-party payers generally have less-stringent requirements, although the concerns are basically the same.

One of the challenges with obtaining billing privileges is that third-party payers may or may not choose to recognize certain healthcare providers. While hospitals and physicians are almost always eligible for recognition, NPPs may or may not be recognized for billing purposes. Also, there are scope-of-practice issues that may arise. Scope of practice is delimited by state laws. Let us join the Apex Medical Center, which has just hired a nurse practitioner to provide a variety of services at the hospital.

Case Study 6.24: Nurse Practitioner Coming to Apex

The Apex Medical Center has been fortunate enough to hire a nurse practitioner (NP). There are a number of different ways in which the hospital wants to utilize this NP. These include being a part-time hospitalist, on call to the ED during certain periods, and seeing patients in one of Apex's provider-based clinics. The NP will be joining the medical staff organization. While clinical credentialing has basically been accomplished, the hospital will now start gaining billing privileges for Medicare and other private third-party payers so that the NP can bill professionally.

The question then becomes, what information and documents need to be pulled together to gain billing privileges for Medicare and other private third-party payers? Here is a general outline of the types of information and documents. In this case, the orientation is that of NPPs.

1. NPP title, definition, and areas of service
2. National certifying/accrediting organization(s)
3. State statutes/administrative laws
4. Licensing board/process (if any)
5. Scope of practice: covered versus noncovered services

---

* See http://www.jointcommission.org/.

6. Site(s) of service: hospital, clinic (provider-based vs. freestanding), physician's office, skilled nursing facility, rural health clinic, other
7. Physician relationship: formal collaboration, agreement, or plan? Does the arrangement have to be approved? If so, by whom?
8. Supervisory requirements
9. Documentation requirements
   a. Physician cosignature necessary?
   b. Documentation reviews
10. Drug Enforcement Agency (DEA) license
11. Professional liability coverage
    a. Medical malpractice liability claims history
12. Professional history, including academic degrees with references

This list is only a general guide, and the specific elements will change depending on the specific type of healthcare provider involved.

Credentialing for both clinical privileges and billing privileges is not a straightforward process in many cases. Some third-party payers may make relatively few demands for allowing billing of physicians or practitioners as long as the individuals are clinically credentialed through a hospital medical staff organization. In other cases, particularly with the Medicare program, enrolling and gaining billing privileges may be a real hassle.

Summary and Conclusion

The adjudication and payment of claims are major parts of any payment system. Adjudication systems can be relatively simple or exceedingly complex. A healthcare payer may pay a hospital on the percentage-of-changes basis. Assuming the billed services are covered, medically necessary, and ordered by a qualified medical person, the calculation of payment on a percentage-of-charges basis is relatively straightforward.

Prospective payment systems tend to have the most complicated adjudication processes. For instance, for DRGs and APCs there is a detailed computer program, called the *grouper*, that is used, including a number of edits that must be passed before the claim can be processed. For contractual arrangements, there may be a combination of payment mechanisms. For instance, in a hospital setting most of the services may be paid under some sort of prospective payment system with significant carve outs for special payment consideration. There may also be cost-based reimbursement for certain expensive items, such as drugs and implantable medical devices (IMDs).

Due to the complexity of the payment systems and the possible use of certain combinations of payment mechanisms, the adjudication process becomes equally complicated. If adjudication of claims is complicated, then compliance also becomes a major issue. Healthcare providers struggle to understand just how claims are to be filed for each of the payers with whom the provider has a relationship. Of course, there are the payers with whom the healthcare provider has no relationship. How will these claims be adjudicated and paid? What compliance standards are in place for these unknown payers?

The basis for compliance standards for both healthcare providers and payers lies with the HIPAA TSC rule. This is a law along with federal regulations that requires the use of standard claim formats and the use of standard code sets to enable electronic data interchange (EDI) for healthcare transactions. While the goal is standardization for healthcare claims processing, this goal is yet to be achieved.

Healthcare compliance breaks down into two areas: statutory compliance and contractual compliance. Statutory compliance resides primarily with the government healthcare programs such as Medicare and Medicaid. Most healthcare providers are extremely sensitive to statutory compliance because the penalties can include criminal prosecutions along with civil monetary penalties (CMPs). Thus, healthcare providers first tend to establish their compliance programs around Medicare and Medicaid issues to avoid possible criminal prosecution. Secondarily, and sometimes quite secondarily, healthcare providers then address their contractual situations for both compliance and reimbursement optimization.

Contractual compliance involves the contracts that the healthcare provider enters into to see covered patients and to be paid by the payer. A physician's office may have a dozen such contracts, while the hospital can have upward of a hundred contracts. Larger integrated delivery systems can have even more. These contracts, including companion manuals, provide for the benefits and obligations of both the healthcare provider and the healthcare payer. These contracts tend to include more than a single payment system or payment methodology. Maintaining full compliance with these contracts becomes an ongoing challenge because different payers may often have significantly different coding, billing, and claims-filing requirements.

To add to the challenges is the *secondary-payer* issue. While there is normally a primary payer and possibly a secondary payer, there may also be a tertiary payer. If we just consider primary and secondary payers, the fact that there are two payers involved means that there may be vastly different payment systems used by the two payers. Thus, providers have the challenge of obtaining primary payment under one set of adjudication rules and then moving to a different set of rules for the secondary payer. Luckily, for Medicare beneficiaries who also have one of the standard Medicare supplemental policies, there is a very smooth interface between Medicare and the supplemental carrier.

Claim adjudication and the concomitant compliance issues really highlight the complexities of different payment systems, different payment methodologies, and the way that payment processes must fit together.

Chapter 7

Summary, Conclusion, and the Future

Healthcare Payment Systems: A Historical Perspective

The fundamental model for healthcare payment involves only two parties: the patient receiving services and the healthcare provider dispensing services. The payment process is quite simple: The provider charges for the services, and the patient pays for the services. This fundamental model is still used for what are termed *self-pay patients*. Over time, a third party was interjected into this fundamental model, and the process became more complex. The third party was generally an insurance company or government program that paid for some or all medical services on behalf of the patient. For the third party to make payment, a claim had to be filed and adjudicated. While the responsibility for filing claims actually lies with the patient, today, for a variety of reasons, healthcare providers file claims on behalf of their patients.

With the involvement of third-party payers, both private and public, the whole concept of developing payment systems to reimburse providers for healthcare services has arisen. These payment systems, embodying a huge variety of payment processes, have evolved over time and will continue to change and become more complex and convoluted.

During the last several decades, the change in healthcare payment processes has involved moving from cost-based and charge-based reimbursement to various forms of prospective payment and fee schedules. Healthcare payers, with the Medicare program leading the way, have looked for ways to constrain the amount that payers expend for healthcare services. The first major change was with Medicare developing the Diagnosis Related Group (DRG) payment system. DRGs represent the first prospective payment system (PPS). Since the development of DRGs, the Medicare program has developed PPSs for hospital outpatient services, home health agencies, skilled nursing facilities, long-term care hospitals, inpatient rehabilitation, and inpatient psychiatric services. More PPSs are being developed by Medicare.

PPSs are characterized by a great deal of bundling of services into a given payment amount. For instance, with DRGs, an inpatient stay groups to a single category for which an averaged or bundled payment is made for all the services. The Ambulatory Payment Classifications (APCs) also bundle certain types of services for payment purposes with the exception that multiple APC categories may result from grouping outpatient encounters. The premise with this bundling or grouping is that healthcare providers will be incentivized to provide the services more efficiently in order for the bundled payment to generate a profit. Whether this approach works can certainly be debated; payers and providers may have very different perspectives on this approach.

One area in which there is generally a single payment system approach is with physician services. While there are exceptions, by and large physicians are paid through fee schedules. The payment process for a given third-party payer, including Medicare, is that the physician is paid the lesser of the fee schedule amount or the charges made by the physician. Fee schedule payment for physicians is really made possible by an extensive classification system using the Current Procedural Terminology (CPT) of the American Medical Association (AMA) with some additional classification from the Medicare HCPCS (Healthcare Common Procedure Coding System). While this is a very refined classification system, for payment purposes the big question involves the origin of the actual fee schedule payment amounts. For the Medicare program, this is the RBRVS or the resource-based relative value scale. For private third-party payers, the payment amounts are derived from the usual, customary, and reasonable (UCR) approach. Again, whether fee schedule payments are appropriate is a point of disagreement between physicians and healthcare payers.

Private third-party payers, such as insurance companies, have followed the Medicare lead to some extent. Modified forms of the different Medicare PPSs are used. Some of the modifications are relatively minor, while other modified payment mechanisms are quite different. Private third-party payers also use a variety of charge-based payment systems or even use the Medicare payment systems as a base and then simply add a percentage above the Medicare payment.

The vast majority of healthcare payment is on a *fee-for-service* basis. This means that the greater the volume of services provided, the greater the payment. With this approach, there is a great tendency to provide any and all services that might be appropriate. The healthcare provider makes more money as the volume of services increases. Capitation is the opposite of fee for service, at least for payment purposes. With capitated payment approaches, the healthcare provider is paid a fixed amount, generally on a monthly basis. The flat payment amount is called per member per month or PMPM payment. For this fixed payment, the healthcare provider is responsible to provide all covered and necessary care for enrolled individuals. Capitation actually involves the shifting of the financial risk from the payer to the healthcare provider. If significant volumes of services are needed, then the provider may lose money; that is, the cost for providing the increased volume of services will be greater than the flat payment. With the fee-for-service approach, a high-volume approach is beneficial (financially) to the provider, with the payer possibly incurring a financial loss. Note that the concept of medical necessity has also shifted. Now, the providers want to provide as few services as possible. Suddenly, the payers are now concerned that all necessary services were provided.

Capitated payment arrangements have been slow to develop. The main reason is that healthcare providers generally do not have the actuarial data and information to assess the risk that is being assumed properly with this type of payment. Insurance companies have developed extensive databases and actuarial analyses concerning the incidence of services within geographical and age ranges. Insurance companies and other payers have done this so that they can understand the risks involved and adjust premiums that are charged to covered individuals or companies.

Another approach is for healthcare providers to band together, such as in a preferred provider organization (PPO). The providers in a PPO can then better negotiate with payers to provide services at a lower cost. Of course, a PPO could also be organized by a payer, or the given payer could develop an organized delivery system. HMOs or health maintenance organizations have been developed to respond to the need of providing payment for healthcare services while managing the provision of services. By managing the types and levels of care provided, costs can be reduced. Of course, patients enrolled in an HMO may disagree with coverage and medical necessity determinations.

Even the Medicare program has embraced the HMO concept. This is through the Medicare Advantage (MA) program. Medicare uses several different approaches with their MA program. There is an HMO approach, a PPO approach, along with some alternatives. Even within specific approaches, there is variability in what is covered, how much the Medicare beneficiaries pay, what happens when an out-of-network provider is used, along with a host of other questions. Generally, the MA approach covers at least what traditional or original Medicare covers, although with the MA program there is no supplemental or Medigap insurance used.

While healthcare payment basically started with the concept of a patient receiving services, the provider then billing for the services, and the patient paying for the services, healthcare payment systems have evolved into increasingly complex processes. Even as we move forward with new approaches and payment mechanisms, the old systems are used to some extent. For example, cost-based reimbursement is currently used by the Medicare program for critical access hospitals (CAHs). Charge-based payment is used through contractual arrangements whereby the provider accepts as payment a percentage of the charges. The list can be extended. Even as we develop new approaches, to some extent the older payment processes are still used.

The bottom line for healthcare payment systems is that we are all on a long journey, with providers, payers, and covered individuals all looking for a way to receive necessary medical services at a reasonable cost.

Extreme Variability in Payment Systems

Currently, there are dozens of different payment systems and payment mechanisms. Some payment systems address virtually all of the services provided by given types of healthcare providers. For instance, physicians and practitioners are generally paid based on a fee schedule arrangement. Or, a hospital is paid a percentage of its charges for both inpatient and outpatient services. In other instances, a given payment mechanism may be applied on a very limited basis. For instance, certain expensive pharmacy items or implantable medical devices are paid on a pass-through basis using either costs or charges converted into costs as the basis for payment.

Because of all the variability, payment system interfaces have become a major concern and operationally a real headache. One of the most obvious interfaces occurs with primary payers versus secondary payers. Sometimes, even a tertiary payer may be involved. If these various payers use different payment mechanisms, then determining how much a secondary payer should pay can become quite complicated. The phrase *coordination of benefits* (COB) is used, and both healthcare providers and payers expend considerable resources in addressing COB issues.

Interfaces between payment systems abound. One of the simplest interfaces occurs when there is a given service that can be provided by different providers or at different facilities. For instance, a surgical procedure might be provided in an ambulatory surgical center (ASC), at the hospital on an outpatient basis, or even at the hospital on an inpatient basis. For most payers, the payment mechanisms for each of these three locations will be quite different. The ASC will cost the least, then the hospital outpatient will cost more, and the inpatient setting will be the most expensive. So, who chooses which location, and what is the justification?

Note: The payment interface for the surgery discussed gives rise to developing a payment mechanism for the surgery itself. The payer will pay a fixed amount for the surgery regardless of where the surgery is performed.

Also, for surgical procedures, there is typically a facility charge and then a physician charge. If anesthesia is required, then there will also be a professional component anesthesiologist charge. What if there was a payment mechanism that paid only a fixed amount for the surgery that then has to be split between the parties involved?

A major Medicare payment system interface was discussed in the second and third books in this healthcare payment series. This is the interface between hospital outpatient payment (i.e., APCs for Medicare) and the physician payment (i.e., the Medicare Physician Fee Schedule). Integrated into this payment system interface is the whole concept of provider-based clinics, typically owned by hospitals, and freestanding clinics, which are typically owned and operated by physicians. The Medicare program has a convoluted process of paying physicians less when their services are provided in an institutional setting (i.e., hospital or provider-based clinic) versus full payment when the services are provided in freestanding clinics. Many compliance issues are generated by provider-based operations.

Compliance Issues

As the type and variety of healthcare payment systems expand, compliance issues also continue to grow and expand. The basic issue is that, due to the complexity of the payment systems, the coding, billing, and claims filing also become more difficult, and errors can be introduced into the process. From the payers' perspective, there is concern about incorrect payments and overpayments to the healthcare providers. While there are also underpayments, the main focus of compliance for coding, billing, and reimbursement generally lies with overpayments. The concept of overpayments presumes that there is a healthcare provider making a best effort to provide services, bill for the services, and be appropriately paid. There are also situations in which purposeful fraud is committed by incorrectly billing or even situations in which no services are provided and payment is still sought.

Healthcare compliance can be divided into two categories:

- Statutory
- Contractual

Statutory compliance involves those payment systems that are established under the laws with concomitant rules and regulations. Medicare and the state Medicaid programs are examples where statutory compliance is of concern. Because statutory compliance involves possible criminal prosecutions as well as civil prosecutions, healthcare providers are very concerned about maintaining appropriate compliance. Even with statutory compliance, the main thrust for auditors is to recoup any possible overpayments. The Medicare program has developed a number of auditing programs, including the recovery audit contractors (RACs).

Contractual compliance results from the contractual relationships established between healthcare providers and private payers. These contracts, along with companion manuals that provide information relative to proper claims filing and payment, should spell out the benefits and obligations for both the healthcare payer and the provider of services. In the vast majority of cases, any sort of conflicts or allegations of overpayment or underpayment can be handled at the civil level, often through arbitration.

For healthcare providers of all types, from the solo rural physician on up to the national hospital network, a systematic approach to compliance is vital. Not only must there be processes in place to ensure correct billing and reimbursement, but also the mere fact that there is a compliance plan can help to mitigate potential liabilities. The most difficult aspect of compliance is to look ahead several years to make an assessment of what may become or be recognized as a compliance issue. If a provider can anticipate compliance issues, then the provider can react in advance to bill properly and develop proper documentation systems to address the anticipated compliance issues.

A special compliance issue is that of proper determination of secondary-payer status. When an individual receives healthcare services, there may be more than one payer involved. While having two payers involved is not unusual, there may even be three payers involved. For a huge governmental program like Medicare, properly determining when Medicare is secondary is a major issue. Medicare has the Medicare secondary payer (MSP) program designed to address this situation. Note that if there are two or more payers involved, then none of them really wants to be primary. Significant savings can be gained by being secondary or tertiary.

As long as the payment systems and associated payment mechanisms are complex, there will always be compliance issues of some sort. Both healthcare providers and payers must work together to make certain that coding, billing, and reimbursement processes are well known and guidance is fully delineated.

Payment Systems: The Future

Cost containment will continue as the driving force for developing new and refined payment systems. This is true for the healthcare providers who seek to provide high-quality necessary services at the lowest cost possible. Cost containment is certainly a goal for healthcare payers as well. Healthcare payers want to reduce overall payments while providing appropriate services for their covered members or beneficiaries.

Over the last decade, quality of services has also become increasingly important, and efforts are being made to integrate the quality of care with payment processes. Medical necessity continues as a major concern for all types of healthcare payment. The quality of services goes beyond that which is medically necessary. However, reporting the quality of healthcare services is not at all straightforward. Much of the effort concentrates on making certain that medical and clinical protocols are being followed. For example, were standard protocols followed in a hospital's emergency department (ED) when an individual presented with a possible heart attack? Or, were standard protocols followed for a patient diagnosed with congestive heart failure (CHF)?

When using this type of quality reporting, the payer will need to decide whether to treat quality of care as an incentive, that is, add on extra payment, or as a penalty, that is, reduce payment. At the time this book was prepared, the Medicare program was diligently working on quality reporting. If a healthcare provider does report on the quality indicators for Medicare, then full payment is made. If reporting requirements are not met, then there is a reduction payment. Note that it is a fact that the reporting is taking place as opposed to the actual assessment of quality that is driving this process.

Quality of healthcare is really a subjective issue relating to clinical outcomes, patient expectations, and then overall patient satisfaction. To document and report quality measures of this type fully requires enormous effort and cannot be readily integrated into payment processes.

As examples of current efforts, we briefly discuss two concepts:

- Accountable care organizations (ACOs)
- Value-based purchasing

Both of these efforts are being pursued by the Medicare program. As usual, private third-party payers may or may not follow the Medicare lead. Also, refinements to these approaches can be used.

ACOs are a result of the Affordable Care Act (ACA) of 2010. While this is a new acronym and title, much of the organizational structuring for ACOs will seem very familiar given all of the different structures that are in use for managed care, capitation, and other delivery system arrangements. The basic idea is that an organized delivery system (ODS) must be established. Typically, this would include hospitals, physicians, clinics, nursing facilities, and other healthcare providers. After the ODS has been established, then the goal is for the ACO to deliver high-quality coordinated care to Medicare beneficiaries. On the payment side, the incentive is for the coordination of care to save Medicare money, and then Medicare will share the savings with the ACO.

Based on our discussions in Chapter 4, this concept of an ACO is straightforward; however, the details of just how this process is to work are very much a different matter. As with HMOs, the ACO assumes a limited degree of risk relative to providing services in such a way that the fee-for-service payments from Medicare will be higher than the costs to the ACO. A key issue in the ACO approach is the coordination of efforts within the ODS. It will take years, and most probably some changes in the way ACOs actually operate, to determine if this approach is feasible.

One of the features of ACOs, depending on the specific arrangements, is to take common conditions on an episode-of-care basis and then have the Medicare program make a bundled payment. At a conceptual level, let us consider three frequently encountered situations with Medicare beneficiaries:

1. **Cataract Surgery with Intraocular Lens (IOL) Insertion.** Cataract surgery is quite common among the Medicare population. The typical cost elements are the facility where the surgery is performed, the ophthalmologist performing the surgery, possibly anesthesiologist services, and the IOL itself. Postoperative care can also be considered.
2. **Knee Replacement.** Unilateral (i.e., left or right) knee replacement is a common procedure. The cost elements are the facility where the surgery is performed, inpatient services posoperatively, anesthesiologist services, and the knee implant. Postacute care can also be considered and may involve skilled nursing or other rehabilitation services.
3. **Simple Pneumonia.** Medicare beneficiaries are often admitted to the hospital suffering from various types of pneumonia. This is generally a medical episode of care involving the hospital facility and the treating physician along with drug therapies. Some concern for postacute care might be considered.

Envisage yourself as an analyst who has been tasked with determining how much your organization should charge for each of these episodes of care. What information will you need? Are there going to be any significant variables? How will you take a single bundled payment and split it between the different healthcare providers that are involved in the services that address the episodes of care?

Because there are different healthcare providers sharing in the bundled payments, it is easiest if providers are employed or owned by the ACO. Negotiating contracts with multiple entities relative to the amount that is to be distributed from such bundled payments requires a great deal of time and effort.

Value-based purchasing (VBP) is a general concept that can be implemented in very different ways. Conceptually, VBP involves allowing the purchasers of health care services (e.g., employers, insurance companies, Medicare) to hold the healthcare providers accountable for both costs and the quality of the healthcare services. Of course, to assess the quality of services there must be some extensive feedback mechanisms. This reporting process involves having the providers report on specific use of clinical protocols and safety measures along with more subjective measures, such as patient satisfaction with nurses and doctors, cleanliness of facilities, and responsiveness on the part of staff. If the quality measures are positive, then the providers will be recognized, and there may be increased payments.

For the Medicare program, VBP is being used initially for hospitals on the inpatient side.* There are specific quality measures for health conditions and hospital-acquired conditions and several measures from the Agency for Healthcare Research and Quality.† On the payment side, what CMS (Centers for Medicare and Medicaid Services) is doing is to reduce the overall reimbursement to hospitals and then allowing hospitals to regain the reductions by meeting the standards established through VBP. Also, CMS is measuring the amount that Medicare pays for beneficiaries for certain services. Thus, on a statistical basis the Medicare program can look at how much is being spent for certain services along with comparative quality data.

The future for healthcare payment systems will certainly involve an increasing emphasis on quality of care and thus the overall value of the care being provided. Given the machinations of just the payment processes, adding in a quality component will increase the level of detail and complexity.

Endnote

The four books in this healthcare payment system series are really just the beginning. In the coming decades, payment systems and processes will continue to evolve. Healthcare payers will attempt to reduce overall expenditures for healthcare services. Healthcare providers will continue to provide services and attempt to remain financially viable under the evolving payment systems. Whatever the case, healthcare is a dynamic industry segment. The one constant is change.

---

* See the November 30, 2011, *Federal Register* for more details.
† See http://www.ahrq.gov.

List of Acronyms

The following is a list of the more common acronyms that are used in connection with healthcare payment systems. New acronyms and terminology seem to arise almost every day. Note that additional references may be made such as specific sections of the Code of Federal Regulations.

837-I	electronic version of UB-04 claim form
837-P	electronic version of 1500 claim form
1500	professional claim form (see CMS-1500)
6σ	Six Sigma (a quality improvement technique)
AA	anesthesia assistant
ABC	Activity-Based Costing
ABN	Advance Beneficiary Notice (*see also* HINNC, NONC)
ACA	Affordable Care Act (2010)
ACC	ambulatory care center
ACEP	American College of Emergency Physicians
ACHE	American College of Healthcare Executives
ACO	accountable care organization
ACS	ambulatory care services
ADA	Americans with Disabilities Act
AFS	Ambulance Fee Schedule
AGPAM	American Guild of Patient Account Managers
AHA	American Hospital Association
AHIMA	American Health Information Management Association
AHRQ	Agency for Healthcare Research and Quality

AIRR	all-inclusive reimbursement rate
ALJ	administrative law judge
ALOS	average length of stay
AMA	American Medical Association or American Management Association
AMC	Apex Medical Center or Acme Medical Clinic (fictitious entities)
AO	advisory opinion
AOAA	American Osteopathic Association Accreditation
A/P	accounts payable
APC	Ambulatory Payment Classification(s)
AP-DRG	All Patient DRG
APG	ambulatory patient group
APR-DRG	All Patient Refined DRG
A/R	accounts receivable
ASCII	American Standard Code for Information Interchange
ASF	ambulatory surgical facility
ASP	average sales price
AVG	ambulatory visit group
AWP	average wholesale price
BBA	Balanced Budget Act (of 1997)
BBRA	Balanced Budget Refinement Act (of 1999)
BIPA	Beneficiary Improvement and Protection Act (of 2000)
BPR	business process reengineering
CA-DRG	Consolidated Severity-Adjusted DRG
CAP	capitated ambulatory plan
CBA	cost-benefit analysis
CBR	coding, billing, and reimbursement
CBRCO	CBR compliance officer
CC (Computer)	carbon copy

CC	coding clinic
CCI	Correct Coding Initiative
CCO	chief compliance officer
CCR	cost-to-charge ratio
CCs	complications and comorbidities
CCU	critical care unit
CDM	charge description master (*see generic term* chargemaster)
CENT	certified enterostomal nurse therapist
CERT	comprehensive error rate testing
CEU	continuing education unit
CF	conversion factor
CFO	chief financial officer
CfP	condition for payment (*see* 42 CFR §424)
CFR	*Code of Federal Regulations*
CHAMPUS	Civilian Health and Medical Program of the Uniformed Services
CHAMPVA	Civilian Health and Medical Program of the Veterans Administration
CHC	community health center
CHCP	coordinated home health program
CHF	congestive heart failure
CIA	corporate integrity agreement
CIO	chief information officer
CIS	computer information system
CM	charge master
CMI	Case Mix Index
CMP	competitive medical plan
CMS	Center for Medicare and Medicaid Services
CMS-855	form used to gain billing privileges for Medicare
CMS-1450	UB-04 claim form as used by Medicare
CMS-1500	1500 claim form as used by Medicare

CMS-2552	hospital cost report form
CNM	certified nurse midwife
CNP	certified nurse practitioner
CNS	clinical nurse specialist
COB	coordination of benefits
CON	certificate of need
COO	chief operating officer
CoP	condition of participation (*see* 42 CFR §482)
CP	clinical psychologist
CPI	consumer price index
CPI-U	consumer price index–urban
CPT	Current Procedural Terminology (Currently CPT-4; anticipated to go to CPT-5)
CQI	continuous quality improvement
CRNA	certified registered nurse anesthetist
CSF	critical success factor
CSW	clinical social worker
CT	computer tomography
CWF	common working file
DBMS	database management system
DEA	Drug Enforcement Administration
DED	dedicated emergency department (*see* EMTALA)
DHHS	Department of Health and Human Services
DME	durable medical equipment
DMEPOS	DME, prosthetics, orthotics, supplies
DMERC	durable medical equipment regional carrier (*see* CMS MACs)
DNS	Domain Name System (Internet)
DO	doctor of osteopathy
DOD	Department of Defense
DOJ	Department of Justice
DP	data processing

DRA	Deficit Reduction Act (of 2005)
DRG	Diagnosis Related Group (*see* AP-DRG, APR-DRG, CA-DRG, MS-DRG, SR-DRG)
DSH	disproportionate share hospital
DSMT	diabetic self-management training
E/M	evaluation and management
EBCDIC (Computer)	Extended Binary Coded Decimal Information Code
ECG	electrocardiogram
ED	emergency department
EDI	electronic data interchange
EEO	Equal Employment Opportunity
EEOC	Equal Employment Opportunity Commission
EGHP	employer group health plan
EKG	*See* ECG. German for elektrokardiogramm
E/M	evaluation and management
EMC	electronic medical claim
EMI	Encounter Mix Index
EMG	electromyography
EMTALA	Emergency Medical Treatment and Active Labor Act
EOB	explanation of benefits
EOMB	explanation of Medicare benefits
EPA	Environmental Protection Agency
EPC	event-driven process chain
EPO	exclusive provider organization
ER	emergency room (*see also* emergency department)
ERISA	Employment Retirement Income Security Act
ESRD	end-stage renal disease
FAC	freestanding ambulatory care
FAQ	frequently asked question
FBI	Federal Bureau of Investigation
FDA	Food and Drug Administration

FEC	freestanding emergency center
FFS	fee for service
FFY	federal fiscal year
FI	fiscal intermediary
FL	Form Locator (*see* UB-04)
FLSA	Fair Labor Standards Act
FMR	focused medical review
FMV	fair market value
FQHC	federally qualified health center
FR	*Federal Register*
FRGs	functional related groups
FRNA	first registered nurse assistant
FTC	Federal Trade Commission
FTP	File Transfer Protocol (Internet)
FY	fiscal year
GAF	geographic adjustment factor
GAO	Government Accounting Office
GI	gastrointestinal
GMLOS	geometric mean length of stay
GPCI	Geographic Practice Cost Index
GPO	Government Printing Office
GSP	global surgical package
H&P	history and physical
HCFA	Health Care Financing Administration (now CMS)
HCO	health care organization
HCPCS	Healthcare Common Procedure Coding System (previously HCFA's Common Procedure Coding System)
HFMA	Healthcare Financial Management Association
HHA	home health agency
HHMCO	home health managed care organization

HHPPS	home health prospective payment system
HHS	Health and Human Services
HICN	Health Insurance Claim Number
HIM	health information management (*see also* medical records)
HINNC	Hospital Issued Notice of Noncoverage
HIPAA	Health Insurance Portability and Accountability Act (1996)
HMO	Health Maintenance Organization
HMOPOS	HMO point-of-service (plans)
HOCM	high osmolar contrast media (or materials)
HPSA	health personnel shortage area
HTML	HyperText Markup Language
HTTP	HyperText Transfer Protocol (Internet)
HURA	health undeserved rural area
HVAC	heating, ventilating, air conditioning
HwH	hospital within a hospital
I&D	incision and drainage
ICD-9-CM	*International Classification of Diseases, Ninth Revision, Clinical Modification*
ICD-10-CM	*International Classification of Diseases, Tenth Revision, Clinical Modification* (replacement for *ICD-9-CM* Volumes 1 and 2)
ICD-10-PCS	*ICD-10 Procedure Coding System* (replacement for *ICD-9-CM* Volume 3)
ICD-11-CM	*International Classification of Diseases, Eleventh Revision, Clinical Modification*
ICD-11-PCS	*ICD-11 Procedure Coding System*
ICU	intensive care unit
IDTF	independent diagnostic testing facility
IDS	integrated delivery system
IG	inspector general
IMD	implantable medical device

IOL	intraocular lens
IP	inpatient
IPA	independent practice arrangement/association
IRO	independent review organization
IRS	Internal Revenue Service
IS	information systems
ISP	Internet service provider
IV	intravenous
JCAHO	Joint Commission on Accreditation of Healthcare Organizations
KSAPCs	knowledge, skills, abilities and personal characteristics
LCC	lesser of costs or charges
LCD	local coverage decision (*see also* LMRP)
LMRP	local medical review policy
LOCMs	low osmolar contrast media (or materials)
LOS	length of stay
LTCH	long-term care hospital (*see* STACH)
LTRH	long-term rehabilitation hospital
MA	Medicare Advantage
MAC	Medicare administrative contractor
MAC	monitored anesthesia care
MAO	Medicare Advantage organization
MCE	Medicare code editor
MCO	managed care organization
MD	doctor of medicine
MDH	Medicare-dependent hospital
MDS	Minimum Data Set
MEI	Medicare Economic Index
MFS	Medicare Fee Schedule
MIS	management information system
MLFS	Medicare Laboratory Fee Schedule

MMA	Medicare Modernization Act (of 2003)
Modem (Computer)	modulator-demodulator
MOG	Medicare Outpatient Grouping
MPFS	Medicare Physician Fee Schedule
MRI	magnetic resonance imaging
MSA	metropolitan statistical area
MS-DOS (Computer)	Microsoft disk operating system
MS-DRG	Medicare Severity DRG (CMS established in 2007)
MSO	management service organization
MSO	medical staff organization
MSOP	market-service-organization-payment
MSP	Medicare secondary payer
MUA	medically underserved area
MUE	medically unlikely edit
MVPS	Medicare Volume Performance Standard
NAH	Nursing and Allied Health
NCCI	National Correct Coding Initiative
NCD	National Coverage Decision
NCQA	National Committee for Quality Assurance
NCQHC	National Committee for Quality Health Care
NF	nursing facility
NM	nurse midwife
NONC	Notice of Noncoverage
NP	nurse practitioner (some variation; for instance, ARNP stands for advanced registered nurse practitioner)
NPP	nonphysician provider/practitioner
NSC	national supplier clearinghouse
NTIOL	new technology intraocular lens
NTIS	National Technical Information Service
NUBC	National Uniform Billing Committee

OASIS	Outcome and Assessment Information Set
OBRA	Omnibus Reconciliation Act
OCE	outpatient code editor
ODS	organized delivery system
OIG	Office of the Inspector General (*see* HHS)
OMB	Office of Management and Budget
OP	outpatient
OPR	outpatient payment reform
OR	operating room
OT	occupational therapy or therapist
OTA	occupational therapist assistant
P&P	policy and procedure
PA	physician assistant
PAM	patient accounts manager
PBD	provider-based department
PBR	Provider-Based Rule (*see* 42 CFR §413.65)
PCP	primary care physician
PE	practice expense
PERL (Internet)	Practical Extraction and Reporting Language
PET	positron emission tomography
PFFS	private fee for service
PFS	patient financial services
PHI	protected health information
PHO	physician hospital organization
PMPM	per member per month
POS	place of service
POS	point of service
PPA	preferred provider arrangement
PPO	preferred provider organization
PPP	Point-to-Point Protocol (Internet)
PPR	physician payment reform

PPS	prospective payment system
PRB	provider review board
PRO	peer review organization
ProPAC	Prospective Payment Assessment Commission
PS&E	provider statistical and reimbursement (report)
PSA	physician scarcity area
PSN	provider service network
PSO	provider service organization
PT	physical therapy or physical therapist
PTA	physical therapy assistant
QA	quality assurance
QFD	quality function deployment
RA	remittance advice
RAC	recovery audit contractor
RAP	Resident Assessment Protocol
RBRVS	resource-based relative value system
RC	Revenue Code (*see also* RCC)
RCC	Revenue Center Code
RFI	Request for Information
RFP	Request for Proposal
RFQ	Request for Quotation
RHC	rural health clinic
RM	risk management
RN	registered nurse
RNFA	registered nurse first assistant
RRC	rural referral center
RUG	Resource Utilization Group
RVS	relative value system
RVU	relative value unit
S&I	supervision and interpretation
SAD	self-administrable drug

SCH	sole community hospital
SDS	same-day surgery
SGML (Internet)	Standardized General Markup Language
SLIP	Serial Line IP Protocol (Internet)
SLP	speech language pathology (*see also* ST)
SMI	Service Mix Index
SMTP	Simple Mail Transport Protocol (Internet e-mail)
SNF	skilled nursing facility
SNP	special needs plan
SOC	standard of care
SOS	site of service
SR-DRG	Severity Refined DRG (HCFA proposed in 1994)
ST	speech therapy (*see also* SLP)
STACH	short-term acute care hospital (*see* LTCH)
SUBC	State Uniform Billing Committee
TLA	three-letter acronym
TPA	third-party administrator
TPP	third-party payer
TQD	total quality deployment
TQM	total quality management
TSC	Transaction Standard/Standard Code Set (*see* HIPAA)
UB-04	universal billing form (2004 revision)
UCC	Uniform Commercial Code (*see* state laws)
UCR	usual, customary, reasonable
UHC	University Health System Consortium
UHDDS	Uniform Hospital Discharge Data Set
UPIN	Unique Physician Identification Number
UNIX (Computer)	Not an acronym, but a play on the word *eunuch*
UR	Utilization Review
URL	Uniform Resource Locator (Internet address)

USC	United States Code
VBP	value-based purchasing
VDP	voluntary disclosure program
VSR	value stream reinvention
W-2	tax withholding form
WWW (Internet)	World Wide Web
XML (Internet)	eXtensible Markup Language
ZPIC	zone program integrity contractor

Appendix: Synopsis of the Medicare Program's Payment Systems

The Medicare program leads the way in developing, implementing, and refining various types of payment systems for a wide variety of healthcare providers and healthcare services. The following provides a summary of the different payment systems and associated payment mechanisms. Each of these systems has been discussed to some level of detail in one or more of the four volumes comprising this series of books. Note that private third-party payers may use these approaches on a modified basis.

Hospital Payment

Inpatient

Short-term acute care hospitals are paid through the MS-DRGs (Medicare Severity Diagnosis Related Groups). MS-DRGs represent a complicated prospective payment system (PPS). There are certain exceptions to the IPPS (inpatient prospective payment system):

- Critical access hospitals (CAHs): Cost-based reimbursement is used.
- Cancer hospitals: Cost-based reimbursement is used.
- Children's hospitals: Cost-based reimbursement is used.

Certain specially designated hospitals receive additional payments. Each of these designations requires meeting certain special requirements. These include:

- Medicare-dependent hospital (MDH)
- sole community hospital (SCH)
- rural referral center (RRC)
- low-volume hospital

There are also a few special cost pass-through payments:

a. Direct Graduate Medical Education (DGME)
b. Organ procurement costs

   c. CRNAs (certified registered nurse anesthetists) for small rural hospitals

   d. Nursing and allied health (NAH) education costs

   e. Hemophilia clotting factors

Generally, for pass-through payment calculation a distinction is made between routine costs and ancillary costs, and different cost-to-charge ratios (CCRs) are used.

The IPPS payment calculation addresses the costs for hospitals in two basic parts:

1. Capital costs
2. Operating costs

A number of other payment issues are involved with payment for cost outliers and transfers of various types (e.g., transfer from PPS hospital to another PPS hospital or transfer from a hospital to a subacute provider such as skilled nursing). MS-DRGs are totally code dependent with the use of *ICD-10* (*International Classification of Diseases, Tenth Revision*) for both procedure and diagnosis coding.

Certain hospitals do not use the IPPS. Instead, they have their own special PPSs. Currently, these are

- psychiatric hospitals or distinct part units,
- rehabilitation hospitals or distinct part units, and
- long-term care hospitals (LTCHs).

MS-DRGs and associated hospital payment mechanisms are discussed in *Prospective Payment Systems*.

Outpatient Services

Payment for hospital outpatient services is more varied than for inpatient payments. This variability simply reflects the enormous range of outpatient services. For lack of a better definition, hospital outpatient services are all those services that hospitals can provide that are not inpatient services.

For many outpatient services, Ambulatory Payment Classifications (APCs) are used. APCs cover surgeries, outpatient diagnostic testing, emergency room (ER) services, therapeutic radiation, chemotherapy, and oncology, to name a few. There are some significant exceptions. For instance, laboratory services are paid through a separate fee schedule, as are durable medical equipment (DME) and ambulance services. Also, physical therapy and occupational therapy are not under APCs and are paid through the Medicare Physician Fee Schedule (MPFS). Services such as speech language pathology (SLP) and pathology may be paid under APCs or through the MPFS depending on the specific service.

APCs have a number of special features, including cost outliers, discounting of multiple services, bundling of inexpensive supplies and drugs, coinsurance, and cost-based pass-through payments for certain items. Both CPT (Current Procedural Terminology) and HCPCS (Healthcare Common Procedure Coding System) coding sets are used for APCs. There is significant use of the CMS National Correct Coding Initiative (NCCI) edits and associated coding policy guidelines.

APCs are also used with outpatient provider-based operations.* For hospitals, these are typically provider-based clinics in which there is both a technical component (i.e., hospital outpatient) claim filed and a professional component (i.e., physician) claim filed. The technical component claim is paid under APCs, while the professional component is paid under the MPFS at a reduced rate. The reduction in payment for the physician claim is called the site-of-service (SOS) differential. The reduction in payment is made because the physicians and practitioners at such provider-based clinics have reduced overhead expenses.

APCs are discussed in *Prospective Payment Systems*.

Skilled Nursing Facilities

For Medicare, skilled nursing facilities (SNFs) have their own PPS, namely, RUGs or Resource Utilization Groups. A patient assessment instrument (PAI) is used to develop different payment levels through the RUGs. In addition, SNFs are subject to extensive consolidated billing requirements that delineate exactly which services are a part of the SNF PPS payments.

See the third volume in this series, *Prospective Payment Systems*, for further information.

Home Health Agencies

Home health agencies (HHAs) have their own Medicare PPS, which uses an extensive patient assessment instrument called OASIS (Outcome and Assessment Information Set) to establish the level of payment. There are HHRGs, which are the Home Health Resource Groups. Episodes of care of sixty days are the units for payment. Adjustments can be made for short periods (less than sixty days) and for cost outliers. Supplies are generally included, although routine and ancillary supplies are separately addressed. DME is not a part of the home health prospective payment system (HHPPS). DME is paid through the DMEPOS (DME, prosthetics, orthotics, supplies) fee schedule.

The HHPPS is discussed in *Prospective Payment Systems*.

Critical Access Hospitals

CAHs are paid on a cost-based reimbursement basis. The basic payment for inpatient and outpatient services is 101 percent of costs. Cost-based reimbursement is also used for swing beds (i.e., skilled nursing beds). Ambulance services can also be paid at 101 percent if the ambulance service is provider-based to the given CAH.

There are two general methods for payment involving a CAH and associated physicians/practitioners.

- Method I payment methodology
  - Hospital inpatient and outpatient services are billed in the normal fashion using the UB-04. The 101-percent payment applies.
  - Physician and practitioner billing is performed in the usual manner using the 1500 claim form. The full 100 percent of the MPFS applies with standard reductions in payment for nonphysician practitioners.

---

* See the Provider-Based Rule (PBR), found generally at 42 CFR §413.65.

- Method II payment methodology
  - Hospital inpatient and outpatient services are billed in the normal fashion using the UB-04. The 101-percent payment applies.
  - For physicians and practitioners who agree to participate (i.e., file an appropriate CMS-855-R for reassignment of payments), the hospital files claims for these professional outpatient services on the UB-04. Payment is at 115 percent of the SOS reduced payment under the MPFS.

Interim payment for CAHs:

1. For inpatient services, payment is based on a per diem cost.
2. For outpatient services, payment is based on charges multiplied by the hospital's CCR as determined from the cost report.

CAH payment is discussed in this fourth volume of the series. Additional information on the MPFS is discussed in the second volume of this series, *Fee Schedule Payment Systems*.

Rural Health Clinics and Federally Qualified Health Centers

Both rural health clinics (RHCs) and federally qualified health center (FQHCs) are cost-based reimbursed. Interim payment is based on visits or clinical encounters. This payment rate is called the all-inclusive rate. There is a final reconciliation with their cost reports.

RHC and FQHC payment is discussed in this fourth volume of the series.

Physician and Practitioner Services

CMS (Centers for Medicare and Medicaid Services) has developed an extensive fee schedule for physician and practitioner payment, the MPFS. MPFS payment is based on the resource-based relative value scale (RBRVS). There are numerous features associated with the MPFS that can affect payment. Here are a few of the more important features:

a. There are bonus payments available for health professional shortage areas (HPSAs) and physician scarcity areas (PSAs). These bonuses apply only to designated geographic areas identified by ZIP code.
b. The relative value units (RVUs) have been developed for CPT and HCPCS codes. There are three different RVUs:
   1. Work
   2. Practice expense
   3. Medical malpractice
   The practice expense RVU is further divided into facility versus nonfacility. The facility practice expense RVU is generally lower than the nonfacility RVU. The difference in these RVUs allows for the application of the SOS differential, by which physician payment is reduced if services are provided in a facility setting.

    c. There is an extensive global surgical package (GSP) that includes three separate parts:
      1. Preoperative
      2. Intraoperative
      3. Postoperative
      For the postoperative period, the length of time is zero days, ten days, or ninety days. These are discrete time periods.
    d. Nonphysician practitioners are also paid through the MPFS, but there are reductions in payment.
      1. Physician assistants: 85 percent of MPFS
      2. Nurse practitioners: 85 percent of MPFS
      3. Clinical nurse specialists: 85 percent of MPFS
      4. Clinical psychologists: 100 percent of MPFS
      5. Clinical social workers: 75 percent of MPFS
      6. Nurse midwives: 100 percent of MPFS
      7. Other limited license doctors: 100 percent of MPFS
    e. There are special payment processes for certain situations:
      1. Assistant at surgery: 16 percent of MPFS
      2. Cosurgery: one-half of 125 percent of MPFS (two surgeons)
      3. Special payment calculation for certain endoscopic procedures
      4. MD anesthesiologist and CRNAs are paid through a special fee schedule arrangement using base units plus fifteen-minute time units.
    f. The NCCI edits and policies are used with MPFS.
    g. Physician supervision for diagnostic services is delineated in RBRVS and applies to both physicians and hospitals.
    h. Surgical complications may invoke additional payment through a return-to-the-operating-room criterion.

See *Fee Schedule Payment Systems*, for an extended discussion of MPFS.

Durable Medical Equipment

DME, or more correctly, DMEPOS, is paid under a fee schedule. A number of unusual items, such as parenteral and enteral nutrition (PEN), surgical dressings, and therapeutic shoes, are included as DME. Note that there are coverage issues for certain items relative to other Medicare payment systems. Accommodations in the fee schedule are made for new, used, and rented DME.

    The DME fee schedule is discussed in *Fee Schedule Payment Systems*.

Clinical Laboratory

Clinical laboratory services are paid under the Clinical Laboratory Fee Schedule. In rare cases, small hospitals may be paid on their costs.

    See *Fee Schedule Payment Systems*, for further discussion.

Ambulance

Ambulance services are paid through the Ambulance Fee Schedule (AFS). Provisions in the AFS do allow for additional payment for rural ambulance services. If a CAH owns the ambulance service and can meet the requirements found in the provider-based rule (PBR), then these ambulance services can be paid on a cost basis.

See *Fee Schedule Payment Systems*, for further discussion.

Ambulatory Surgical Centers

For Medicare, ASCs are paid through a combination of APCs and the MPFS. Only approved surgical procedures may be performed at an ASC. Generally, ASCs are paid approximately 65 percent of the APC payment unless the surgery can be performed in a physician's office; then, the payment is the lesser of:

a. 65 percent of the APC payment or
b. the nonfacility practice expense (PE) RVU from the MPFS.

See *Fee Schedule Payment Systems,* and *Prospective Payment Systems*, for further discussion.

End-Stage Renal Disease Facilities

End-stage renal disease (ESRD) facilities are paid on a composite rate that includes the dialysis treatments, certain drugs, lab tests, and supplies. The composite or bundled payment rate is geographically adjusted.

Pharmaceuticals and Implantable Medical Devices

Drugs and various implantable devices are paid through most of the other Medicare payment systems. Often, inexpensive drugs and routine supply items are bundled for payment purposes. For relatively new implantable devices, there may be a period of several years in which the devices are paid on a pass-through basis by converting charges into costs. After a transition period, the payment for the implantable devices is included in the prospective payment process. See further discussions of device dependent APCs and MS-DRGs in the third volume of this series, *Prospective Payment Systems.*

Medicare Managed Care: Medicare Advantage

Medicare Advantage or MA programs can be established in one of several ways. The four approaches are:

a. Health maintenance organization plans,
b. Preferred provider organization plans,

c. Private fee-for-service plans, and
d. Special needs plans.

A given MA plan may cover not only what traditional Medicare covers, but also additional coverage and benefits can be provided to the Medicare beneficiaries enrolling with such a plan. This includes Part D drug coverage. Note that Medicare beneficiaries who do enroll in such a plan do not use the Medicare supplemental or Medigap coverage.

MA programs are included in this fourth volume of the series.

Appendix: Case Study List

Throughout this book, small case studies are used to illustrate various issues and information provided. This is intended to assist readers in more fully understanding some of the complex and interlaced issues surrounding healthcare payment systems. This appendix provides a listing of the various cases within each of the chapters. Note that in some instances, a given case may be repeated from a different perspective.

Chapter 1

Case Study 1.1: Emergency Department Visit Involving Finger Splint
Case Study 1.2: Injured While Visiting a Neighbor
Case Study 1.3: Expensive Pacemakers
Case Study 1.4: Supply Item Payment
Case Study 1.5: Contracting for Surgical Services
Case Study 1.6: Clinical Nurse Specialist versus Nurse Practitioner
Case Study 1.7: Critical Access Hospital Use of Nurse Practitioner
Case Study 1.8: Nurse Practitioner and Clinical Nurse Specialist
Case Study 1.9: Freestanding Clinic inside the Apex Medical Center
Case Study 1.10: Hospital-Owned and -Operated Clinics
Case Study 1.11: Orthopedic Specialty Hospital
Case Study 1.12: Per Diem Payment for Inpatient Services
Case Study 1.13: Long-Term Care Hospital inside a Short-Term Acute Care Hospital
Case Study 1.14: Apogee Healthcare System
Case Study 1.15: Competing DME Suppliers
Case Study 1.16: Private Pay Home Health Services
Case Study 1.17: IDTF Billing for Radiology Services
Case Study 1.18: IDTF Acquired by Apex and Converted to Provider-Based
Case Study 1.19: ASC across the Street
Case Study 1.20: Cataract Surgery ASC

Chapter 2

Case Study 2.1: Dr. Brown, a Sole Practitioner
Case Study 2.2: Pharmacy Items at the Apex Medical Center
Case Study 2.3: Volume Purchasing of Pharmacy Items
Case Study 2.4: High-Technology Pacemakers
Case Study 2.5: Expensive Stent Wastage
Case Study 2.6: Acme Medical Clinic Examination Room
Case Study 2.7: Apex Medical Center Operating Room
Case Study 2.8: Expensive Pacemakers
Case Study 2.9: Increasing Costs at the Apex Medical Center
Case Study 2.10: Pass-Through Payments for Intraocular Lenses
Case Study 2.11: Advantage of Cost-Based Reimbursement
Case Study 2.12: Provider-Based Ambulance Services
Case Study 2.13: Acme Medical Clinic Conversion
Case Study 2.14: Differences in RHC Visits
Case Study 2.15: Two Visits on the Same Day

Chapter 3

Case Study 3.1: Charge Sensitivity for Insured Patients
Case Study 3.2: Charge Sensitivity for Medicare Beneficiary
Case Study 3.3: Negotiated Payment for Services
Case Study 3.4: Mixed Charge-Based and Cost-Based Arrangements
Case Study 3.5: Charge-Based Payment to Medicare Plus Percentage Payment
Case Study 3.6: Realization Rate
Case Study 3.7: Conservative Hospital Pricing
Case Study 3.8: Setting Clinic Charges
Case Study 3.9: Setting Hospital Charges
Case Study 3.10: Comparing Hospital Charges
Case Study 3.11: Surgery Charges for Different Hospitals
Case Study 3.12: Specialty Orthopedic Hospital
Case Study 3.13: Variable Payment for Supply Items
Case Study 3.14: Routine Supply Items
Case Study 3.15: Charging for Unusual Nursing Services
Case Study 3.16: Intravenous Solution Pricing
Case Study 3.17: Contractual Difference for Drug Reimbursement
Case Study 3.18: Low Reimbursement for Drug-Eluting Stents
Case Study 3.19: Proper Pricing of Pacemakers
Case Study 3.20: Percentage-of-Charge Payment Contract
Case Study 3.21: Preferential Laboratory Fee Schedule
Case Study 3.22: Sports Therapy Preferential Charges
Case Study 3.23: Setting a Charge for a New Procedure
Case Study 3.24: Pricing Drug-Eluting Stents
Case Study 3.25: Packaging Pricing at the Apex Medical Center
Case Study 3.26: Reducing Prices at the Apex Medical Center

Chapter 4

Case Study 4.1: Acme Medical Clinic Contracts
Case Study 4.2: Hospital Remittance Advice
Case Study 4.3: Hospital Per Diem Payment
Case Study 4.4: Venipuncture Payment
Case Study 4.5: Skilled Nursing Services
Case Study 4.6: Variable Claims Filing Requirements
Case Study 4.7: Expensive Dermatologist
Case Study 4.8: Copayment for Physician Visit
Case Study 4.9: Construction at the Apex Medical Center
Case Study 4.10: Aquatic Therapy at Hotel Swimming Pool
Case Study 4.11: Terminated Contract during Episode of Care
Case Study 4.12: Bundling of Low Osmolar Contrast Media Payment
Case Study 4.13: Hydration Preceding Cardiac Catheterization
Case Study 4.14: Special Medication Regimen
Case Study 4.15: Compounded Dermatology Prescriptions
Case Study 4.16: Hospital Inpatient Stay Changed to Observation
Case Study 4.17: Location of Service
Case Study 4.18: Payment Averaging
Case Study 4.19: Establishing an MA Plan
Case Study 4.20: Out-of-Network Services under an MA Plan

Chapter 5

Case Study 5.1: Headache in the Emergency Department
Case Study 5.2: Capitated Contract for the Acme Medical Clinic
Case Study 5.3: Employer Reducing Healthcare Payments
Case Study 5.4: Dermatologist Specialists under Capitation
Case Study 5.5: Access to Specialty Care
Case Study 5.6: Capitated Health Coverage

Chapter 6

Case Study 6.1: Out-of-State Patient
Case Study 6.2: Out-of-State Patient Fall in a Parking Lot
Case Study 6.3: Improper Payment by the Payer
Case Study 6.4: Injections Provided during Surgery
Case Study 6.5: Shortage of Skilled Nursing Beds
Case Study 6.6: Back-End Processing System
Case Study 6.7: Apex Medical Center Auditing Program
Case Study 6.8: Acme Medical Clinic Auditing Program
Case Study 6.9: Correlating Hospital and Physician Coding
Case Study 6.10: Apogee Home Health Auditing Program
Case Study 6.11: Clinic Visit Coding Audit

Index